When the Secular Becomes Sacred

Other Works by This Author

Ernest J. Zarra III has authored thirteen books, including the additional Rowman & Littlefield titles:

- *Detoxing American Schools: From Social Agency to Academic Urgency* (Rowman & Littlefield, 2020);
- *America's Sex Culture: Its Impact upon Teacher Student Relationships Today* (Rowman & Littlefield, 2020);
- *The Age of Teacher Shortages: Reasons, Responsibilities, Reactions* (Rowman & Littlefield, 2019);
- *Generacion Z: La Generación con Derechos* (Narcea/Rowman & Littlefield, Spain 2019);
- *Assaulted: Violence in Schools and What Needs to be Done* (Rowman & Littlefield, 2018);
- *The Teacher Exodus: Reversing the Trend and Keeping Teachers in the Classrooms* (Rowman & Littlefield, 2018);
- *The Entitled Generation: Helping Teachers Teach and Reach the Minds and Hearts of Generation Z* (Rowman & Littlefield, 2017);
- *Helping Parents Understand the Minds and Hearts of Generation Z* (Rowman & Littlefield, 2017);
- *Common Sense Education: From Common Core to ESSA and Beyond* (August 31, 2016);
- *The Wrong Direction for Today's School: The Impact of Common Core on American Education* (Rowman & Littlefield, 2015);
- *Teacher-Student Relationships: Crossing into the Emotional, Physical, and Sexual Realms* (Rowman & Littlefield, 2013).

When the Secular Becomes Sacred

Religious Secular Humanism and Its Effects upon America's Public Learning Institutions

Ernest J. Zarra III

ROWMAN & LITTLEFIELD
Lanham • Boulder • New York • London

Published by Rowman & Littlefield
An imprint of The Rowman & Littlefield Publishing Group, Inc.
4501 Forbes Boulevard, Suite 200, Lanham, Maryland 20706
www.rowman.com

6 Tinworth Street, London SE11 5AL, United Kingdom

Copyright © 2021 by Ernest J. Zarra III

All rights reserved. No part of this book may be reproduced in any form or by any electronic or mechanical means, including information storage and retrieval systems, without written permission from the publisher, except by a reviewer who may quote passages in a review.

British Library Cataloguing in Publication Information Available

Library of Congress Cataloging-in-Publication Data

Names: Zarra, Ernest J., 1955- author.
Title: When the secular becomes sacred : religious secular humanism and its effects upon America's public learning institutions / Ernest J. Zarra III.
Description: Lanham : Rowman & Littlefield, [2021] | Includes bibliographical references and index. | Summary: "From educational philosophy to classroom practices, this book exposes and analyzes tactical intersections between secular humanism and religious self-worship"— Provided by publisher.
Identifiers: LCCN 2021010702 (print) | LCCN 2021010703 (ebook) | ISBN 9781475858525 (cloth) | ISBN 9781475858532 (paperback) | ISBN 9781475858549 (epub)
Subjects: LCSH: Public schools—United States. | Secular humanism—United States. | Religion in the public schools—United States. | Education—Aims and objectives—United States. | Education—Philosophy. | Secularization—United States. | Individualism—United States. | Self-worship.
Classification: LCC LA217.2 .Z37 2021 (print) | LCC LA217.2 (ebook) | DDC 370.973—dc23
LC record available at https://lccn.loc.gov/2021010702
LC ebook record available at https://lccn.loc.gov/2021010703

This book is dedicated to my former high school teachers, present and departed. I owe a deep sense of gratitude to you all for not giving up on this academically challenged, shy student from South Bloomfield, New Jersey. I also dedicate this book to my former professors, each of whom saw raw ability in a young man and shaped it through investments of professional and personal time. Thank you Drs. John Warwick Montgomery, Walter Martin, Dallas Willard, David Marsh, James Bjornstad, and John Carruthers. Your marks on my life, academic development, and personal abilities, including the development of character, will never be forgotten. Last, I dedicate this book to all of my former colleagues, students, families, and fellow worshipers at the many schools, colleges, and churches, where I both worked and attended. Life is not merely a sum of experiences. Life is also a product of significant exponential influences and importance.

Contents

Preface	ix
Acknowledgments	xxiii
Introduction	1
1 Humanism: Secular and Religious	7
2 Education as Religion	37
3 The God of Self	69
4 Cracks in the Ivory Towers	95
5 Seeking Converts	123
6 Is Public Education Too Far Gone?	153
Index	183
About the Author	193

Preface

To begin, after extensive Amazon and Google searches of several key words, there has been found no book on the market that focuses on the specific themes I intend to address in my book. For decades, it appears from the literature that secular humanism had been viewed as distinct from anything religious. After all, the word "secular" does imply something distinct from qualitative sacredness. Nevertheless, since the Supreme Court ruled in 1961, in *Torcaso v. Watkins*, that secular humanism may be referred to as a religion, each passing decade reveals more and more that secular humanism does indeed present itself as religious. While many of its advocates deny this assertion, this book will reveal how the so-called secular belief system and practices affect American culture as these comprise the religion of America's public-learning institutions.

HISTORICAL OVERVIEW

According to some, American culture has long veered from its traditional and historical moorings. There is a distinct convergence of the secular and the sacred. Ironically, a part of this convergence seems to be historical in nature. Scholars in the United Kingdom are having to decide how best to display the remaining copies of the Magna Carta.[1] Apparently, many in the public have ascribed a certain sacredness of the documents. That being said, much of history is lost on the American public, as a result of focusing more on social issues over academic ones.[2]

Public-learning institutions in the United States are largely responsible for this shift. However, they are not alone. Traditional religious groups are also involved. Even some groups that refer to themselves as Christian have moved into the secular, joining many Jewish sects and mainline liberal Christian church denominations. This movement will also be chronicled in the book. The observation that the secular more greatly affects the sacred and the latter gravitates toward secularism. The evidence of this is seen in the liberalization of mainline denominations. Lowering views of the integrity of Holy Writ, replacement of mandates and traditions of religious groups, and the expectations that there are no consequences to be had beyond this life, are just a few examples.

The marginalized nature of politics is reminiscent of what occurs between those of different faiths. Ironically, even with the American tradition of the separation of church and state, certain secular figureheads are acting as religious leaders. They preach right and wrong, often shaping personal morality to political reality, manifested in actions that support the progressive liberalization of both.

A recent example of this was the 2008 election of President Barack Obama, with headlines and photographs touting the "new messiah," and Oprah Winfrey directly commenting on the candidate Obama as "the One." Not only are leaders within politics today the new religious icons of humanistic culture, but religious icons are also becoming more political and secular.

An example of this is the evangelical push of support for President Donald Trump, and the Christian leaders willing to overlook some of his words and behaviors, in order to advance a narrative on select issues. Political leaders and expert voices are now worshiped in ways that founders of religions were idolized, whether these leaders are denominational or party-affiliated. The rise of social media platforms means that they can disseminate information directly to people, with the mere click of a mouse.

Changes in culture have direct impacts upon schools in America, since their implications are realized in policies that shape what is taught in schools and how the curriculum is written. The impacts are also clearly visible in teacher training institutions, which are often the places that state policies manifest themselves prior to their impacts in American classrooms. As a result, schools have become places of impassioned social and political agency rather than competitive institutions of learning. Again, this is purposeful and advanced by progressive educational institutions and support groups.

In an overt and demonstrable likeness to religious outreach, social programs and targeted activism are the conscious evangelistic tools used to promote activities of a secular belief system, hence a religion. The evidence is that students are both the recipients of indoctrination and followers trained to exhibit expected traits, such as those of any new believers and disciples associated with religious faith. The concern for this is that students are directly in the cross hairs of both.

Students from elementary school through college arrive home with a great deal more fervor for their newfound, personal beliefs, including their new identities. They are told they are the center of the education universe and are energized by this sense of entitlement. Furthermore, this type of religious fervor is reminiscent of the *Hippie Anti-War* movements of the 1960s and 1970s, the eventual *me movement* of the 1970s, and beyond. The nation is now in the midst of the *identity and entitlement movement* that has many of the earmarks of the establishment of a new religion.

The notion that something claims to be secular, albeit humanist, can simply be called out, as religious is far too simplistic. There must be some overriding evidence, or at least acknowledgment from multiple sources, not the least of which are courts, researchers, and even humanists themselves, in order for such an assertion to be affirmed. There are certain tenets that appear in secular and religious institutions that are amazingly correlated. For example, the belief in oneself and the idea that a person can exercise control over his or her destiny, is as religious a belief as one can find.

Attributing higher power to oneself or to a God is still attribution of power from one source, a human being. But secular humanism and religion are much more than this. The focus here will be mostly on Christianity, the dominant religion in America. I refer to the pairs of humanism as secular humanism as one, and the same for religious humanism and religious secular humanism throughout the book.

The term *secular humanism* no longer triggers widespread negative responses as it once did. Just a few decades ago, battle lines were drawn between conservatives and liberals, over the issue of religion and the state. The negative connotations have dissipated, somewhat. This alone should be indication enough that there has either been a discontinuation of the fight between marginalized groups or that the extremes have more in common than each was willing to admit in the past. It appears that the latter is the case, especially with the newest of cult groups that have emerged in gender and racial circles.

THE PROBLEMS DEFINED

Certainly, not every institution has the exposure of students to harmful ideologies as the focus of the faculty meetings. However, to have bought into the dogma of twenty-first-century American psychology, some educational philosophy, social-emotional learning theory, gender theory, social justice practices—or any one of several others—may mean conversions to the goals and acceptance of the secular religion have already taken place.

For example, the terms *inclusive environment* and *tolerance* are today code to advance understanding and acceptance of Black Lives Matter and LGBTQ+ among students at all levels. Required sex education classes and required race/ethnic studies classes are just the beginning. This begs the multi-part question as to whether the groups in question are religious, what it means to be spiritual, and if they are not religious, why are they trying hard to affect students and proselytize them toward racial and sexual/gender acceptance?

In the past, America's public education institutions had been labeled everything from places of enlightenment[3] to dens of indoctrination,[4] and even as places of atheistic secular humanism.[5] Marginalization has worsened in America over many issues, and coarsened rhetoric has not been helpful.

What is not being discussed openly today is that the newest construct for American public education has eerie similarities to American evangelical history,[6] particularly the overt push practiced by the emerging evangelical movement of the 1970s. American secular humanism claims to see the world through a humanistic lens, while using religious methods to change mindsets and win over converts. An example of this is Howard Zinn's history of the United States. Different aspects of the Zinn Educational Project and *A People's History* are discussed and critiqued in chapters 2 and 6.

Consider the public school student, or college students, who comes home one day and mentions to one or more adults at home that he or she is a Marxist, and that the adults in question are racists. Furthermore, the adults might be taken back by an additional claim that it is the student's generation that intends to overthrow America as it is known, because of its colonization, genocide, and historical White Supremacy. The adults would no doubt consider that the mind and belief system of the student had been deeply affected, given the fact most American homes are not geared toward Marxist ideology, and their heroes are not Saul Alinsky or Che Guevara. Where would the adults conclude this radical conversion had occurred in the being of their child, or young adult?

Now, consider that this same student comes home and declares a new personal identity. The student has found his or her true self and wants the support of the entire family, as a result. He or she wants to grow in experiences with the newfound identity, begin to go to places where people share the same identity, develop relationships, and study more about those that share in this newness of reality.

The exploration of the depths and joys is a main goal of the student and the excitement of what lies ahead is most exhilarating. Essentially, the student claims not to be the same person as before and proclaims there is no desire to live as the person everyone knew before the conversion and emergence of the new identity. The student changes names and declares an old name a dead name.

Which of these two experiences classifies as secular and which can be deemed religious? Both include a radical change from inside the student. Both share goals of newness of personhood, and both attribute changes to the ways of life, before and after conversion. There is a sense of mission and passion to drive forward with newfound identities. Inasmuch as religions seek to convert souls, minds, and hearts, the teachings of modern secular religion are meant to produce similar results. Curriculum and instructional materials are available at all levels to ensure the dictates of humanism are drilled into the minds of students. It is at this point *the secular becomes sacred*, which is the overarching idea behind this book.

There is a highly competitive battle being waged for the minds and hearts of the younger generations. The evidence of this is the growing number of people leaving traditional religions and adopting a mode of spirituality that encompasses personal identity and a litany of secular and/or doctrinal tenets that are the mysteries and keys to being a successful educator today. Professional development is full of these types of seminars. There seems to be something about finding oneself in emerging fads of culture that appeals to the same emotions that play into being recognized on social media, the place to express one's beliefs. But today's movement is so much more than a passing fad. One's identity is based upon it.

REASONS FOR WRITING THIS BOOK

There are many reasons for this book. The *main purpose* is to addresses the movement and intersection of religion and humanism. Most people remain unaware that the secular humanism of the 1970s was classified in the beginning as a religion, but mostly in name only. Some fifty years later, entire generations have been affected by the teachings of humanism in 2020. The rise of religious humanism comes with all the characteristics that earmark an actual religion. These will be addressed in the book.

A *second purpose* for this book is to point out that throughout history, American education has developed and changed, and along with it the philosophies that prompted these changes. One of the philosophical debates is whether education in America has become the victimizer by emboldening radical groups and fringe organizations, or remains the savior to millions of young people. In this book, the reader will discover that today there is a merging of the two. Education is portrayed as one—it is as salvific inasmuch as it is victimizing.

To the religious and political left in our nation, education is proclaimed as the savior of people, the epitome of personal enlightenment, and the gatekeeper to economic success. To those on the political and religious right, education tends to come across today as indoctrination of students, and as a blatant force to redefine society from the values upon which the United States is founded. But there is another major point to consider, which is a *third reason* for writing this book.

Students today from K–16 are being influenced by religious humanism and social activism. Groups whose main goals are to win converts have made students their cultural targets. Not only do these groups bring a "you are in charge of your life" message, they also claim students can change their identities at any time they choose. Thus, race, sexuality, and gender have become the dominant focal points in humanism today. These are addressed in the book.

There are points at which American culture is intersected by education and religion. There are also close parallels where the two seem to stream alongside each other, almost interchangeably. Today, unlike any other recent times in American education history, the lines separating education and religion are blurred.

BASIC QUESTIONS ADDRESSED IN THE BOOK

The following list comprises ten basic questions that are addressed in the book from multiple perspectives.

- What are the definitions of secularism, humanism, and religion?
- How is modern education like a religion?
- What characteristics of modern public education appear as indoctrination and as a cult?
- In what ways do schools today convert students to belief systems?
- Why should some themes and topics be deemed off-limits for students and teachers?
- Why are teachers allowed to teach materials that are offensive to some groups of students, their families, or to the communities in general?
- What spiritual, emotional, and psychological harm could result in children dismissing their biological identity?
- Why should schools be allowed to teach American students that America is a racist nation and that Whites are racists by birth?
- What are parents to do when their children reject their faith, moral foundations, personal identities, and are converted to a religion within the classrooms, or assemblies at their schools?
- Are public schools too far gone to save, in their current form?

SCOPE OF THE BOOK

When the Secular Becomes Sacred: Religious Secular Humanism and Its Effects upon America's Public Learning Institutions is an analysis of the culture of American public-learning institutions from a unique and different perspective. The thesis extends to what today amounts to America's K–16 students being overtly proselytized in order to convert a generation to humanistic religious beliefs.

The analysis underscores competing worldviews in culture and the struggles faced by institutions and educators, as education policy is shaped by national figures. Essentially, our nation's schools are implementing religious-type indoctrinating paradigms and attempting to effect changes upon the spiritual and affective domains of students as they develop and mature. The aim of the advocates is unabashed conversions of students, which is the ultimate goal.

This book will provide the reader a realistic look into the effects of *uncanny parallels and intersections* between secularism and religion. It will challenge readers to contend with the notion that the separation of church and state concept has been compromised and is being used to the political advantage of some. Furthermore, the reader will be presented with the argument that self-worship of the individual is attracting more and more students away from historical and traditional religious teachings to a secular religion—one in which the self becomes simultaneously the worshiper and the object of this worship.[7]

When the Secular Becomes Sacred explores the causes and effects of secular humanism throughout the history of American culture and the shifts that result in cultural changes. These impacts have led to an education *reformation* of the public-learning institutions in the United States. This exploration (1) takes the reader into this reformation, as it examines the doctrines and tenets of the modern secular education movement, and (2) lays out a cogent and concise set of arguments as to why modern secular humanism is much more like a religion today than at time ever before.

An increasing number of contemporary professors and teachers act more like culture-changers than academic instructors. This is especially true of some academic disciplines. They bring their personal beliefs into their lessons, pressure students who dissent, and avoid primary voices of dissent. Students are sometimes shamed into being quiet because of the risk of a grade, and therefore acquiesce, or even mobilize as advocates for social change.

For example, under the guise of social-emotional learning, some K–12 students may be instructed contrary to the values they have learned at home. For example, the thrust of the social-emotional focuses on several key elements, according to its authors.

Certain aspects of learning proper behaviors and cultural norms that vary from life at home are often perceived as social conditioning, which are also traceable elements to both motivational instruction and brainwashing activities. This book will highlight some of these examples. Inasmuch as some cultic religions offer ways of thinking about the world, and then ask converts and protégés to apply the principles to this world, the same approach can be found in America's public education curriculum and instructional methods. It is especially insidious when doctrinal statements are used as facts and not open to dialogue or discussion. Gender and sexuality, as well as anything dealing with Black Lives Matter, are today approached from a doctrinal and forcible evangelistic approach in America's public schools.

Teachers are trained in implicit bias, and how to identify it in themselves and others. The identification of such bias is predicated on the assumption that it exists in all teachers, both about other adults and about the ways teachers view students, work with them and their families, and set expectations. This type of training usually is coupled with the fragility of Whites, in that the assumption is that they are unable to deal with their own implicit bias and demonstrate this inability when they hear about how racist current America is as a nation.

Every religious figure expects that he or she can motivate their followers. But what must be asked is motivated from what to what else? Changing the mindsets of students is the first step to changing the culture of a generation. Toward this end, students are being instructed to put on and practice a growth mindset and apply it to all they think and do.

There is growing evidence that teachers and professors today are more biased and identifying as more partisan in the process. This bias alienates and attracts. By the time students finish college, there is a "diploma divide,"[8] in terms of education and voting, based primarily on the political and moral exposure experienced throughout students' college tenure. Why is it said that parents fear sending their young adult children away to college?

The notion that public schools are the same today as they were just a decade ago is erroneous. Public education institutions are now places of overt and purposeful advocacy for beliefs and practices that, just a decade ago, would be considered aberrant to families and off-limits in classrooms. Social media has helped to break down moral barriers in culture and provides tempting new viewpoints for today's students. There is much evidence of this, as this book will demonstrate.

Therefore, what was wrong a generation ago is fast becoming a norm of its own. When a subjective truth replaces another, which truth is true? The secular humanist sees little concern with such a question and perceives even less concern by its supported practices.

STRUCTURE OF THE BOOK

Contemporary learning institutions resemble places of worship in several ways. This book will explain how this is the case, by examining educational philosophies and classroom practices.

Particularly for Generation Z and the Millennials, ideological lines have been blurred by politicians, activists, and even by some religious figures, and this blurring is intentional and tactical. State schools are more like religious institutions as they are intentional in presenting humanistic doctrinal tenets, as they are intentional in making converts. Their intentions can be found in programs such as civic, citizenship participation, health and sexual education, and involvement as activists in social activism.

Several strategies employed are frighteningly similar to those used by cult figures in training, meant directly to affect the minds and hearts of their followers. These are addressed below, and will be more detailed in the book.

The secular education institutions have taken on sacred features today, in tandem with vacuum created by the progressive political movement. Essentially, this vacuum replaced what had occupied the sacred and educational spaces in American culture: God and the Bible

There is strong evidence to support the notion that worship of the *self, the individual*, has usurped the historically sacred place reserved for a transcendent deity. In a twist of irony, students are now taught they can fluidly grow beyond the self and arrive at the point of self-worship. The fact is that this worship of the individual is certainly more fashionable and attractive than traditional orthodoxy or evangelical theology across American society.

With these things in mind, the layout of the book is as follows. Chapter 1 examines humanism from secular and religious perspectives. It presents brief histories of humanism and religion, defines major terms, and lays out arguments as to why humanism is religious. The chapter also presents a case for some of the causes and effects of humanism as they relate to people leaving their faith, replacing it with another faith as their chosen belief system.

Chapter 2 addresses education and its philosophies as a new religion and schools as the places of worship. In addition, examples of worship at public schools are also included in the chapter. The chapter also contains information on the impacts of Horace Mann, John Dewey, and others on public education over the years. The chapter also presents analyses of the philosophies behind humanism and humanistic doctrines, and the practices associated with both, as it defends the thesis that the secular becomes sacred.

In chapter 3, the reader will come to understand the *god of self idea* and how this belief is accomplished through emotions, moral programming, and the principle of *losing oneself to find oneself*. These and other principles and practices of *identity* affect the minds of children and young adults. Included also in this chapter are critiques of critical theories on race and gender and the notion of White Fragility.

The places where many cultural isms are invented are the Ivory Towers of academe. Chapter 4 is a deep dive into some of the teachings that have emerged from colleges and universities that have turned hard left politically and, in doing so, have pulled young people toward activism. A discussion is also included, in terms of free speech and where it has been disallowed on campuses as well as in certain churches.

Chapter 5 details the messages and strategies of humanists in seeking to convert students' minds, hearts, and souls. Also addressed is the nature of *wokeness* and its religious implications. The chapter compares religious humanism and other religious cults and how exposure to both affects students in schools. There is an analysis of sex education and gender legislation that is being mandated for many K–12 schools, and why parents should be concerned about this direction. Several other key discussions occur in this chapter, including whether religious humanism is replacing Christianity in America, the cult of race, and how religion has become secular.

The last chapter of the book, chapter 6, poses the question as to whether public education is too far gone to be saved. In answering this query, the chapter delves into utopian concepts, sloganeering, and the motivations of today's students in America's K–16 public-learning institutions. The chapter asserts that humanists believe their worldview is salvific and that belief in the self is the proper application of a humanistic perspective. An examination of revisionism of American history is included in the chapter to inform the reader how bias and worldview present nearly seamless agreement. In the final analysis, the claims of humanism are analyzed and the reader is left with the challenge of the newest cults rising to the top in American culture and their evangelism in American schools.

INSPIRATION FOR WRITING THIS BOOK

Alarm bells sounded in my mind when the riots of 2020 occurred. Students with backpacks and facemasks, skateboards and placards paced the streets in protest. The rhetoric which most of the young adults were driven by began to sound reminiscent to periods of the past. There were some differences in what was being said. The alarming rhetoric that caught my attention made its way into my heart.

Students inspired me long before the summer of 2020. Yet, there was something different, in that two revolutionary groups were taking to the streets with the students. Leaders spewed anti-American and hateful speech, unlike anything I ever experienced, dating back to the Vietnam Protests of the 1960s. What I was observing was a transformational religious movement taking place right before my eyes. This inspired me to look backward in time, and deeper into the ideas that have now made their ways into K–12 schools, after being handed down from the Ivory Towers of academe. Having spent a career in both, I perceived that many of the teachings that students are exposed to today emerged from those Ivory Towers. As a result, I was inspired to analyze these teachings, the reasons for students following them.

Next, since I am an evangelical Christian and have a graduate degree in Christian Apologetics, I began to see how twenty-first-century humanism began to mimic religion and how two groups in particular began to have so much influence upon children and young adults. This inspired me to look a lot deeper into the groups.

Churches are being affected by the teachings of both BLM and the LGBTQ+ movement, and I wondered whether there were any correlations between the flighty form of evangelicalism to more liberal denominations that teach humanism and support the two cult groups in question.

The fundamental inspiration for this book is twofold: (1) I am concerned about the hearts, minds, and souls of today's children and young adult college students, and (2) I want to discover reasons why humanism has become a substitute religion for these same groups.

NOTES

1. Barry Ardley and Richard Voase. "Magna Carta: Repositioning the secular as sacred." *International Journal of Heritage Studies*. 2013. 19(4): 341–52. Retrieved May 24, 2020, from https://www.tandfonline.com/doi/abs/10.1080/13527258.2012.663780.

2. Ernest J. Zarra III. *Detoxing American schools: From social agency to academic urgency.* 2020. Lanham, MD: Rowman & Littlefield Publishers.

3. Matt Emerson. "Do schools educate for enlightenment?" *America Magazine.* January 13, 2014. Retrieved December 25, from https://www.americamagazine.org/content/ignatian-educator/do-schools-educate-enlightenment.

4. Colleen Flaherty. "'Lost generation.'" *Inside Higher Ed.* July 25, 2016. Retrieved December 25, 2019, from https://www.insidehighered.com/news/2016/07/25/academics-fact-check-pervasive-idea-liberal-academics-indoctrinate-their-students.

5. Staff. "Humanist common ground: Atheism." *American Humanist Association.* 2019. Retrieved December 25, 2019, from https://americanhumanist.org/paths/atheism/.

6. Rousas J. Rushdoony. *The messianic character of American education.* 1976. Nutley, NJ: The Craig Press, p. x.

7. Susan Jacoby. "The White House is tearing down the wall between church and state." *New York Times.* July 5, 2018. Retrieved December 26, 2019, from https://www.nytimes.com/2018/07/05/opinion/sunday/church-state-supreme-court-religion.html. Cf. Andrew L. Seidel. "The Supreme Court case that could bring down the wall of separation between church and state (updated)." *Rewire News.* November 12, 2018. Retrieved from https://rewire.news/article/2018/11/12/the-supreme-court-case-that-could-bring-down-the-wall-of-separation-between-church-and-state/.

8. Adam Harris. "America is divided by education." *The Atlantic.* November 7, 2018. Retrieved January 24, 2020, from https://www.theatlantic.com/education/archive/2018/11/education-gap-explains-american-politics/575113/.

Acknowledgments

I would like to acknowledge the many supporters of this project for their input and commentary on the manuscript. There are too many to name, but please know that I am extremely grateful for your discussions online, our Zoom critiques, and the email comments. Your input has made this a better book in so many ways. You have made me, yet again, a better writer.

There are a few people who do deserve special recognition. Thanks go to a friend of thirty-five years, Roger Oakley, and Daryl Martin whose apologetic minds and depths of reason are surpassed only by their humble hearts and lifelong encouragements.

Also, special recognition goes to Pastor Chris Rogers, Graham Marshall, Bob Renckly, and Jason Stearns, whose wisdom and zeal for God during our online Christian Conversations Forum touched on the core of many issues and helped to refine the themes of this book.

Thanks also go out to Amjad Hussein, a young millennial man whose personal testimony of faith and political efforts to rein in so much of what this book addresses have not been lost.

Next, I would like to recognize Professors Daymon Johnson, and Peter Wood, whose efforts to stem the tide of radicalism are ongoing, and whose knowledge of history and philosophy are not only great benefits to their students, but very handy for authors when needed. Our online exchanges were quite helpful. Your students are blessed to call you their professor.

Last, I acknowledge the following physicians: Drs. Christopher Green, Myung Park, Ed Libby, Claudius Mahr, and Jamie McCabe. They know why and so do I. But without their assistance, this book would have never been written.

Introduction

When my wife and I first began our teaching careers in our early twenties, schools were very different places. There was much more parental support of the complete education process. Parents were generally helpful in our classrooms, and volunteered for a variety of responsibilities delegated to them. Most were supportive of teachers also and understood that the actions of their children were to be owned by the children, themselves.

If some of our students needed to be disciplined, phone calls home usually brought swift responses, for the most part. Often with the phone calls there came guarantees that we would see differences in the students on the following days.

In terms of my four-decade career in education, there have been some very noticeable changes in the direction of schooling. There were huge paradigm shifts, and these differences lacked subtleties in expectations. Changes were handed down by those who had little or no experience in education. This is no surprise, since politicians and other elected and appointed officials rarely understand the goings-on in school rooms in their towns and cities.

Liberal and conservative lobbyists were responsible for many of the changes that busied teachers and increased accountability across the board. Rather than removing previous requirements from their plates of teacher's responsibilities, states and the federal government just provided larger plates. These additions did not lead to anything but marginal improvements in student learning, and barely helped teachers, given the fact that during these expansions of responsibilities there were explosions of professional development seminars. I know this personally because I was a professional development leader for a district of approximately 40,000 secondary students.

After thirteen years, I resigned from the professional development position when I was told I had to teach teachers how to implement the Common Core State Standards for California. This was not the right direction, in my opinion, for the nation or for my state. It was shortly thereafter that I wrote an award-winning book titled, *The Wrong Direction for Today's Schools: The Impact of Common Core on American Education* (Rowman & Littlefield, 2015).

Parents have generally supported teachers over the years. However, since the year 2000, and with each passing year, I noticed a clear slippage of parental support. It seemed the more energy I expended on classroom management and parental contacts, the less it benefited my classroom. It became exhausting.

Now, all these decades later, after surviving data teams, Professional Learning Communities, *No Child Left Behind*, *Race to the Top*, the *Common Core*—as well as the changes in educational psychology legitimizing identities that were categorized years earlier by these same institutions as emotional and psychological problems, the larger context of American education has become a place of aberration and indoctrination.

To be fair, education is vastly different during a pandemic. This is something no one could have fathomed. K–12 schools in almost every state had to develop platforms for online classrooms using Canvas, Blackboard, and other learning and management systems. Teachers are working now from early morning to late in the evenings, just prepping and staying on top of the hours they anticipate spending during the next day of instruction. Zoom had to become a friend to teachers and college faculty. In short order, the popular video-chat platform had become both a noun and a verb.

Many colleges had to develop complete online teacher education programs because of teacher attrition, which occurred for several reasons. In addition, alternate credentials became available, and many states now employ teachers with just their bachelor's degree, as long as they will enter a teacher training program sometime during their employment. On that topic, I wrote another highly acclaimed book titled, *The Age of Teacher Shortages: Reasons, Responsibilities, Reactions* (Rowman & Littlefield, 2019).

The differences between earning a credential now and then are stark. During the early days of my pursuit of a teaching credential in the state of New

Jersey, we had to forego a full year of employment and salary and sacrificed much to earn that glorious piece of paper called the state teaching credential. My, how times have changed. I chronicle these changes in my book *The Age of Teacher Shortages*.

Teaching is just a profession in name only. There are no clients, no white jackets with teachers' names on them, and no appointments scheduled with patients. Teachers are generalists in K–8, and somewhat more specialist in single subjects in secondary. But that knowledge and any bit of expertise in content takes a back seat to classroom management today.

A teacher today would be fortunate to avoid being blamed for their student's poor grades, their bad behaviors, and the lack of discipline in the classrooms. Giving a student "that look," when causing a disturbance, now brings parents to classroom doors to challenge the teacher as to why he or she is picking on their child. The tools to discipline have all been removed for a "social worker approach to discipline." This approach is not focused on discipline. Rather, it is focused exclusively on restoration.

When it comes to classroom issues, if the students in question are (1) persons of color, or (2) of a different sexual orientation, or (3) self-proclaimed new gender identity, teachers now run the risk of being called racists with phobias, all because of administering discipline. Just by doing their jobs, they might be slandered and libeled across social media platforms by parents, social activists, and hordes of anonymous student supporters. These groups might even show up in protest at teacher's houses and harass the teachers' children, in order to bully them at their schools. This is another reason for this book. Informing teachers of the risks associated with speaking out is one thing, but empowering them to do so is quite another. Teachers need to know someone understands them and has their backs.

Classroom discipline has changed dramatically over the years. Schools in many states do not allow teachers to send students to the office for infractions, the kind that would have resulted in student suspension, or possibly expulsion, in previous years. Misbehaviors and disrespect are now tolerated for at least three reasons: (1) society has become more coarse and caustic, (2) so that social justice activists do not picket, and (3) to assuage parents so that they do not sue the school district.

Teacher education programs at colleges underwent major changes throughout the decades. Programs became more stringent and academically rigorous.

Then when demand was greatest, during the economic Great Recession of the early 2000s, teacher education classes swelled because of job layoffs. As the recession eased, fewer people chose to become teachers and, when the demand for teachers increased again, states were looking for teachers to fill their classrooms. As a teacher educator for a university at that time, I was kept very busy. There were more openings than teachers being trained by most teacher training programs.

Within the last few years, teacher attrition has increased. Retirements, geographic relocations, along with a large number of disenchanted teachers are reasons responsible for what is now a sustained teacher shortage nationally. As a result, states loosened the requirements for teacher training once again.

When I have asked teachers what had them so disenchanted, the responses were almost predictable and matched my own personal experiences. Teachers are no longer enjoying the amount of sacrifice and the increased lack of support. Instead of tickets out of poverty, schools are now labeled pipelines to prison. Teachers hear this and feel like their efforts are often sometimes hopeless.

In the decades since I began my career, the teacher has gone from professional to facilitator, to classroom monitor. They take abuse on a regular basis. Some of them are assaulted by violent students. A growing group of teachers complain about parents discussing them online in not-so-glowing terms. Teachers are unable to defend themselves against verbal and physical assaults, without getting placed on leave or even fired. They have very little recourse, even if they are members of their unions. Refer to my book *Assaulted: Violence in Schools and What Needs to be done* (Rowman & Littlefield, 2018) for first-hand accounts.

Humanism has become the new religion in schools, and parents and students are on the prowl for micro-aggressions, and teachers with good intentions and boundless energy on behalf of their students are now labeled racists because of their skin color. The students have risen from being the focal point to little deities shaping their destinies as they wish. They think they now call the shots in the classrooms and flex their attitudes to the disadvantage of many.

Schools are just not what they used to be just five years ago. They have become tribal and intolerant of anything that circumvents the modern humanistic narratives of the empowered social, racial, and ethnic groups. Any vestige of either patriotic allegiance or the Judeo-Christian ethic and heritage has been replaced with a religious humanism that is affecting all aspects of society. We have created a moral vacuum in the nation and with this creation have brought about a cementing of narcissism in students' psyches. Students' race, gender, sex, and identity are no longer set by a roster of students. Calling the name of a student, when that student now goes by a different name, is equivalent to a micro-aggression and can bring swift action against the teacher. This has happened before and will continue to happen.

The book is friendly to those who are not aware of the current humanism that has become its own religion in their children's schools—both public and private. It is meant to be a wake-up call to parents whose lives keep them busy from digging into the mind-altering that occurs in their children. I provide details in the book as to how the secular has become quite sacred and how this sacredness has led to outright confusion in schools.

In order to inform the reader, the following themes are addressed throughout the book:

(1) *There is a violation of the separation of church and state by the inclusion of new religious cults in schools*; (2) *schools are establishing a religion by the promotion of these cults*; (3) *religious humanism is affecting education as its status is elevated.* This new philosophy is the foundation of a new religious movement that has not only affected schools but has attracted many from their traditional faiths as a substitute.

(4) *K–12 Public-learning institutions in America are too far gone to save in their current form.* Educational reform has been tried for years and the band-aid approach no longer is able to shield the problems in schools. (5) *Colleges and universities are points of origin of cultural upheaval in American society.* Proponents of Critical Race and Gender theories advance the notions that America is both racist and gender-phobic. (6) *Race has become a central point for the redefining of America's national history and there are serious errors and distortions to the American history to which the nation's students are exposed.* The Zinn Educational Project and the *New York Times 1619 Project* are two examples of bias and liberties taken with history to advance a deceptive narrative.

To review, after forty-two years in the profession, which includes many years at a large secondary school district serving as teacher and professional development leader, fifteen years as both adjunct and full-time college professor of teacher education, student mentor, former assistant principal in a private school, author of thirteen books on education issues—and even as an associate pastor of Christian education, I can honestly say I have seen many changes in the career to which I dedicated so many years. But I regret none of my experiences. I do not hear this spoken by many teachers today. In all candor, many of them cannot wait to exit the blue-collar institutions they once called a profession.

The benefits of this book extend to those who desire knowledge about the moral slippage of what is happening in America's K–12 public schools, and in America's college and universities. Indoctrination and calls for actual and literal revolution are happening right before the nation's eyes. Some of these calls originate in the Ivory Towers of academe.

Every American of good conscience should be concerned about racial and gender cults leading children astray. Those who woke up recently to question "what happened to our family, our community and our schools—and even our nation" must read this book. I strongly recommend passing one on to parent groups, board members, and politicians.

Teachers who see and understand the direction of education in this nation, but either are too fearful of speaking up or unable to do so at this time, I appeal to you to allow this book to speak for you. As a husband, father, grandfather, and now full-time author, I cannot sit back and watch an entire generation wander aimlessly in confusion, believe in errors, and be led by a few popular social and political cult leaders in this nation.

Chapter 1

Humanism
Secular and Religious

Secularists are known for dismissing religion as merely espousing a set of blind beliefs without any evidence to support them. The crudest among them will often do it in a snide and sneering way, holding that religious belief is imaginative and fantastical—like a childhood fairy tale—in contrast to the scientific view that they espouse.[1]

Norman Geisler and William Watkins define the term *worldview* as "a way one views the world. And since people have vastly different views of the world, depending on the perspective from which they view the world, it is clear that one's world view makes a world of difference."[2] It makes a difference how a person views the world because it affects how a person views reality. In fact, a worldview is an "interpretive framework through which or by which one makes sense out of the data of life and the world."[3] Humanists would have American society believe there is only one valid lens through which to view the world, and of course it is theirs.

There are differences in the types of filters used to determine reality and truth, which is associated with one's worldview. What is clear is that reality is true—and so is the denial of reality. Whether using a personal lifestyle lens to filter or thinking something is real when it is not, both draw forth truth statements, but such lenses prompt errors in numerous places.[4]

For example, much has been made over the years about the rise of secularism, albeit separate and apart from religion. Our nation likes to echo the rhetoric that there is a constitutional wall of separation between church and state, based largely on the 1802 Thomas Jefferson letter to the Danbury Baptists. In that letter, Jefferson stated, "I contemplate with sovereign reverence that act of the whole American people which declared that their legislature should make no law respecting an establishment of religion, or prohibiting the free exercise thereof, thus building a wall of separation between Church & State."[5] The actual phrase of addressing this separation appears nowhere in the Constitution.

The idea of the separation of church and state and additional clarification also stems from the Supreme Court case *United States v. Reynolds* (1879),[6] among others. Reynolds is a case involving the Mormon Church, with Reynolds attempting to defend polygamy as a First Amendment right. Reynolds' conviction of marrying another woman, while he was already married, was upheld. In addition, although the belief in polygamy was left alone with Reynolds, the court decided that it could not uphold the correctness of the practice of polygamy and that people cannot void a law due to their religion.

There occur regular debates as to whether religion and secularism are somewhat tied historically, particularly in relation to the Reynolds case. For example, in 1879, would Reynolds have had a better chance in Utah by marrying a second wife civilly, apart from religion? Relying on his Mormon faith, he attempted to appeal to the freedom of religious expression provided in the First Amendment.

In terms of actions that stem from beliefs, actions always seem subject to higher levels of scrutiny by the public and especially between those with dissimilarities. As a starting point, it is best to revisit the first clause of the First Amendment to the U.S. Constitution. It states that "Congress shall make no law respecting an establishment of religion, or prohibiting the free exercise thereof."[7] This is the foundation of religious liberty, and it comes with clear prohibitions on the federal government—specifically the Legislative Branch of the U.S. government.

With that foundation established, what exactly is the meaning of the terms *humanist, secular, and sacred*? Do the beliefs and practices of each have to be tethered to an actual, recognized church or religious organization in order to be considered *religious*? Throughout this chapter and the book, this author will refer to the terms *secular* and *humanist/humanism* interchangeably, as American history and culture have come to understand the terms accordingly.

HUMANIST/HUMANISM

A humanist is a person who believes in humanism; that is, a humanist believes that the needs of humans and the values espoused by humans exceed those of any postulates and practices associated with religious faith. There are three basic types of humanists: (1) Strict secular humanists, who want to apply similar levels of importance to family, but without holding to a stated religious or biblical meaning. (2) Functional humanists—those that allow humanism to function when it is expedient for them, and the results are what humanists would consider good works.

(3) There is a third group that are religious humanists and incorporate a blend of both non-religious and religious actions in their practices. These view their actions as religious and civil. An example is the choice of abortion.[8] Without a belief in God, the religious humanist would have to make a rational argument that supports a functional position on life and abortion.[9] In other words, the support for or against abortion would be developed apart from a belief in God.

SECULAR

That which is secular is generally described as attitudes and activities which have no particular religious basis to them. During the European Renaissance, this period of great enlightenment resulted in the reshaping of the old ways of culture and helped shape new ways of thinking about life and reality. Inventions, formulas, experiments, and scientific theories arose and made their marks on westernized cultures. This included the early mindsets of those that colonized the fledgling new world of the Americas.

Albert Mohler describes this period and its subsequent impact on American learning institutions. He explains, "At the heart of this great intellectual shift is a secular reframing of reality . . . secular, in terms of contemporary sociological and intellectual conversation, [and] refers to the absence of any binding theistic authority or belief. . . . The closer one gets to most American colleges or universities, the closer one gets to a secular public space—an intellectually secular place."[10] But it must be added, what is secular in name only may well be religious by actions.

SACRED

Gordon Lynch defines sacred as "what people collectively experience as absolute, non-contingent realities which present normative claims over the meanings and conduct of social life."[11] Lynch notes that something which carries the label of sacred does not necessarily pertain to some sort of exclusive "religious category."[12] However, in general, anything to do with God or gods, or is dedicated to a venerated purpose, is deemed sacred.

Some humanists claim that Christianity was the basis of humanism during the Renaissance,[13] and thus formed part of the understanding of the sacred. Marcia Pally views the defined terms through the lenses of politics and power, and adds the contrast between government institutions and the citizenry. Pally explains:

> "Secular" and "neutral toward religion" are taken to mean neither governments antagonistic to religion nor societies devoid of religion. Rather they refer to institutions whose authority to develop concepts and implement policy is not seen as coming from the divine. The authority of neutral, liberal, democratic government, for instance, comes from citizen consent, common law, and constitutions. It is the governmental and legal systems that are secular and neutral, not societies, which may include many believers. The purpose of neutral, liberal democracy is not to be more antagonistic toward believers than toward other citizens but to allow sectarian and nonsectarian ways of life to develop freely. . . . In sum, what liberal democracy strives for is fair, unbiased procedures in government and the judiciary, as well as pluralistic freedom of conscience to criticize the state.[14]

HUMANISM AND RELIGION

Throughout history, American education has had charges leveled against it. Depending on the location, community, and general political culture at the time, education in America has been categorized as both the victim of a failed mission and the savior to millions of young people. The odd part of this seemingly strange pair of opposites is that the current state of education demonstrates an interesting overlap of the two.

Despite efforts to denounce the fact, education is portrayed today more comprehensively as a large umbrella rather than as one entity. In some ways, American education manifests itself as salvific to life,[15] while at the same time accessing and recruiting souls for its continued mission.[16]

Education as Savior

To the religious liberals, religious humanists, and political left in our nation, public education is proclaimed as the savior of people, the epitome of personal enlightenment, and the gatekeeper to economic success.[17] Yet, many of these place their children in private schools, revealing an elitist hypocrisy. To those on the religious and political right, public education tends to comes across as an indoctrination of students and as a nefarious force to redefine society away from the values upon which the United States was founded.[18]

The rise of private religious schools and charter schools should tell us something about K–12 public-learning institutions and their subsequent direction. What is equally as telling is the number of articles and books that are being written in the post-religious era in America.

Scholars are revisiting the supposed boundaries between the sacred and secular. One of the reasons is that many Americans struggle over the loss of what used to be a finer point of "knowing who we are."[19] This can be attributed to the fact that what has been "mightily diminished during the past several decades"[20] is one's religious affiliation and membership. Yet people claim to be religious in beliefs and actions, which amounts to a most interesting form of post-Christian spirituality.

THE INFLUENCE OF RELIGION

Mainline denominations have been hemorrhaging members for decades,[21] while congregations and professions extolling agnosticism and atheism have peaked.[22] Evangelical churches are sensing a slippage away of their members.[23] The *good news* does not seem to have the same impact it once had. Maybe this is because it is not presented as it once was presented. For example, when religion and good news are secularized, it becomes feel-good teachings and less theological absolutes. The theology of Joel Osteen is a prime example of religion packaged in religious humanistic feel-good wrappings.[24]

In 2019, membership in the Southern Baptists, the largest protestant denomination in America, "fell to 14.8 million, which is the first time the number dipped below 15 million since 1987."[25] Groups of younger people seem to be paying more attention to secular culture these days than they are teachings of the church. And there are many reasons for this. One of these reasons is the interest and rise of *secular religionism*. But this trend has a historical precedent.

Educational Messianism

Rousas Rushdoony, the late editor of the *Philosophical and Historical Studies of the International Library of Philosophy and Theology*, traced messianic directive through the history of education. He discovered:

> The messianic character of American education received its direction from Horace Mann (1796–1858), aptly called the "Father of Common Schools." It would be easy to point out that European educators have surpassed Mann in maintaining that the schools are the means, instruments, vehicles, and true church by which salvation is given to society. The marked difference between continental and American educational theory has been that continental Europe often developed its schools with either a specifically anti-Christian impetus or a post-Christian concept of society, whereas in America, for some time, both because of inherent developments and as a result of Mann's work, education presented its aims as the fulfillment of Christianity.[26]

This comes as no surprise that Rushdoony would perceive the nature of education as salvific to American culture. As a dominionist, this is to be expected. Advocates of the dominion theological position believed that "the state has a duty to serve God, or to be Christian, to be a part of God's kingdom, or else it shall be judged by him."[27] It is dominion they have always been after—a dominion that will be a conquest of the entire world.[28] Secularism has now adopted the dominionist's refrain, and humanism has become influential in American society. This is also found in the teachings of Islam. Religion still persists in American society today.

Religion and Replacement

Religion has always had an influence in the affairs of the world. Politics and diplomacy are close seconds. The impact of religion upon International Relations (IR) is a good example of secular religionism, the extent to which religion impacts secular thinking and decision-making. For example, Samantha May, Erin Wilson et al. trace religious influence upon the political state in the west, by examining the use and justification of Treaty of Westphalia. The treaty is examined in terms of the spread of European and other nation-states, previous wars and violence, and the impact upon international relations.[29]

The authors maintain that "separation of the public and private—and religion's relegation to the latter domain"[30] sets the tone for understanding what is viewed as the "general undermining of religious beliefs,"[31] which was intended to limit and eventually diminish religion's social significance. Basically, Westphalia focused on two wars and the resulting political powers and religious rights that were established afterwards. The following is a brief summary describing the Peace of Westphalia.

- The Peace of Westphalia was a series of peace treaties signed between May and October 1648 in the Westphalian cities of Osnabrück and Münster. The treaties ended both the Thirty Years' War and the Eighty Years' War.[32]
  - The Thirty Years' War was a series of wars in Central Europe between 1618 and 1648. Initially a war between various Protestant and Catholic states in the fragmented Holy Roman Empire, it developed into a conflict involving most of the great powers.[33]
  - The Eighty Years' War, or Dutch War of Independence (1568–1648), was a revolt of the Seventeen Provinces against the political and religious hegemony of Philip II of Spain, the sovereign of the Habsburg, the Netherlands.[34]

History is quick to remind the interested that religion has been used and manipulated by both state and non-state actors. Religion has been used to influence outcomes that would affect both secular and sacred-based institutions. Among the entities in America that came under this influence were public-learning institutions. Accordingly, May writes, "Religion is not simply concerned with supernatural entities and the nature and existence of a transcendental realm. It is also, crucially, a framework through which to interpret and respond"[35] to world and local occurrences. Through these responses, and with purposeful means, the use of "symbolism, rhetoric, images, narrative, histories, myths, values and experiences, religious ideas and influences continue to intervene in, and unsettle, the supposedly ordered rational nature of secular politics."[36]

Religion as Education

In the past, America has had religion *as* education for centuries, and generations have graduated from many such denominational and church-based educational institutions. Education is become more like a religion today and amounts to one of the major reasons for the eventual development of religious secular humanism.[37]

American "society is distanced from Christian theism as the fundamental explanation of the world and as the moral structure of human society."[38] But in religious humanism, there is the replacement of a foundational religious teaching with another foundation just as religious. This replacement mitigates the explicit reliance upon Judeo-Christian teachings. In fact, in this new religion "Christian truth claims have lost all binding authority in the culture."[39]

The loss of Christian claims affected even the most basic of social relationships in America. Mary Eberstadt explains. "The diminution of active Christianity, in particular, has other consequences that no one has even begin to map. Secularization also means that many people no longer experience the opposite sex as those with a religious background are instructed to do—as figurative sisters and brothers united in fellowship. Once more people have been deprived of a familial, nonsexual knowledge of the opposite sex, and another healthy bond between the sexes has been frayed."[40]

Actions as Religion

Marcia Pally adds:

> By the turn of the twentieth century, significant numbers of evangelicals felt that a Social Gospel movement was expending too much time on charity and not enough on saving souls. The concern was basically a shift from a *this-worldly* to an *otherworldly* emphasis, in terms of the sense that a choice had to be made between the two.
>
> This emphasis grew, and along with the influence of Romanticism, the shift to social welfare activities became a religious staple. While some Christians interpreted Romanticism and came away with a focus on a loving, fatherly God who forgives (leading to charitable activity), others were captured by the drama of Romantic apocalypticism.[41]

As an example, we turn to the late American literary critic, Meyer Howard "Mike" Abrams. In section five of his essay, *Apocalypse: Theme and Variations* characterizes Romantic apocalypticism as an "apocalypse of consciousness: the mind of man possesses the power, by an interior revolution, to transform his intellect and imagination, and by so doing transform his perception of the everyday world into a new earth in which he will be thoroughly at home."[42] In Abrams, there is an obvious allusion to the humanistic elements of mankind's pursuit of internal change. What is discovered is that the practice of religious humanism focuses on actions as theology.

During the 1960s, there was a surge in the influx of eastern religions, some of which were made attractive by the Beatles' experimentation. Even Satan became a modern object of worship at the time, as a result of the formation of the Church of Satan by Anton Szandor LaVey. Evangelicalism changed in the 1960s with the Jesus Movement and the Hippie-era, Jesus counter-culture.

Nevertheless,

> What perhaps best characterizes post-sixties evangelicalism is irony. In well-meaning effort to reassert anti-authoritarianism, self-reliant moral conduct, evangelicals lost sight of self-reliant, church-state separation and hitched themselves to the authority of the state. The irony emerged as early as 1947, when the Supreme Court ruled that church-state separation applies not only to the national government but also to the states. This put evolution into public schools (*Everson v. Board of Education 1947*) and took prayer out (*Epperson v. Arkansas 1968*).[43]

Currently, there is a strong advocacy for the teaching of both creationism and intelligent design in public schools. The popularity remains high despite Supreme Court cases limiting the scope of what has been categorized as religious in nature.[44] Incremental attempts by some to bridge the secular and the sacred accelerated into areas of science and history. This acceleration can be viewed in contrast by examining the Intelligent Design movement, the establishment of *Seattle's Discovery Institute*, the *New York Times* 1619 revisionist history project, and the *Thomas More Society*, among others.

Anyone having come through the competitive, *religious menu movement* of the 1970s remembers the "I Found It" evangelistic era, the "I Never Lost It" response, and the Hare Krishna at America's airports. There were also Jim Jones and the People's Temple of San Francisco, the Moonies, the Billy Graham stadium evangelism, and the rise of several eastern religions that parallel various American-born philosophies. Simultaneously, the rise of televangelism and the cult of personality seemed to dominate radio and television airwaves.

There is a certain luxury in being able to compare decades and follow trends. Trends are things that change in cultures and usually result in the establishment of temporary, but memorable norms. That being said, there is an uneasy feeling from the current activist paradigm that is affecting many in American schools today.

Altar calls are now offered by activist teachers in classrooms, and by special sensitivity training sessions at school district meetings and assemblies across America. The *good news* messages today are packaged in racial, gender, and identity movements' doctrinal tenets, as these have profound impacts upon educational philosophies and in K–12 school curricula. Post-Christian, secular America is captured in the words of Jacques Ellul.

Darrell Fasching describes Jacques Ellul's post-Christian theology, in terms of global ethics. He writes, "For Ellul, the sacred makes a virtue out of necessity in which our utopian hopes deliver us into some literal apocalyptic self-descriptive destiny. Today, technique replaces nature as that new realm of necessity that surrounds and overwhelms us and on which we depend for our very existence. It takes the place of nature as the realm of the sacred—the object of our fascination and dread."[45]

Fasching continues and further explains Ellul's de-emphasis of the sacred: "If we follow Ellul's sociological analysis, in a sacred society one expects to find God at the center, in the sacred temple what reinforces ethnocentric identity. In such a society, all who are the same are sacred and human, all others who are different are profane and less than human.... But the biblical tradition of the holy is anti-ethnocentric. It decenters our expectations and insists that God cannot be found at the center of our society, or even at the center of our religion, but only outside of it—in the stranger, the one who is not like us.... Hospitality is the direct embodiment of the holy."[46]

HUMANISM IN POST-CHRISTIAN AMERICA

Humanists prefer the use of terms that do not imply luck, a deity, or superstition should be outside the realms of any discussion involving human experiences. Humanists also claim they are "analytical by nature,"[47] and that words are to be taken seriously.[48]

As a replacement paradigm in post-Christian America, this assertion necessarily comes under some scrutiny. The humanist is truly selective in what words are acceptable and germane. For example, any person claiming there is a Creator of the universe is ruled as fanciful and entertaining myth, and immediately discarded from rational discourse. In other words, anything that does not fit the narrow framework of humanist thinking is canceled. When this occurs, the humanist provides evidence that not *all* words are taken seriously. This illustrates Ellul's sociology.

An example of humanists' undertaking in post-Christian America is evident in the use of the term *miraculous*. This term has no place in referring to childbirth because the humanist cannot completely analyze the event to which the term may be applied. Therefore, the truth of the matter is actually that humanists believe in and trust their *own* words, not just anyone's words. They take their own words seriously and prepackage an acceptable and established vocabulary. Thus, the humanist exemplifies the meaning of what can be construed as *high-brow cancel culture*.

Legal Battles

In the federal district court case, the *American Humanist Association v. United States Federal Bureau of Prisons (2014)*, the court found that humanism should be "treated like . . . religions, such as, Christians, Muslims, Rastafarians,"[49] etc. The court also found a place to declare that secular humanism is a religion for Establishment Clause purposes. The court went even futher and determined that "humanism should be treated as *religion* for purposes of the Equal Protection Clause, which prohibits religious discrimination."[50] The federal courts seem to be moving in the direction that humanism is to be treated as any other religion, for purposes of establishment and free exercise.[51] What should be made of this?

One of the downsides of being defined as a religion is the type of scrutiny the federal courts apply to cases involving religious practices of the group. If the courts ever decide that theoretical teachings such as evolution, or atheism, are closely connected to religious humanism, then there has been a substantial violation of Jefferson's wall of separation of church and state. The humanists might have to sacrifice their theories from being presented in K–12 public-learning institutions, because of the Establishment Clause of the First Amendment.

Post-Christian America is not meant to be taken as an era of post-religious beliefs and post-religious practices under the First Amendment. What has arisen in this era is that Christianity has come under liberal fire by the advocates of American cancel culture because of Christianity being labeled as a

White man's religion. Reducing the faith of an estimated 2.5 billion because of race is an interesting ploy, which is addressed in other chapters in this book. As it stands, many other nations do not view it in a similar manner.[52]

The Shape of Humanism

Humanism is a belief system shaped largely over time by ideas originating during the Enlightenment period and has grown by way of liberal *religious denominations*. The values espoused by humanism are stated as non-religious. Humanism rejects any notion of the supernatural, yet elevates "human dignity, and places trust in the ability of cooperative human effort to create a better future."[53]

The challenge for humanists is to explain the origin of individual human dignity over animals and nature, and square this with the notion of personal dignity, as it relates to human cooperation. Although humanism claims it is not religiously dogmatic by design, its three Manifestos are evidence of its dogma. The truth is humanism is flexible and changes due to the nature of its progressivism and liberal associations.

Humanists stand firm on their three Manifestos as beliefs that represent "a consensus view of what Humanists believe at a particular time. . . . Humanism does not stand still."[54] Humanists try to create barriers not only toward what may be viewed as the establishment of religion but also to the free exercise of religion—even among students at school. But, as has already been established, humanism itself is religious. The reality is these barriers helped to "lay the legal and cultural groundwork for eventually substituting atheism for Christianity as the religion of U.S. schooling."[55] Joy Pullman, writing for The Federalist, asserts:

> The truth is that there is no neutrality about religion. To not believe in God is a religious belief, just as believing in God is a religious belief. To include the Bible in curricula is a religious decision, just like not including the Bible in curricula is a religious decision. To pray or not to pray: both are religious questions. . . . Either we are all allowed to educate our children according to our religious beliefs, or some get to impose their religious beliefs on others. . . . U.S. public schools impose religious beliefs on children. According to young Americans who have abandoned the family's faith, they did so on average before leaving high school. One of their top reasons for abandoning the faith is

the scientism they are taught in their schools. The other top reason is the sexual relativism they are taught in their schools.[56]

Pullman had some of her concerns addressed in the recent U.S. Supreme Court case of *Espinoza v. Montana Department of Revenue* (2020). The issue was whether parents and taxpayers had any choices about the kinds of religion their children were taught. Albeit, this was more narrowly decided through whether "private donations may support schools that make their religious beliefs explicit."[57]

Nevertheless, the question raised was whether such donations and state tax deductions for the donations were allowed to be distributed by the state to religious schools. Previously, "Montana's tax agency . . . banned religious schools from accessing these private donation[s] on the grounds that would violate the state constitution's ban on using public funds for sectarian schools."[58]

In a blow to humanists, the Supreme Court held, "The application of the Montana Constitution's 'no-aid' provision to a state program providing tuition assistance to parents who send their children to private schools discriminated against religious schools and the families whose children attend or hope to attend them in violation of the free exercise clause."[59] The judgment was 5-4, and the decision of the lower court that held aid could not be distributed back to students who attended religious schools was reversed and remanded back to the lower court.[60]

There is a certain attractiveness to the ideas of modern humanism. These ideas have found their way into classrooms and lecture halls across America. The popularity of humanistic religious teachings in schools does not appear to be on the wane. There are clear efforts to convert students, and this is discussed in chapter 5. Attention is now turned to why humanism is religious.

WHY HUMANISM IS RELIGIOUS

The Dutch philosopher Hans Kelsen argued against what he called "secular religion."[61] Secular religion, as an idea, "boils down to the negative thesis that secular transcendence is an oxymoron." He maintains that there is no religion without transcendence; likewise, there is no religion without a God.

Bert van Roermund explains, Kelsen's "central tenet, repeated over and over again, is that secular transcendence is a self-defeating concept. . . . He explains time and time again that concepts like progress, perfection, redemption, salvation, sovereignty, and their ilk, are perfectly understandable in secular terms and should be assessed by secular criteria."[62]

How does Kelsen's thinking relate to the topic of religious humanism? *First*, humanism promotes mankind as an arbiter of decisions but uses religious terminology by which to express human authority. In short, people are in control of their own destiny. Essentially, humanism is an attempt to incorporate reality with potentiality, human existence, experience, and choice. The humanist has a dilemma with the fact that nothing human has arrived into existence by itself. Nevertheless, the humanist ascribes innate power of control to humans.

Second, if one's humanist and intolerant ideology is a substitute for traditional religious authority, then Kelsen's ideas and the modern identity theories are interestingly coalescent. For example, if people can assert unique and unfettered authority over their identities, then they can justify identity without biology. If this be the case, then what is to stand in the way of a religion without God? All one needs to do is exercise autonomous authority in words and belief. *If there is identity without biology, then there can be religion without God.*

Whether modern humanists agree there are religious aspects to their humanistic positions and beliefs is not at issue. For those humanists that would make it an issue, the essential argument today then sounds more like a validation of Eric Voegelin's conclusion that humanist notions are "religious ideologies in disguise."[63]

Pippa Norris and Ronald Inglehart view the western world as having been so potently affected by the push for social transformations that this push has "reduced the salience of religious belief."[64] Thus, the result is secularization. The contrast to this is the religious believer's understanding that "ultimately, secularism is an illusion about the world, presumably because it denies the believer's faith in the truth of God."[65]

Along with acknowledging that many Christian activists complain that secularism has exceeded its place in American culture, the authors assert "that which is holy is actually quite sacred . . . and it can be sacred and holy without reference to a supreme God."[66] Thus, humanism fits the qualifications of at least religious teachings, if not a religion itself.

Humanism and Shared Characteristics

While it is true that humanists generally do not consider themselves as religious, it is clear that some of them "consider Humanism to be a religion."[67] There are two distinct camps in modern humanism: religious humanists and secular humanists. Religious humanists "are still humanists—they are atheists or agnostic, skeptics . . . they are secularists, and they reject the supernatural. If there is a difference between secular and religious Humanists it is how they express and practice their Humanist life-stance, but the life-stance is the same in both cases."[68] Humanism cannot be labeled areligious. The evidence is mounting that it has always had religious elements, regardless of the denial by some adherents.

Austin Cline writes about the growth in diversity in modern humanism. He asserts, "Because Modern Humanism is so often associated with secularism, it is sometimes easy to forget that humanism also has a very strong and very influential religious tradition associated with it. Early on, especially during the Renaissance, this religious tradition was primarily Christian in nature; today, however, it has become much more diverse."[69]

In fact, religious humanism "shares with other types of humanism the basic principles of an overriding concern with humanity—the needs of human beings, the desires of human beings, and the importance of human experiences. For religious humanists, it is the human and the humane which must be the focus."[70]

Whether the object of worship is the self, or whether it is a social group cause, the religious elements persist. These elements find ways into institutions throughout society, and churches and educational institutions are no exceptions.

HUMANISTIC RELIGIOUS AWAKENING

The title of this section is not an oxymoron. A growing number of today's students are intoxicated with religious zeal in their self-expression and emotionally based identities. However, amidst their stupor, they actually remain emotionally vulnerable in their confusion. The students' brains and emotions are nowhere near fully developed, which is one reason why so many are easy targets for the shifting winds of cultural change.

An example of this confusion in our young adults comes by way of an unscientific ideology based on narrow identity politics. The acceptance of this ideology may be expressed in terms of the fluidity of personal identity, occurring over the course of one's lifetime. What has not changed—and probably never will—is that at whatever juncture or in whatever transitional phase students find themselves, these same students fully expect others to recognize them in ways they recognize themselves.

This expectation is a byproduct of thinking that (1) identity is larger than life itself and that (2) fluidity can somehow replace firmness. When these are challenged, the result is student disappointment and anger. Some react by name-calling. Others fall into self-loathing, and some even consider self-harming actions as a result.

One of the more humanistic beliefs in American education institutions is that biology and science have little to do with a person's claimed identity and internal convictions concerning one's *defined personage*. The argument is that such definitions are the results of personal choices. Can this be humanistic without having met the criteria of self-analysis? Austin Cline explains, "Whatever our problems might be, we will only find the solution in our own efforts and should not wait for any gods or spirits to come and save us from our mistakes."[71]

Humanistic Evangelism

Schools are being used to spread modern humanist beliefs. For example, in centuries past, the basic fundamental truth about gender was accepted at face value. Such determinations were left unchallenged. The nuclear family, human biology, and religious faith were sacred territories in culture. This is not necessarily the case any longer.

Today, these sacred territories have been either redefined or dismissed. Staying true to form, each is now merely a choice in the minds of humanists. Notice the shift in authority. Gender and sexual fluidity is now multiple choice, and it is quite appealing to young people seeking more empowerment over their lives. In humanism the *self* is now the deity over all things. What could be more god-like than the idea that one can create his or her own identity by will?

Recognition of a human as one who would be as a god is to determine that life is controlled through personal logical choices and outcomes. Such gods mandate religious devotion and tolerance from others, for their personal decisions. Such requirements are actually secular mandates for worship. This has led to a cult of personality.

Many religious cults of the past sought to ensnare with their own brands of appeal. Cults still ensnare today by uplifting celebrations of self through the worship of one's identity. It sounds circular, and it is. From Shirley McClain's *Out on a Limb* statement of *I am god . . .* to the current *I am god and my choices are my self-worship*, the seat of personal authority has not changed all that much.

The reality is, as history goes, the tombs are full of the self-deified and others claiming their own alternate identities. Lurking in the background is this ultimate reality of the absolute of death that swirls like a vortex over the religious and non-religious alike. Are generations still considering their mortality these days?

Detached Generation

Self-expression can be a numbing intoxicant. For example, the fact that Generation Z has had many things handed to them without struggle, and that they view themselves as entitled, means they are already confused about their place in the real world.[72] The movement toward self-identification does have its genesis, partly in the social and emotional constructs presented to them while in school. But it is also derived from removing any foundation of belief in God, where the purpose and value of personhood originates, outside of feelings. *Generation Z wants feelings of religious connectivity, but without religious connections.*

Suicide rates and opioid drug addictions are evidence that something is not right in the land of new identities. Drugs have long been a part of religious cult groups and will probably remain as such. Yet, there seems to be a terrible epidemic of children being treated medically today with opioids. Why are so many students suffering from this major problem?

According to the Schaeffer Center for Health Policy and Economics and the Keck School of Medicine at the University of Southern California, researchers found that nearly 40 percent of the time, young people, including young adults seen in a general emergency department, "are three times more likely to be given an opioid prescription compared with similar young people treated in pediatric emergency departments."[73] A serious question needs to be answered by advocates of identity politics. If students are supposedly finding themselves, why then are they working so hard to remove themselves from their stated identities by drug use?

There is cause for great concern in terms of the ease at which the younger generation is prescribed addictive pain killers. In fact, the authors of the Schaeffer and Keck study are greatly concerned about what increasing opioid prescription drugs are doing to the developing brains of adolescents, given their vulnerability in the development of their fragile brain chemistry, and the long-term addiction and effects well into adulthood.[74]

All over America, growing numbers of young people are dealing with one addiction or another, and attending school under the influence of drugs. This adds a new level of concern to the landscape. In other words, students might not be in the best shape, or have the capacity these days to weed out truth from error, and be able to evaluate what they hear and see. Still, they are adamant that in their confusion they have found their true identities and that they are steady and mature enough to make their own life-altering decisions. One should question whether drugs have any part in students' confusion.

What is of great concern today to physicians, educators, and parents had a peculiar advocate in the 1960s. The late Harvard professor, Dr. Timothy Leary, encouraged students to turn on with LSD and tune in to themselves, while dropping out of the traditional and cultural expectations placed upon them. There is a peculiar sense that Leary's encouragement was somewhat prophetic and is finding renewed interest among the present younger generations.

In real terms, today's students have listened to people who claim they should look deep within their confused souls and allow the confusion to work itself out by experimenting with a variety of cultural, gender, or sexual expressions. In so doing, they are told they can arrive at determining their own personal destinies by self-reflection, a philosophy taught by many religions today.

Alleviating confusion for students and coming to terms with internal discord, in a sense, is similar to a type of religious or spiritual conversion. The distinction is that such a conversion enables a person's mind to feel free from what determined the old identity, and no one but the person knows whether such a conversion is genuine or not. The problem arises when the new identity faces the same challenge of the previous identity.

Evangelicals Turn Left

Has humanism affected the church to move farther left theologically, or has the church affected humanism by pulling it rightward? The term religious humanism implies both. Around 2010, there was a shift in what could be called a conscious effort by evangelicals to involve themselves in social and issues. "One sign of this change was the way evangelicals viewed church involvement in elections."[75] The majority considered that it was not within the roles of the church to become involved in supporting political candidates. So, they began supporting issues instead. In fact, "evangelical concerns were broadening from abortion, gay marriage, and electoral wins to poverty relief, environmental protection, and immigration reform."[76]

The shift in action led to a split, essentially between those who bore the titles of conservative and liberal evangelicals. The mainline Christian denominations began to veer more to the left politically, and adopted more secular tenets on social and moral issues. The more conservative evangelicals moved somewhat farther to the right on these same issues, but adopted some humanist practices in the process.

Specifically, Black evangelical churches began moving away from their religious traditions, which served as the underpinnings for the twentieth-century Civil Rights Movement. In the words of John Lewis, "We were in Selma that day because of our faith."[77] It is true that the Black churches hold to some of the more conservative views on abortion and same-sex marriage, but they are more active liberally on social and racial issues. It is also true that they hold on to some of the more liberal views on the economic issue, government assistance, race relations, and civil rights.[78] Some very progressive individuals in churches of all denominations even advocate for government to replace reliance on God in the lives of people.[79]

For over one-half century, most evangelicals have claimed association with the Republican Party. The delimited political tenets to social issues were defined by the pro-life and pro-traditional nuclear family platform. During George W. Bush's two terms in office, the Republican Party added the concerns of poverty, faith-based social programs, and began to favor stewardship of the environment.[80]

During the Obama years, several progressive evangelical mega-churches burst onto the scene with a post-seeker emphasis. Sharing more in common with liberal mainline denominations, the emerging neo-evangelicals renewed an active focus on alleviating poverty. In fact, these emergent churches began to use similar progressive rhetoric, as they waded into more pacifistic positions on the use of violence against other nations and military intervention.

One emergent church pastor, Shane Claiborne, proclaimed that the United States is the greatest "purveyor of violence"[81] across the globe. According to Claiborne, this is what led some in the Arab world to blame American aggression and violence for the radical Muslim terrorist tragedy on September 11, 2001.

At the same time, the new evangelicals are taking notice of other areas upon which to apply *good stewardship*, some of which are typically assigned to more liberal-minded denominations. Marcia Pally observes, "Many more evangelicals look to market systems and civil society activism, donating to renewable energy research, running church programs to insulate home in poor neighborhoods or outfit them with solar panels, and reforesting land and purifying water supplies overseas.

Evangelicals who work with governmental agencies unsurprisingly give greater importance to government; role in protecting the environment, both through legislation and incentives for environment-friendly construction and other programs."[82] So, which entity, humanism or religion, has moved more closely toward the other?

THE PLACE OF FAITH IN HUMANISM

Humanism has made serious inroads into the evangelical community. It seems that both the humanist and the evangelical are more than willing to bypass facts of science and human logic, while at the same time placing trust in their *culturally adapted faith*. In other words, "Secular humanism is invigorated by the best that atheism and religious humanism have to offer—through naturalistic, yet infused by an inspiring value system."[83]

The debate between humanism and evangelical thought is contrasted by Stephen Krason, as he asserts, "Evangelical secularists embrace a narrow incomplete definition of science as just involving empirical study. They can't fathom that philosophy is also a science, which operates from evidence and sound reasoning. . . . They also can't grasp that other principles that they embrace—such as a defense of human rights and a rejection of racism—could not possibly be derived from empirical science."[84]

Krason continues, "Both the evangelical secularists and those in American institutions who have reflexively embraced their mindset—like the public-school officials who think that, say, chastity education violates the separation of church and state—can't distinguish philosophy from theology."[85]

There is a certain blind faith attributed to evangelical Christians by critics. But the same is also ascribed to religious humanists. The gospels of humanism and evangelicalism display an uncanny religious parallel. These are "beliefs that often have no basis in the empirical science they claim to be devoted to, and sometimes even defy reason. We can find these blind faith beliefs everywhere in the secular culture. Christians have even unthinkingly accepted some of these because they have heard them so often."[86]

The following is a short list of ten accepted and shared beliefs,[87] into which both the religious humanist and the evangelical place large quantities of what Krason describes as *blind faith*: (1) Global warming is real, climate change is real, and both are exclusively caused by humans. (2) Humans have evolved from lower forms of life treating the theory of evolution as a law of scientific certainty. (3) There are many forms and types of families and it makes no difference into which a child is born and reared. (4) Same-sex attraction is intrinsic and grows from birth, making change unlikely, if not impossible. (5) Men and women are essentially the same and biology has little to do in determining one's gender. (6) Gender constructs are determined by doctors, parents, or by other cultural agents. (7) It is not healthy for a child to feel as if he or she is one gender, while the parents promote another. (8) Gender is fluid and can be chosen throughout life. (9) Western democracy and capitalism are evils that demonstrate greed and the system only works for those in the top 1–2 percent. (10) Systemic and institutional racism exists in America and is part of White Supremacy, which is part of the DNA of Whites.

Placing faith in these tenets, without an understanding of the philosophical foundations that undergird each—while at the same time disregarding science that provides contrary evidence—is a blind faith. Finding a scientific study to support one's tenets and then using such a study to prove a point is akin to the evangelical finding a verse or two from Holy Writ to substantiate a belief.

This practice is also a common element between religious humanists and evangelical Christians. There is an unfortunate mindset that pervades twenty-first-century American culture. That is, winning at all costs, and the gaining of likes and accolades on social media pages is necessary for emotional and spiritual support.[88]

REDEFINING NORMS

Kim Knott, from Lancaster University in the United Kingdom, writes, "Those forging social identities in secular contexts—who draw on non-religious commitments and beliefs including atheism, humanism and secularism—mark as *sacred* those occasions (such as marriage), persons (a lover), things (a ring), place (a registry office) and principles (equality and justice) that they value above all others, and that they see as set apart and inviolable: those things that may be deemed to be both secular and sacred."[89]

Marriage. Another interesting point about humanists is the seriousness at which the majority of them desire sacred norms for themselves, yet claim no necessity to recognize the source of sacredness from a Supreme Being. It appears that marriage and other rituals and practices are quite sacred to the humanists, because they are special and elevated by human experiences.

The sense of apprehension to attribute one's experience with sacredness is somewhat revealing. Yet, would a humanist place a similar value on marriage, akin to those of religious groups, as if it is something beyond a civil union performed by a legal entity within a state?

Family. Why is a family unit so sacred, if children are mere biological productions? Both marriage and family are institutions with religious origins. For example, Genesis 2:18, 24 include the following statements: "Then the Lord God said, it is not good for the man to be alone; I will make a helper suitable for him. . . . For this cause a man shall leave his father and mother, and shall cleave to his wife; and they shall become one flesh."[90] These statements are reiterated in the New Testament in the words of Jesus Christ in several places, and by the Apostle Paul and other New Testament writers. Two of the numerous examples include:

- And He answered and said, have you not read that He who created them from the beginning made them male and female, and said, for this cause a man shall leave his father and mother and shall cleave to his wife, and the two shall become one flesh? Consequently they are no more two, but one

flesh. What therefore God has joined together, let no man separate. (Matthew 19:4–6)[91]
- For this cause a man shall leave his father and mother, and shall cleave to is wife; and the two shall become one flesh. (Ephesians 5:31)[92]

The Value of Life

The laws regarding abortion have come a long way since those early years, after *Roe v. Wade*, in 1973. Today, some public school districts, in conjunction with liberal local administrations and Planned Parenthood, have placed clinics on public school campuses.

At first glance, the abortion advocate is probably applauding such placement. But drill down into the placement and application of the services provided and the story line changes. Make no mistake about it, abortion is a sacrosanct religious practice to most humanists. The recent passing of Supreme Court Justice Ruth Bader Ginsburg emphasized the level of importance of this societal practice to both pro-choice and pro-life advocates.[93]

For example, in Los Angeles County, Planned Parenthood is set to open 50 school health and well-being centers, right on public high school campuses.[94] Again, the abortion advocate would examine this and consider that planning a family is not bad, and getting advice from counselors about sexuality is all right, and so on. Again, drilling down more deeply, the truth of the matter is revealed. Children will be offered "more extensive birth control options including intrauterine devices and arm implants." And because "California law allows minors older than 12 to obtain confidential treatment and birth control, students can access the services at these clinics without parental consent."[95]

Furthermore, counselors from Planned Parenthood will be on campuses a certain number of hours, and nurses from the organization can give physical exams, dispense conception control to children, and offer the "another set of caring adults to whom they can come with those strange life questions."[96] It remains to be seen the effects that the COVID-19 pandemic will have on Planned Parenthood's on-campus clinics, if schools remain shuttered for too long a period of time. The coronavirus may have something to do with long-term choices by children thinking about having sex.

But not all is well with Planned Parenthood's sex clinics and sexual well-being programs. A former Planned Parenthood sex educator has come out and revealed that the program is damaging to children and encourages increased sexual activity among teenagers.

Monica Cline, a woman who formerly worked as a Title X training manager for Planned Parenthood, writes, "I got a close-up view into the world of Planned Parenthood and sex education."[97] She is "speaking out against the organization's teachings."[98] When asked to help her to train young girls not to have sex, Cline was told, "No, dear . . . We're not going to teach them not to have sex. We're going to teach them how to do it safer."

The sex education training shares a variety of explicit sex acts and are geared more toward curiosity than protection. In fact, one of the biggest issues for the former trained was the secrecy of what was taught. Cline writes, "Parents are purposely left out. . . . Parents are a barrier to service. . . . This type of education does not protect our youth. It only serves to encourage them to explore all sexual activities and places a burden on them that they are not prepared to bear. . . . Their answer to happiness and empowerment is to have sex, use a condom, get tested, treated, and have an abortion."[99]

The religious humanist might see that life has certain extraordinary traits that come with the territory. Religious humanists often refer to these as human essentials. Austin Cline contrasts the relationship between religious and secular humanism. Cline writes, "The nature of religious humanism and the relationship between humanism and religion is of profound importance for humanists of all types. According to some secular humanists, religious humanism is a contradiction in terms. According to some religious humanists, all humanism is religious—even secular humanism, in its own way."[100]

To The humanist reason is king.[101] Therefore, if a person reasons that "humanism is religious in nature for someone, then that is their religion. We can question whether they are defining things coherently. We can challenge whether their belief system can be adequately described by such terminology. We can critique the specifics of their beliefs and whether they are rational. What we cannot readily do, however, is assert that, whatever they might believe, they cannot really be religious and humanists."[102]

Humanists and Truth

In a progressive world, truth is reasoned as not absolute. But in the process an absolute has been created. One very important thing to remember about postmodern, post-Christian America—whether within politics or religion—is that yesterday's truth does not necessarily have to be today's truth. This is why progressive politicians have little trouble sounding contradictory to the average person.

The fact is that *selective truth* still comes across as truth. Selective truth is as subjective and humanistic as it is progressive. If selective truth is not truth, then what about the absolute claims that love is love and that gender is fluid? Are these subjective or absolute to the humanist?

This type of secularization of truth has given birth to a form of deconstructionism "bent on the casting down of any religious or theological authority."[103] Unfortunately, this has taken up residence in the evangelical church in America, and philosophy and science have often nudged theology to the side. Nevertheless, with its own suggestions as absolutes, there can be no pretense that a certain religious element does not exist among them.

Josh Hammer demonstrates the confusion surrounding humanist suggestion as absolutes: "Cultural progressives, who reject the very humanity of unborn children but confidently assure us there are upward of 70 distinct genders, tend to have an uneasy relationship with the truth. And the proliferation of transgender pronouns—the use of biologically inaccurate pronouns to describe those afflicted with gender dysphoria—is among the more pernicious tools in the broader arsenal that progressives use to have us question that truth."[104]

American culture has been inundated with images and information that support the transition from a traditional understanding of humanity to ideas that involve more emotions than science. When it comes to humanist views on sexuality and gender, humanists ask others "to yield to the soft tyranny of transgender pronouns is to pretend that gender dysphoria is an anodyne lifestyle on which societal legitimacy should be conferred, not a psychological malady requiring compassion and psychological treatment."[105] As with fundamentalist Christians who join recovery groups, one can only ponder how long before humanist recovery groups assemble for similar group therapy.

NOTES

1. Stephen M. Krason. "The blind faith beliefs of secular culture." *Crisis Magazine*. May 5, 2014. Retrieved May 10, 2020, from https://www.crisismagazine.com/2014/the-blind-faith-beliefs-of-secular-culture.

2. Norman L. Geisler and William D. Watkins. *Worlds apart: A handbook on worldviews*. 2003. Eugene, OR: Wipf and Stock Publishers, p. 11.

3. Ibid.

4. Ibid.

5. Thomas Jefferson. "Letters between Thomas Jefferson and the Danbury Baptists." *Bill of Rights Institute*. 1802. Retrieved August 13, 2020, from https://billofrightsinstitute.org/founding-documents/primary-source-documents/danburybaptists/.

6. *Reynolds v. United States* (1879). *Justia Supreme Court Center*. Retrieved August 13, 2020 from www.oyez.org/cases/1850-1900/98us145.

7. First Amendment to the Constitution. Retrieved August 13, 2020, from https://constitutioncenter.org/interactive-constitution/amendment/amendment-i.

8. Mary Ziegler. "Abortion opponents think they're winning: Have they set themselves up to fail?" *New York Times*. May 15, 2019. Retrieved August 15, 2020, from https://www.nytimes.com/2019/05/15/opinion/alabama-abortion-supreme-court.html.

9. Austin Cline. "Religious vs. secular humanism: What's the difference?" *Learn Religions*. February 11, 2020. Retrieved May 27, 2020, from https://www.learnreligions.com/religious-vs-secular-humanism-248117.

10. R. Albert Mohler, Jr. *The gathering storm*. 2020. Nashville, TN: HarperCollins Christian Publishing, p. 5.

11. Gordon Lynch. *The sacred in the modern world: A cultural sociological approach*. New York, NY: Oxford University Press, p. 29.

12. Ibid., pp. 15, 26, 29.

13. Austin Cline. "What is religious humanism?" *Learn Religions*. March 16, 2019. Retrieved May 22, 2020, from https://www.learnreligions.com/what-is-religious-humanism-248118.

14. Marcia Pally. *The New Evangelicals: Expanding the vision of the common good*. 2011. Grand Rapids, MI: Wm. B. Eerdmans Publishing Company, pp. 30–31.

15. Patrick Kobler. "Education saves lives." *George W. Bush Presidential Center*. August 10, 2012. Retrieved December 26, 2019, from https://www.bushcenter.org/publications/articles/2012/09/education-saves-lives.html.

16. H. L. Schacter, and J. Juvonen. (2015). "The effects of school-level victimization on self-blame: Evidence for contextualized social cognitions." *Developmental Psychology,* 51(6), 841–47.

17. Kim Parker. "The growing partisan divide in views of higher education." *Pew Research Center*. August 19, 2019. Retrieved December 26, 2019, from https://www.pewsocialtrends.org/essay/the-growing-partisan-divide-in-views-of-higher-education/.

18. Auguste Meyrat. "How public schools indoctrinate kids without almost anyone noticing." *The Federalist*. October 26, 2018. Retrieved December 26, 2019, from https://thefederalist.com/2018/10/26/public-schools-indoctrinate-kids-without-almost-anyone-noticing/.

19. Mary Eberstadt. *Primal screams: How the sexual revolution created identity politics*. 2019. West Conshohocken, PA: Templeton Press, p. 57.

20. Ibid.

21. Staff. "In U.S., decline of Christianity continues at rapid pace." *Pew Research Center*. October 17, 2019. Retrieved June 24, 2020, from https://www.pewforum.org/2019/10/17/in-u-s-decline-of-christianity-continues-at-rapid-pace/.

22. Ibid.
23. Peter Wehner. "The deepening crisis in Evangelical Christianity." *The Atlantic.* July 5, 2019. Retrieved June 24, 2020, from https://www.theatlantic.com/ideas/archive/2019/07/evangelical-christians-face-deepening-crisis/593353/.
24. Matthew Sheffield. "People like Joel Osteen are a big reason why Americans are dumping religion." *Salon.* August 30, 2017. Retrieved August 13, 2020, from https://www.salon.com/2017/08/30/religious-leaders-like-joel-osteen-are-a-big-reason-why-americans-are-dumping-religion/.
25. Mohler, *The gathering storm*, p. 190.
26. Rousas J. Rushdoony. *The messianic character of American education.* 1976. Nutley, NJ: The Craig Press, p. 18.
27. Rousas J. Rushdoony. *The Kingdom Come: Studies in Daniel and Revelation.* 1978. Fairfax, VA: Thoburn Press, pp. 39, 194.
28. Pally. *The New Evangelicals: Expanding the vision of the common good*, pp. 53, 220–21.
29. Samantha May, Erin K. Wilson, Claudia Baumgart-Ochse, and Faiz Sheikh. "The religious as political and the political as religious: Globalization, post-secularism and the shifting boundaries of the sacred." *Politics, Religion, & Ideology.* August 21, 2014. 15(3): 331–46. See especially pp. 332–38. Retrieved June 3, 2020, from https://www.tandfonline.com/doi/pdf/10.1080/21567689.2014.948526.
30. Ibid., pp. 338–39.
31. Ibid., pp. 338–39.
32. Staff. "The peace of Westphalia and sovereignty." *State University of New York-Herkimer County Community College.* 2019. Retrieved June 3, 2020, from https://courses.lumenlearning.com/suny-hccc-worldhistory/chapter/the-peace-of-westphalia-and-sovereignty/.
33. Ibid.
34. Ibid.
35. May, Wilson, Baumgart-Ochse, and Sheikh. "The religious as political and the political as religious: Globalization, post-secularism and the shifting boundaries of the sacred." *Politics, Religion, & Ideology*, p. 339.
36. Ibid.
37. Staff. "Federal court decides secular humanism is a religion." *Christianity Today.* November 5, 2014. Retrieved December 26, 2019, from https://www.christiantoday.com/article/federal-court-decides-secular-humanism-is-a-religion/42653.htm. Cf. Ilya Somin. "Atheists and secular humanists are protected by the First Amendment regardless of whether their beliefs are 'religions' or not." *The Washington Post.* November 19, 2014. Retrieved December 26, 2019, from https://www.washingtonpost.com/news/volokh-conspiracy/wp/2014/11/19/atheists-and-secular-humanists-are-protected-by-the-constitution-regardless-of-whether-their-belief-systems-should-be-considered-religions-or-not/.
38. Mohler, *The gathering storm*, p. xiii.
39. Ibid.
40. Eberstadt. *Primal screams: How the sexual revolution created identity politics*, pp. 57–58.
41. Pally. *The New Evangelicals: Expanding the vision of the common good*, p. 53.

42. Leah Bromberg. "Romantic apocalypticism in John Ruskini's 'traffic.'" *The Victorian Web*. February 18, 2011. Retrieved August 14, 2020, from http://www.victorianweb.org/authors/ruskin/bromberg.html.

43. Pally. *The New Evangelicals: Expanding the vision of the common good*, pp. 57–58.

44. Ibid., p. 83.

45. Darrell J. Fasching. "The sacred, the secular and the holy: The significance of Jacques Ellul's post-Christian theology for global ethics." *The International Jacques Ellul Society*. April 2014, p. 5. Retrieved June 2, 2020, from https://journals.wheaton.edu/index.php/ellul/article/download/414/16/.

46. Ibid.

47. David Niose. "Humanism is a religion? Why even anti-religion humanists should celebrate." *The Humanist*. November 10, 2014. Retrieved May 26, 2020, from https://thehumanist.com/commentary/humanism-is-a-religion-why-even-anti-religion-humanists-should-celebrate.

48. Ibid.

49. Howard Friedman. American Humanist Association v. United States of America. *Scribd*. October 30, 2014. Retrieved May 26, 2020, from https://www.scribd.com/document/245271872/American-Humansits-v-US?ad_group=xxc1xx&campaign=VigLink&medium=affiliate&source=hp_affiliate.

50. Niose. "Humanism is a religion? Why even anti-religion humanists should celebrate." *The Humanist*.

51. Friedman. American Humanist Association v. United States of America. *Scribd*.

52. Rev. F. L. Sackitey. "Is Christianity a Whiteman's religion and has it destroyed African culture?" *Modern Ghana*. January 21, 2011. Retrieved August 14, 2020, from https://www.modernghana.com/news/313167/is-christianity-a-whitemans-religion-and-has-it.html.

53. President and Fellows of Harvard College. "Humanism as a belief system." *The Pluralism Project*. 2020. Retrieved May 23, 2020, from https://pluralism.org/humanism-as-a-belief-system.

54. Ibid.

55. Joy Pullman. "Supreme Court to decide if atheism can keep its monopoly on K-12 schools." *The Federalist*. January 22, 2020. Retrieved January 23, 2020, from https://thefederalist.com/2020/01/22/supreme-court-to-decide-if-atheism-can-keep-its-monopoly-on-k-12-schools/.

56. Ibid.

57. Ibid.

58. Ibid.

59. Staff. "Espinoza v. Montana Department of Revenue." *SCOTUS Blog*. June 30, 2020. Retrieved July 17, 2020, from https://www.scotusblog.com/case-files/cases/espinoza-v-montana-department-of-revenue/.

60. Chief Justice John Roberts. "Kendra Espinoza, et al., petitioners v. Montana Department of Revenue et al." *Supreme Court of the United States*. June 30, 2020. Retrieved August 15, 2020, from https://www.supremecourt.gov/opinions/19pdf/18-1195_g314.pdf.

61. Bert van Roermund. "Kelsen, secular religion, and the problem of transcendence." *Netherlands Journal of Legal Philosophy.* 2015. 44(2): 100. Retrieved May 22, from https://www.bjutijdschriften.nl/tijdschrift/rechtsfilosofieentheorie/2015/2/NJLP_2213-0713_2015_044_002_002.

62. Ibid.

63. Ibid.

64. Sam Crane. *"Ancient Chinese thought in modern American life." The Useless Tree Blog.* July 16, 2005. Retrieved May 25, 2020, from https://uselesstree.typepad.com/useless_tree/2005/07/the_secular_as_.html/.

65. Ibid.

66. Ibid.

67. President and Fellows of Harvard College. "Humanism as a belief system." *The Pluralism Project.* 2020. Retrieved May 23, 2020, from https://pluralism.org/humanism-as-a-belief-system.

68. Ibid

69. Cline. "What is religious humanism?" *Learn Religions.*

70. Ibid.

71. Ibid.

72. Ernest J. Zarra III. *The entitled generation: Helping teachers teach and reach the minds and hearts of Generation Z.* 2017. Lanham, MD: Rowman & Littlefield Publishers.

73. Stephanie Hedt. "Kids treated in general ERs are more likely to be prescribed opioids." *HSC News of the University of Southern California.* October 21, 2019. Retrieved October 26, 2019, from https://hscnews.usc.edu/kids-treated-in-general-ers-are-more-likely-to-be-prescribed-opioids#:~:text=%E2%80%9CWe%20found%20that%20young%20people,at%20the%20Keck%20School%20of.

74. Ibid.

75. Pally. *The New Evangelicals: Expanding the vision of the common good*, p. 107.

76. Ibid.

77. J. Meacham. *American Gospel: God, the Founding fathers, and the Making of a Nation.* 2006. New York, NY: Random House, p. 192.

78. Pally. *The New Evangelicals: Expanding the vision of the common good*, p. 108.

79. Candace Owens. "Liberty University Convocation." *YouTube.* September 26, 2018. Retrieved July 7, 2020, from https://www.youtube.com/watch?v=rrKOnp1dcoo.

80. Pally. *The New Evangelicals: Expanding the vision of the common good*, pp. 114–16.

81. Ibid., p. 193.

82. Ibid., p. 223.

83. Scotty Hendricks. "Why secular humanism can do what atheism can't." *Big Think.* August 14, 2019. Retrieved July 17, 2020, from https://bigthink.com/culture-religion/what-is-secular-humanism.

84. Krason. "The blind faith beliefs of secular culture." *Crisis Magazine.*

85. Ibid.

86. Ibid.

87. Ibid.

88. Sonica Rautela. "Spirituality and social media: Connecting the dots." *International Journal of Interactive Mobile Technologies*. September, 2019. 13(9):81. Retrieved August 16, 2020, from https://www.researchgate.net/publication/335647132_Spirituality_and_Social_Media_Connecting_the_Dots.

89. Kim Knott. "The secular sacred: In-between or both/and?" In Abby Day, Giselle Vincent, and Christopher R. Cotter, Editors. *In social identities between the sacred and the secular*. 2013. Surrey, UK: Ashgate Publishers, passim.

90. Genesis 2:18, 24. *New American Standard Bible*.

91. Matthew 19:4–6. *New American Standard Bible*.

92. Ephesians 5:31. *New American Standard Bible*.

93. Sarah McCammon. "Ginburg's death a 'pivot point' for abortion rights, advocates say." *NPR*. September 19, 2020. Retrieved September 23, 2020, from https://www.npr.org/sections/death-of-ruth-bader-ginsburg/2020/09/19/914864867/ginsburgs-death-a-pivot-point-for-abortion-rights-advocates-say.

94. Sonali Kohli. "L.A. County and Planned Parenthood to open 50 high school sexual health and well-being centers." *Los Angeles Times*. December 12, 2019. Retrieved January 14, 2020, from https://www.latimes.com/california/story/2019-12-12/50-new-sexual-health-wellbeing-centers-in-l-a-high-schools.

95. Ibid.

96. Ibid.

97. Monica Cline. "I was a sex educator trained by Planned Parenthood; here is what I taught your kids." *Washington Examiner*. September 5, 2019. Retrieved July 17, 2020, from https://www.washingtonexaminer.com/opinion/op-eds/i-was-a-sex-educator-trained-by-planned-parenthood-here-is-what-i-taught-your-kids.

98. Heather Clark. "Former Planned Parenthood sex educator says program damages kids, encourages sexual activity among youth." *Christian News*. May 14, 2020. Retrieved May 15, 2020, from https://christiannews.net/2020/05/14/former-planned-parenthood-sex-educator-says-program-damages-kids-encourages-sexual-activity-among-youth/.

99. Cline. "I was a sex educator trained by Planned Parenthood; here is what I taught your kids." *Washington Examiner*.

100. Cline. "Religious vs. secular humanism: What's the difference?" *Learn Religions*.

101. Ibid.

102. Ibid.

103. Mohler, *The gathering storm*, p. 14.

104. Josh Hammer. "The fifth circuit rejects the lie of transgender pronouns." *National Review*. January 27, 2020. Retrieved May 6, 2020, from https://www.nationalreview.com/2020/01/transgender-pronouns-fifth-circuit-rejects-them-and-lie-they-stand-on/.

105. Ibid.

Chapter 2

Education as Religion

If church, community, and family have all weakened markedly during the past half century, as measures indicate overwhelmingly, might any substitute institutions have emerged to take their places?[1]

If there is no higher law than human law, then one must logically be a stick-in-the-mud conservative. Logically, atheists must worship the State, or, in a democracy, "consensus," for there is nothing higher. If religion dies, politics takes its place.[2]

There are at least as many definitions for education as there are for religion. The interesting thing is there are elements common in both definitions. The fact is most people associate education with schooling. However, education is the noun, while schooling is the verb. The former is the product, and the latter is the process. The same can be said for religion. Religion is the noun, and practice is the verb. Beliefs, worldviews, and practices are common to both—even if viewed through different lenses.

In general, religion is defined as "a set of beliefs concerning the cause, nature, and purpose of the universe . . . a specific fundamental set of beliefs and practices generally agreed upon by a number of persons or sects . . . the body of persons adhering to a particular set of beliefs and practices . . . something one believes in and follows devotedly; a point or matter of ethics or conscience."[3] Education is both formal and informal, but refers to the "process of teaching or learning, especially in a school or college, or the knowledge that you get from this."[4] It is at this juncture where teachers and professors have the most impact.

Chapter 2

PUBLIC EDUCATION AS RELIGION

Public education institutions in America are now substitutes for other houses of worship. If religion is the opiate of the masses, then secular religion is a new version of the daily fix for the secular addict. One need not mention the divine or a god to be religious, as pointed out in chapter 1.

Borrowing from some key passages of ancient scripture, an understanding of the importance placed on teaching becomes clear. This importance of these scriptures was carried over to the American colonies, into schoolhouses, and the founding of colleges up and down the eastern seaboard, during the colonial era.

While imprisoned, the Apostle Paul wrote the following passage to the Church at Ephesus. "And He gave some as apostles, and some as prophets, and some as evangelists, and some as pastors and teachers."[5] Many of these roles, usually reserved for the church, church schools, and Ivy League seminaries, are now filled by secular leaders in America's public-learning institutions.

Today's learning institutions employ very different manners of worship. Among other things, children are lifted up as figures of adoration. Programs exist in K–12 schools that aim to direct the souls and emotions of younger students in the paths they should go. Likewise, encouragement toward social activism has become the main thrust of contemporary civic education for older students. As a result, actions based on deeply held beliefs are manifested by students. Public education now shows more like an institution seeking converts and disciples.

Public schools act like religious institutions in the ways they care about families and attempt to save American students from a litany of societal ills. The schools have become modern-day social-gospel satellites. Mary Eberstadt affirms this when she states, "Schools now serve for many as substitute, substandard families. Whether government run or otherwise, even the best schools amount to forced packs and . . . produce winners and losers depending on the adaptive strategies of their institutionalized members."[6] But there is a point of beginning for much of this. The "messianic character of American education received its direction from Horace Mann (1796–1858) . . . Mann's stand was basically this, that true religion would best be served by the schools, and that the churches were in error in their interpretation of their faith and its realm."[7]

The emphasis on the whole child and what appears as student worship had its beginnings also in the philosophy of Mann. His focus on natural law, as well as identifying "protestant Christianity with freedom,"[8] led Mann to the conclusion that it is "clearly legible in the ways of Providence as those ways are clearly manifested in the order of Nature and in the history of the race, which proves the absolute right to an education of every human being that comes into the world."[9] Mann incorporated these views into his educational philosophy, which still impacts school communities to this day.

Many colleges and universities are modern seminaries for secular humanism, with vestiges of Mann's educational philosophy undergirding current secular thinking. According to Mann, "the Common School is the greatest discovery ever made by man,"[10] and became the "cure-all for sin and crime."[11] In addition, in these schools "the pupil is . . . a person with rights rather than responsibilities. Instead of being accountable to God, parents, teachers, and society, the pupil can assert that God, parents, teachers and are responsible to him."[12]

A good example of this thinking is found in the debate over the theory of evolutionary origins of life. The biblical account of creation is dismissed as a myth. Students are instructed that out of nothing but chaos came everything, as if universal confusion formed its own identity over time. The organization of systems and life out of chaos without an overseer is to celebrate choiceless and purposeless creation.[13]

This chaos and purposeless is yet apparent in modern American society. Eberstadt adds, "The plain fact is that the relative stability of yesterday's familial identity could not help but answer the questions at the heart of identity politics—*Who am I?*—in ways that many men, women, and children can't answer anymore."[14]

However, as critical as this is, it is not the only concern. Richard Kirk, in *American Thinker*, adds, "The #MeToo movement exposed what perceptive observers already knew, that the dissolution of the family had led to profound ignorance not only about the opposite sex but also about one's own sexual nature."[15] The correlation to discovering one's personal, human identity and the falling apart of the nuclear family is quite stark. Simple matter does not make choices. Complex humans are the choice makers, and the gap between chaos and universal order is just as stark.

HUMANISM IN EARLY AMERICAN EDUCATION

Examples of what students are taught about humanism include, "We deplore efforts to denigrate human intelligence, to seek to explain the world in supernatural terms, and to look outside nature for salvation,"[16] and "We affirm humanism as a realistic alternative to theologies of despair and ideologies of violence and as a source of rich personal significance and genuine satisfaction in the service to others."[17]

These statements of beliefs, appearing to minimize traditional religious teachings, are actually religious in-and-of-themselves. Mann would agree. "Mann was not interested in the Bible as a means toward promoting godliness but rather social efficiency. Religion should be used because it is productive of civic virtue.... The basic reference in religion is therefore not to God but to society."[18] Excluding religion as an underlying purpose of civic education is an excellent illustration of religious humanism.

Referring to Mann, Rushdoony asserts, "In terms of Mann's presuppositions, what he envisioned was a new religion, with the state as its true church, and education as its Messiah. Mann's heirs were to make this implicit faith explicit,"[19] and "his stand was basically this, that true religion would be best served by the schools, and that the churches were in error in their interpretation of their faith and its realm."[20] Dewey reaffirmed Mann's humanism in his book *Problems of Men*. According to Dewey, "the purpose of the schools is to create a faith in the one world of man,"[21] while at the same time fitting in with "membership in a single family."[22] This was early *it-takes-a-village* rhetoric.[23]

Theodore Bramfeld, like Dewey, was an advocate of religious humanism, with emphasis on its relativism,[24] but he did not end there. Bramfeld maintained that it was more than relativism that was key, especially when considering political structures, such as democracy. Majority rule, or consensus, comprised the basic framework of his Bramfeld's religious humanistic philosophy.[25] This is reminiscent of the deists of the American colonial period.

The secularization of American education replaced God with its own deity. Rushdoony illustrates this transition:

> In the United States, and throughout the Western world, there has been an equally strong emphasis on the group or the state, and on education in terms of utility to the state or group, as against the traditional faith in education in terms of utility to God. Man has ceased to regard himself as created in the image of

God and insists on seeing himself materialistically as a social animal and a creature of the state. The forms of faith differ, but the essence remains the same. The roots of this new concept of man are in part in Darwin and Freud, whose influence have led to anti-intellectualism in a variety of forms.[26]

THE LENSES OF HUMANISM AND CHRISTIANITY

Humanism addresses the basics of Christian doctrine by countering that Christian doctrines are myths. Therefore, by negating Christian doctrine, there must necessarily be a replacement set of doctrines by which to live. Humanism claims not only its validity as a belief system but also its superiority to Christianity. Humanism replaces God with human reason and logic. The *God of humankind* is now *humankind is God*. But how does this work in the real world? In secular schools, where real students have disagreements, and when teaching and learning is often dissimilar, how does humanism play out?

When a belief system such as humanism does not allow students the opportunity to express different beliefs on a level playing field, such a system should be ruled as intolerant. But that is not the case. That being said, all over the nation, students, teachers, and parents are fearful of speaking out against things they view as unfair or improper in schools. Unfortunately, even with the humanistic statement of human reason and logic as the pinnacle of human solutions, it is anathema to speak up against the system by using these very tools.

Consider for a moment the following. Imagine a system based on a theocentric concept of creation, and not evolution. It would be expected that creation would be embedded in all that would be taught. Essentially, creationism would affect an entire worldview and pervade academic curriculum. So it is with the theory of evolution and the humanist teachings. According to the Humanist Manifesto I, humanism is the lens through which all of American society should be viewed.

The following quote from the Humanist Manifesto I (1933) reveals exactly the nature and goals of twentieth-century religious humanism.

> In order that religious humanism may be better understood we . . . desire to make certain affirmations which we believe the facts of our contemporary life demonstrate. There is great danger of a final, and we believe fatal, identification of the word religion with doctrines and methods which have lost their significance and which are powerless to solve the problem of human living in the Twentieth Century.[27]

Nicholas Murray Butler was a contemporary of John Dewey and was a vocal advocate of educational conservatism. Critics quickly dismissed his views as untenable. An example of the struggle Butler had with the state over property ownership reveals his concerns. "In Christian terms, in the Reformed interpretation, the issue is simply this: is it man, the church, or the state who is created in God's image? If it be man, then it is idolatry and a violation of the first commandment to kneel before or bow down to the church or state."[28]

Butler was conflicted about the empowerment of the state over the individual. Butler concluded that "democracy and the conviction that the support and control by the state is a duty, in order that the state and its citizens may be safeguarded, have necessarily forced the secularization of the school."[29] Butler delineates between church and state.

Paul Kurtz brings a religious tone to soften Butler's contrast. He states that humanists believe "in optimism rather than pessimism, hope rather than despair, learning in the place of dogma, truth instead of ignorance, joy rather than guilt or sin, tolerance in the place of fear, love instead of hatred, compassion over selfishness, beauty instead of ugliness, and reason rather than blind faith or irrationality."[30] Kurtz's statement could have easily been taken from a political candidate's speech.

Consequently, what does humanism have to offer when the despairs of life become real? It relies on seeking individual answers through exploring the universe and often flawed human reason. Therefore, the ultimate answers of life and death for the humanist are answered by human endeavors, and certainly not by the Christian teaching of reliance on God and man's efforts. Regrettably, the problems faced by humans are not all solvable by someone's logic and reasoning, and a quick view of a 7-minute YouTube clip.

The faith placed in religious secularism has its inception in the worship of the individual. The bottom line is rather than Christian dogma, humanism relies on its own dogma. This reality should be affirmed by all humanists, especially after the outcome for secular humanism in the Supreme Court case *Torcaso v. Watkins*.[31]

The Philosophy behind Humanism

The advocates of the philosophy behind humanism promote side-taking and exclusivity. For example, according to the adherents of humanism, followers of traditional religions—namely evangelical Christians, are culturally ignorant, uneducated, and uninformed.[32] Conversely, the educated are supposedly the truly enlightened, proclaimed elitist leaders. Such exclusivity based on subjective claims, and personal practices by humans, leads to a religiously secular class society.

Rushdoony calls out the humanists by asserting, "If education is in any sense a preparation for life, then its concern is religious. If education is at all concerned with truth, it is again religious. If education is vocational, then it deals with calling, a basically religious concept. It would be absurd to reduce preparation for life, truth, and calling to an exclusively religious meaning in any parochial sense, but it is obvious that these and other aspects of education are inescapably religious."[33] Alfred North Whitehead agrees that "the essence of education is that it be religious."[34]

Religions and beliefs have disciples and mentors, as well as many devotees and followers. The teachings of humanism span the length of the curricula which are also undergirded by a religious philosophy emphasizing that humans can determine their own truth.

Regardless the shifts in philosophy throughout the years, education as a religion is not a new idea.[35] Subjective statements and human feelings form much of today's religious experiences.[36]

To the religious humanist, mankind is both the center of the universe and simultaneously its deity. The lens through which the universe is viewed shifts from Almighty God to mighty mankind. But one thing is clear. The tribal factions within this secular religion deem themselves worthy of worship in the classrooms of America's public-learning institutions. Moreover, this type of thinking has also found its way into the pews of America's churches. This is adding further evidence to the perception that there are less differences, over time, between what is considered secular and what is deemed as sacred.

EDUCATION AS SPIRITUAL FORMATION

When secularists speak of developing children spiritually, they are using religious language. Certainly, secular spiritual formation, at first, seems like an oxymoron, but only until the reality of today's humanist educational proximity to religion is realized. In seeking to formulate something spiritual, humanists cozy up to soteriology and insert humans as their own saviors from social evils and injustices.

Human spirituality to the humanist does not necessitate a belief in God, as orthodoxy would define. To the religious secularist, spirituality comes from human endeavors in terms of the pursuit of realizing personal divinity. Again, that which is spiritualized is humanized.

Humanism actually attempts to replace centuries of biblical and spiritual foundations by elevating humans to the status historically afforded to God. If God is not necessary to form any semblance of spirituality, then certainly human efforts to generate the capacity toward spirituality empower humans. A good example of this is the demythologizing of the divinity of Jesus Christ. As one humanist writes:

> I find that I am better able to love and appreciate Jesus as a humanist imagining him as a man than when I was a Christian and imagined him as a God or a spiritual presence. Jesus was a man therefore he is one of us and we can truly become like him.
>
> I feel that I have lost nothing by rejecting the doctrines of Christianity. Rather, I have rediscovered what it means to have true faith and true understanding by embracing humanism and science. Humanism then does not reject Christianity, it completes it.
>
> Paul was wrong. Our faith is not foolish if Jesus is not literally and physically risen from the dead. We know our faith is true, because we know that death has not defeated him. As a humanist, I do not discard the rich legacy and richness of the Christian tradition, rather I claim to be the true heir to the Christian patrimony.
>
> Christians embrace a shallower version of Jesus. I know this because I continue to be transformed by Jesus's love and he continues to inspire my humanist faith—faith that there is yet some good in this earth, that we can all be redeemed by love, and that we should all choose life and should try to live it fully in a spirit of peace and brotherhood with all mankind.
>
> It makes no difference to me whether Jesus was born of virgin or rose bodily from his grave after three days. These are signs that the wicked demand because they do not have the heart to see the divine in Jesus and in all of us without such signs. Blessed are those who follow Jesus not having seen and without any need for signs and wonders.[37]

Researchers into the life of Jesus Christ are coming to terms with the belief of a relationship with Jesus is tantamount to the vernacular of other relationships, in terms of *wokeness*. The demythologizing of Christ into a good man then leaves the level of belief in Christ up to the humanist.

Humanists assert the assumption that there cannot be any compromise with other perspectives, particularly if they are blatantly religious. They view such viewpoints as fiction and based on wrong logic. This author recalls a debate with a humanist, which was held at a local college. The topic was "Does God exist?" The opening statement of the atheistic humanist was *if Santa Claus exists, then God exists. Since there is no Santa, there is no God. Both are myths.* Shortly after, what was pointed out was that *"God did not have to exist for Santa Claus to exist, and neither did Santa have to exist for God to exist. But the atheist exists as a person either by his own Santa Claus of evolution, or by intervention of a power high than sperm and egg."*

The Humanists believe the best life is here and now, and people have certain power to make it so, regardless of the state or condition. Humanists and their efforts then comprise the totality of spiritual formation for themselves and the children they educate. But are these works truly spiritually transforming or emotionally formative?

THE SECULAR BECOMES SACRED

The phrase *the secular becomes sacred* pertains foremost to the replacement of one form of religion with another. It also represents the blurring that occurs as a result of the intersection of the two in American culture. Humanists have become absorbed in the philosophy of self. In the midst of this fervor, "It never occurs to these . . . that the concepts they took for granted of a good society were purloined from the Christian heritage that they have studiously ignored or denied."[38] Becoming one with Christ is not the aim of the humanist. The only oneness for the humanist is personal and more complete understanding of one's identity. The object of the mission is different.

The bottom line is that common opinion states one's secular education is far superior to one's education in their faith. Also common is that humanism is an intellectually and accurate lens through which to view the world.

Political Correctness as Religious Expression

One of the hallmarks of a religious cult is that the only truth that exists comes from the group making the claim. A second and equally important characteristic is that there is anger and distrust expressed toward those who would challenge the veracity of the group and its teachings.

Americans are embroiled in a battle over what is true and what is right. There is nothing new about this. Members of society are also caught between having the right to speak one's mind and disagree, as well as practice this right against the doctrine of political correctness. The actions taken toward those rejecting political correctness are harsh. They now result in the disallowance of freedom of speech and much more.

Students are taught today what they can and cannot say. There are certain off-limits words, concepts, and even *people groups* are no longer addressed as they were. Teachers reinforce this status quo while indoctrinating followers in the subtle art of shaming those not on board. In this sense, teachers that find themselves in the position of disagreeing personally, while professionally supporting the status quo, find themselves impaled on the horns of a dilemma. Political correctness has become a sacred practice for the humanist.

Political correctness has become cult-like, both in idea and practice. Aaron Ames argues that public schools and secular institutions of higher education are not places for traditionally religious groups—especially Christians.

> Let's get right to the point: many Christians throughout history shared the idea that God is the fundamental source of all truth, whether religious, academic, or otherwise. But what are we to make of a student who has spent 15 to 20 years studying academics without ever considering God's relationship to these fields of knowledge? Does this kind of education not actually imply that God is *not* the source of all knowledge and truth?
>
> It should really be no wonder that students so quickly abandon the faith after a year or two of university schooling. God has been left out of every meaningful field of knowledge by the end of high school, so it does not take much more prodding to decide that God never really fits in the first place.[39]

One of the reasons for concern over the lack of tolerance of Christian beliefs is the pull of religious humanism upon them. This pull fuels rebellion and is similar to the means used in the 1960s–1970s in the United States when children ran off to join up with the faddish fringe religions and cults that invaded American society. The difference today is that by attending public schools, students are a captive audience. Ames is exactly correct. Evangelization occurs regularly, and new devotees are pumped out each June.

Competition over Sacred Beliefs

In the past, schools recognized the basics of morality and the underlying principles of the Judeo-Christian heritage. Consider that within secular education, much of what is claimed as truth is often derived from decisions made by political forces and elitist reasoning—all of which is deemed far superior to religious pretexts as seats of life and judgment.

The fact is that with today's version of secularism in schools, one religious set of tenets has been replaced by another, and this replacement is reflected in the philosophies and curricula that show up in the classrooms. As the argument goes, *why believe in a God, when destiny is shaped by the individual and truth becomes the masterpiece constructed by personal experiences?*

Rushdoony puts it well and his words square with current educational philosophy. To reiterate, "The pupil is therefore a person with rights rather than responsibilities. Instead of being accountable to God, parents, teachers, and society, the pupil can assert that God, parents, teachers and society are responsible to him."[40] If one strips away the political and legal forces behind today's entitled generation,[41] all that exists would be a group of students staking claims to personal divinity and demonstrating this by autocratic but inconsequential actions.[42]

Public education has been the source of some lofty philosophical expectations. These expectations are communicated by way of secularists presenting their wares as they hit the education market with the newest and purest versions of pragmatic truth. The ultimate goal is to convert school districts to their programs.

For example, a few years ago, there was no training in White Fragility. The LGBTQ+ lobby was just gaining political traction, and Black Lives Matter was barely a phrase. The accusations of *systemic institutional racism* have now become a society-wide household phrase, and so has the term *racist*. Within a short period of time, schools, businesses, corporate board rooms, and others were required to take implicit bias and sensitivity training for employment. Now they are commonplace.

Evangelists for these groups make every effort to convert people to their beliefs and causes. Some of the more radical fringes, such as factions within the domestic radical group BLM and the Antifa domestic terrorists, have enlisted thousands of new members, the vast majority of which are ages twenty-one to thirty-five.

The founders of these groups all have one thing in common, the destruction of the systems that comprise America. This commonality is a set of beliefs based on radical teachings, ranging from anarchists to communists. The founders are referred to as gurus, masters, harbingers of truth and universal mysteries by their followers. In many cases, the words of the leaders are considered the impartation of *divine wokeness*. These radical changes happened quickly. But that is how radicalism operates in counting on sudden, widespread impact and seeks to blunt any and all other messages that are contrary.

WORSHIP AT PUBLIC-LEARNING INSTITUTIONS

What does worship in public-learning institutions look like? Worship at these institutions is blended with political, social, and racial platforms. Religious humanists approach worship with a conscious effort not to connect their actions to traditional religious teachings.

Traditional religion, especially conservative evangelicalism, is not tolerated much on K–16 campuses in America. Regardless of one's race, conservatives of all persuasions are met with horrible intolerance.[43] There are outcries of intolerance toward people of certain religious faiths. This intolerance is more against the practices of these religions, more than their beliefs. Sadly, tolerance seems to only cut in one direction.

Religious schools of the past are now unrecognizable, as they have adopted more humanistic approaches to their institutions. State schools have become even more secular, if that is possible. But both the historically religious private institutions and the state universities apply types of monergism and synergism,[44] for who is credited for their lives and accomplishments.

Ivy League universities, such as Harvard, Yale, and others were established as schools of divinity, and were dedicated to training young men for the ministry. Today, they are so very different. Schools where their origin was founded on worship of God have caved to where they now worship humans, worship education, and worship politics and social activism. These comprise much of the humanists' actions of religious expression.

Students as Objects of Worship

The object of worship in K–16 schools and colleges is students, and the expression of this worship is the student and his or her empowerment for self-worship.[45] Teachers have become facilitators, often being guided by the students themselves. Classroom instructors are mere recipients of the whims of students.[46]

Nearly all public institutions have now become completely sold out to the social agency model of education.[47] Civic education is now little more than reform and indoctrination and when students attend college, they are indoctrinated again by the leftist ideas resident in some of their liberal arts and undergraduate humanities classes.[48]

Students may go into their first year of college with certain viewpoints about life, but so very many emerge from the process taking sides, even against their parents. Those in political science and sociology fields refer to the phenomenon as "affective partisan polarization" . . . [where] each side demonizes the other . . . implicit or unconscious biases are now at least as strong across political parties as they are across races."[49]

On its face, the notion that caring for a student in every way possible sounds like the most responsible thing to do. This is definitely the axiom used to promote humanist philosophy. In a perfect world, perfect children make perfect choices. However, we do not live in a perfect world. The empowerment of students has led students to place trust in themselves and their changing emotions, often disregarding those whose wisdom is actually best.

Love and Hate as Worship?

Value creep is real and is part of the humanists' understanding of love. Love is a most sacred expression of commitment, but it is based on much more than feelings. America's sex culture has diminished the sacredness of love to various degrees.[50] One of these degrees is the philosophy that the sacredness of love is now attached to one's self-identity. Love of self and identity are often used as evidence of the purest of love and the essence of spiritual awareness.

Secularists go out of their way to continue to promote the faddish moniker that *love is love*, but it refers only to LGBTQ+ advocates. Humanists proclaim that their definition of love is more tolerant and considerate of humanity. But is this really accurate?

Erotic love is not brotherly love, and is also not necessarily unconditional, sacred love. Yet, to believe that feelings and expressions of love are all the same can become problematic in an environment when the understanding of love and its expressions are different. Religions have their books, and religious humanism is no exception to this. Students hear a mantra and process it internally, which raises the emotional level of the belief. Today's political beliefs are incorporated into the curriculum and the daily interactions on school grounds and on college campuses.

Psychiatrist Kurt Smith asserts: "Most of us tend to focus on falling in love and use the feeling of love to determine the duration of the relationship. Falling in love is easy to do, almost effortless, but losing that loving feeling is not that hard to do, either. . . . Feelings, however, can be fleeting. No one seems to want to talk about how those loving feelings can fade . . . and that choosing to stay in love is a choice we all have to make. . . . Love is all about choices."[51]

Speaking of choices, an Iowa State University professor forbid her students from criticizing groups with which she agrees. She wrote, "Any instances of othering that you participate in intentionally (racism, sexism, ableism, homophobia, sorophobia, transphobia, classism, mocking of mental health issues, body shaming, etc.) in class are grounds for dismissal from the classroom."[52] Essentially part-time professor, Chloe Clark limited free speech and created a class as a political safe space for her personal views. She warned students, "you cannot choose any topic that takes at its base that one side doesn't deserve the same basic human rights as you do (i.e.: no arguments against gay marriage, abortion, Black Lives Matter, etc.). I take this seriously."[53] She was more intent on punishing those who would speak up about the policies and practices of those groups.[54]

Professors like these demonstrate biased support for political, social, and racial groups, while punishing any disagreement. Affection for extremism and emotion over a right to free speech is not tolerant. It is prejudice. Humanists that support such practices are not being true to the beliefs that human reason and logic are the pinnacle of the search for solutions. They are autocrats seeking to cancel students' versions of truth and free speech.

Beware of Truth That Changes

Ear-tickling philosophies that pose as statements of truth appear revelatory to the young generations and are thereby tantalizing and tempting. Some of these philosophies are accepted because the axioms, mantras, or monikers fit a preconceived set of beliefs that resonate with an already established group of supporters. When accepted, these ideas offer no room for serious reflection, and none is required. The beliefs become wrapped together with feelings, both of which may prove over time to be fleeting.

An interesting point to consider here is that humanistic and progressive moral and social philosophies usually go unchallenged most days in classrooms. These ideologies find their way into students' brains by teachers and are reinforced by slanted social media and political platforms, or newsfeeds and online reports. Entertainment and athletic icons (a religious term) also sway the young in their beliefs. Clear and divergent worldviews are challenging America's students, but religious nonetheless.

COMPETITION BETWEEN WORLDVIEWS

No one should be surprised the practice of one's faith is largely acceptable in public school K–12 classrooms, unless its practice is tethered conspicuously to Christianity or Judaism. Even though protected under the First Amendment, certain religious expressions have come under fire in recent years, with Christians and Jews singled out. The reason for this is that historically, these religions have competed with other atheistic and humanistic beliefs on some key social and religious issues. What this amounts to is the intolerance of others' intolerance.

Today, children in the United States are pressured to choose between their faith and the religion of humanism.[55] The pressure to choose the latter is increasingly accompanied by shaming and ridicule. Social change agents and strong pushes of mental images by social media platforms and social media influencers help to shape the minds and hearts of children.[56]

The socialization of children into a worldview is a gradual and continual process. Moral changes in thought processes are considered as brain-based. So, the more exposure a child has to an ideology, the more likely the child will feel tempted to explore the ideology, or try out a moral practice to discover its appeal.

Primarily, Christian students are challenged to reconsider their family's beliefs and traditional faith practices. Joel Thiessen addresses this socialization and explains the competitive aspects of competing world views. Thiessen writes:

> Socialization is an ongoing process informed by primary and secondary mechanisms. Primary socialization refers to a child's first socialization experiences

in their family. Parents filter through and pass on an array of attitudes and behaviors to their children. This process is informed by one's social location based on characteristics such as race, socioeconomic status, or religion, and social scripts on socialization content and timing. *Secondary socialization involves institutions like schools, the media, religious organizations, or the government who socialize individuals into other arenas of the outside world.* In these settings, individuals recognize, perhaps for the first time, that not every person, family, or social institution views the world the same way. *When primary and secondary groups conflict in their reality-defining narratives—a common occurrence in societies with a complex division of labor and higher levels of pluralism—individuals must parse through competing worldviews. People are aided in this process by significant others whose worldviews they tend to favor.*[57]

Teachers holding strong religious beliefs are told to leave their beliefs at the doors of their classrooms. Religious humanism has exclusive claims and forbids any disagreement or alternative viewpoints to expressions arising from within the new teachings on human sexuality and gender expressions are considered hateful. The exclusion is most unfair.

By favoring one religious group over another, a selective religious environment is established. Clearly, religious humanism is favored over other religions. After all, *intolerance is intolerance.*

Competition over Classrooms

There is great risk in marshalling adversaries to challenge the party-in-power. Economic punishment has been meted out by politicians legislating economic punishment toward other states because of those states' contrary political or economic positions. Taking sides has resulted in competition over schools. Sadly, the political results are often hatred or acts of violence. Both of these have increased since 2005.

Where do students learn to shame others, and grow up to riot and cause destruction of property? The philosophies that fill their heads and fuel their actions are obvious during personal interviews with them. As an example, in schools, favoring and allowance of messaging associated with the attire of one political party, but ridiculing and not allowing others, indicates clear partisan bias. Likewise, when red hats are banned as triggers, yet communist images are allowed, something is deeply wrong in our nation's schools.

Students have been attacked in class by others and verbally assaulted by teachers favoring unpopular political philosophies on issues such as sex and gender. Politics has always been controversial, but scandals and personalities have elevated disagreements to hate and vitriol, including physical altercations. Harming and/or labeling any students that disagree is wrong on every level.

REDEFINING FAMILY AND BELIEFS

The traditional family is the bedrock of all societies. In order for it to be redefined, humanism must necessarily denigrate the historical traditional family. According to Judeo-Christian and other religious theology and history, the family unit was instituted by the Almighty. Yet, humanists believe it can be redefined with no damage to society-at-large, since there is no supernatural deity required.

Humanistic efforts to usurp what religions teach are accomplished by inserting their own definitions. By doing so, they demonstrate how foundational religion truly is in humanism. One cannot simply reorganize something as foundation in religion, as the family, without also claiming its replacement is just as sacred.

Secular humanism states that any group of people staying together, or merely identifying as family, is the same as any family. To coin a phrase, *family is not family*. The–anything-is-family construct denies the truth that that is the bedrock of all human civilization for millennia. Dating back to thousands of years, religions have recognized the basic makeup of family was given by God and not constructed by some westernized culture.

The claim that this had been handed down through time by a Creator, and modeling it by a first family is treated as fact by many people of faith, and cannot be dismissed by mere humanist disbelief. As evidence, people groups of all races and backgrounds around the world recognize the nuclear family as the foundation of any society. So, why the redefinition at all? The answer is because the traditional family as a norm makes those outside the norm *feel* bad.

A traditional religious definition of nuclear family, one which recognizes a marriage, and a mother and father with children, comprises anathema to the humanist because it is a standard that excludes new forms. Yet, the humanist is not loathed to practice the historical, traditional form, which is interesting.

Students from elementary school through college have become embroiled in emotional arguments over what it means to be a family. This is to be expected when delving deeply into students' social-emotional natures and what they value. In the hands of teachers, unafraid to bring personal beliefs into their classrooms, one can see how the acceptance by a child of one set of beliefs can be contrary to those from home. This may lead children to doubt their parents. Teachers have a lot of sway over what students believe. And this is a concern, especially among those within the ranks of social activists, organization advocates, as well as their supporters.

Children being read stories about alternative family lifestyles is a direct attempt to soften them toward accepting changes in their beliefs and traditions. The new traditions are presented in good light and with emphasis.

This author has been present at several of the readings of literature that are contrary to many students' upbringings. Students are told to sit quietly and learn something new. A major problem arises when a student disagrees with what he or she has heard in these new readings. Some families are more vocal than others about these experiences for their children. Some teachers warn students in advance about different beliefs, and especially are on guard for religious objections. Older elementary students are told to keep these beliefs to themselves.

When students feel threatened, or when they are triggered by someone with different beliefs about life, some are provided safe sanctuary spaces for time-outs, so as to protect their feelings. Disagreements among students and teachers can cause emotional stirs. Schools are now the new families for many children, with teachers adopting new roles as surrogate parents. Schools have become sanctuaries for students and protecting students' emotions is of paramount importance.

Confusion and Illusion

Secondary teachers and college professors at some institutions have been instructed not to use terms such as mothers and fathers, men and women, or even refer to boys or girls. Gender has been redefined by secularists and even students are bring warned about referring to each other as they once did.

What else could it be but confusing to a child, especially now with the knowledge that there are dozens of genders from which to choose and pronouns they are told that are acceptable and unacceptable. There is moral confusion, and children are caught in the middle of it all. To many parents, the speed at which culture has changed over the past few years appears illusory. At school, children hear one thing and at home most likely another. Both worlds are not compatible, and emotional chaos reigns as a result.

Children have a natural tendency to trust those in authority. But when children arrive home bearing conflicting messages from someone they trust, the child again is confused. What are children to think when their parents and teacher(s) are on opposite sides of issues? What are parents to think? Parents have the right to expect teachers not to subvert the values by which parents rear their offspring.

Imagine the atheist child arriving home to his atheist family with the good news that his teacher says that God exists in him and his emotions—or that she is her own god. How would this news be received? Frankly, the identity movement that has infected America's public-learning institutions is all about elevating the self. If the atheist parents are *woke* they would celebrate their god-like child's new identity. People actually believe if they feel something strongly enough, they can create it in themselves. Humanists celebrate this type of thinking.

Another area in which humanism impacts is biology. Human biology is minimized in contrast to psychological theories on emotions. Biology became of the greatest importance during the COVID-19 pandemic. And that is exactly the point! The irony is that in today's gender identity confusion, one's birth biology means little. However, when COVID-19 patients were treated, chosen personal identities were overlooked and the patients were treated by the science and biological identities. When taught that choice is the highest form of self-expression—the ultimate worship of self—biology is removed from the conversation. When everyone was told to trust the science, those in the identity movement trusted themselves. When common sense is removed, faith is placed in feelings.

Humanists believe they are the center of the rational universe. To put it candidly, *humans are gods of choices—their own*—thinking they can select for themselves what science, physicians, parents, and families—as well as thousands of years of history, faith, and human norms—have already decided. Robert Jastrow, in his book *God and the Astronomers*, captures the essence of the humanist's authority. He writes, "For the scientist who has lived by his faith in the power of reason, the story ends like a bad dream. He has scaled the mountains of ignorance; he is about to conquer the highest peak; as he pulls himself over the final rock, he is greeted by a band of theologians who have been sitting there for centuries."[58]

HUMANISTIC THEMES AND TENETS

In April 2020, JoBeth Hamon raised a few eyebrows when she used Howard Zinn's *A Young People's History of the United States*, "in place of the customary Bible in her swearing-in to the Oklahoma City Council." Rachna Sizemore Heizer did the same thing as she was sworn-in for her seat on a school board in Fairfax County, Virginia.[59] The substitution of another book for the Bible, which was long revered as the standard for bearing oaths, provides evidence that another book holds a place of greater importance to some progressives elected to political positions. In these cases, progressives willing to elevate a negatively biased view of history speaks volumes about the content of the book and intent of the elected official.

The Religion of Zinn

More and more, public schools are adopting social studies *programs* and leaving history instruction behind. This means students are being programmed to learn from history revisionists for their understanding of American history. The story becomes quite a contrast to what historians have taught for decades. For example, students are now being exposed to an interpretation of history that is meant to serve as an activism and cause racial and social anxiety over the founding and maturation of America.

The focus is primarily on slanted aspects of history, and by sometimes leaving out facts, events are embellished to lead students to predetermined conclusions. The controversy surrounding the supposed evil colonizer and conqueror, Christopher Columbus, is one such example. Other examples will be included in the following sections. But there is another project gaining attention and finding support in education.

The 1619 Project

The 1619 Project, supported by the *New York Times*, assails U.S. history and its founding. The 1776 Declaration of Independence is largely dismissed as a

White man's document and evidence of White Supremacy. In fact, the 1619 Project originally claimed that America was founded the same year as the project title, when slaves first came to the New World shores. However, the historical premises upon which the project is based are false. So, the project's founder and the *New York Times* quietly changed the project's website.[60]

When the project went public in August 2019, the print version which children all across the United States read, included one statement. The revised version of the student print version changed the original statement, some four months later.[61] Millions of students all across America were falsely led to believe America was founded by the arrival of Black Africans to America.

Both the original introductory statement and the revised introductory statement appear side-by-side below. The motivation for changing such a critical piece of the document was left unspoken. The example in table 2.1 represents just one of several key errors in the 1619 Project.

Both the Zinn and 1619 projects are severe revisions of American history. Wilfred McClay writes that Zinn has affected two generations of Americans with his People's History text, by causing people to "believe their nation is among the most culpable and unjust nations in human history."[62] McClay adds, the 1619 Project, "the pet of the *New York Times* contains patently untruthful . . . inaccurate and tendentious scholarship to defame the American Founding and support a political cause—reparations for slavery."[63]

Advocates of both programs are not in favor of traditional U.S. history. It is criticized for being too White. In stark contrast, both offer a "tendentious,

Table 2.1   1619 Project Statements

August 2019: Original School Print Version	December 2019: Revised School Print Version
The 1619 Project is a major initiative from the *New York Times* observing the 400th anniversary of the beginning of American slavery. It aims to **reframe the country's history, understanding 1619 as our true founding,** and placing the consequences of slavery and the contributions of Black Americans at the very center of the story we tell ourselves about who we are.	In August of 1619, a ship appeared on this horizon, near Point Comfort, a coastal port in the English colony of Virginia. It carried more than twenty enslaved Africans, who were sold to the colonists. **No aspect of the country that would be formed here has been untouched** by the years of slavery that followed.

simplistic, and relentlessly negative view of the American past."[64] They view history through the lenses of original sins of Americans, and any aspect of human ills, or imperfections, are cast across the entire landscape of American history and the American people. This is what is meant by the term systemic racism and White Supremacy. Lines are errantly drawn between dates and events to justify the narrative that *America is sinful*.

Thou Shall Not Debate

The content of the projects in question is not to be tested. The project developers are not to be questioned. More and more schools are using both Zinn and the 1619 Project as replacements for traditional American history. Questioning the projects leads to only one conclusion: A person's White Supremacy and implicit bias are in the way of understanding. The translation of this means such people are part of the problem with America. It is in this light that young people are motivated to tearing down monuments and defacing monuments to American history. Such actions are directly related to beliefs, and these beliefs trace back to what students have been taught.

Along with the anger that is intentionally fomented, there is an activism component to both Zinn's work and the 1619 Project. In the hands of activist teachers, including those of BLM and racial resistance movements, the actions taken by the young are tantamount to a religious crusade in the name of social justice, where race and identity politics are at the top of the list of attention. The younger generations of adults now approach civil disobedience with a fervor similar to a religious crusade, often accompanied by verbal abuse and physical violence.

Nevertheless, the crusade is so much more than political. The destruction of evil is the aim of each purveyor of each project. America's past is evil, and it is being perpetuated even today. The overthrow of America's long-standing history is a victory that awaits, after which the victors intend to remake the nation in their own image.[65] As BLM likes to remind people, the time for revolution is now.

THEMES THAT TRIGGER

There is a major weakness of humanism in the nature of humanism. The nature of humanism is that it changes with culture. This means any truth stated by humanists is open to change. Any statement found to be in conflict with previous truth can be easily discarded. Progressives can revise or discard past truth statements by *new revelations* in areas such as science or history. Some tenets which comprise truth to humanists and progressives are included in the following section. Each of these is already affirmatively positioned in America's public-learning institutions.

The list of themes below are considered triggers that may be considered taboo to some. Many on the list of themes are current and have already made their way into school curriculum and literature. There are differences in teaching *about* topics and teaching *within* topics. Activist teachers instruct from within a topic, as they choose live out their beliefs in the environment for which they advocate.

Good educators teach about topics and do so from various perspectives, in fair fashion. For example, the teaching of reading is wonderful. Selecting literature which embeds a targeted theme and lobbying for a subjective practice as truth is another. Parents should protest the arrogance that bureaucrats know best when it comes to what children learn in schools.

The fact that they do not protest enables what children are taught as part of their curriculum. Once established, it becomes ingrained in the heads and hearts of the young people. Over time, parents begin to hear the new ideas shared by their children in a variety of ways, which eventually may result in the taking of action.

Parents that do not stay involved with their children's education and check in with their schools and their children's teachers should not be surprised when, as adults, that which was incubating in their children's minds for years in public schools presents itself at home at some of the oddest times.

Thou Shall Not Trigger

Teachers entertaining a contrary view to any one of the following themes in American public schools brings the risk of being marginalized, disciplined, or even released. One of the reasons for this is because political correctness prompts the direction of the conversations with the terms.

For example, a secular humanist may attempt to exclude any discussion of these from any position that expresses a political, moral, or religiously conservative view. He or she might do so under the banner of the possibility of triggering someone to bad feelings or an emotional outburst.

The following list of triggers comprises themes that, when criticized or not taken seriously by students in schools, may result in highly emotional student and family responses in schools.

- Abortion
- Alternative Genders
- Antifa
- Black Lives Matter
- Cancel Culture
- Colonialism
- Common Core State Standards
- Evolution
- Feminism
- Free Speech
- Gender Fluidity
- Implicit Bias
- Latent Bias, Systemic Racism
- LGBTQ+
- Mansplaining
- Manspreading
- Normal Culture
- Nuclear Traditional Family
- Patriarchy
- Politics
- Public Education
- Racial, Cultural, Gender Appropriation
- Racial, Sexual, Gender Identity
- Racism
- Reference to Pronouns
- Relationships Between Teachers and Students
- Restorative Justice
- Same-Sex Marriage
- School-to-Prison Pipeline
- Sexual Identity
- Social Justice
- Social-Emotional Learning

- Student Discipline
- Subjective Truth
- Toxic Masculinity
- Traditional Religions
- Use of Terms such as Mother and Father
- White Fragility
- White Privilege, White Supremacy

All Words Matter

The fact that an educator would even mention the word "norm" today, when speaking of mothers and fathers and nuclear families, is often enough to evoke anger and social media chastisement. Such an educator may be classified as encouraging hatred of those practicing alternative lifestyles, which are not of the teacher's *norm*. Changing what has always been a norm is unwise. But for the humanist, change is always required when the culture shifts. For example, reading stories to first graders about alternative lifestyles without balancing the reality of most families as the societal norm is fine for the activist.

This type of evangelistic outreach as an activist seeking converts is as religious an action as those of any other religion (see chapter 5). Each are attempts to persuade children that any structure is the same as any other. *Families are families* is as general as *love is love* and without details and explanations the phrases are as shallow as bumper sticker philosophies.

Teachers can be excommunicated from the classrooms, professional athletes can be fined, and actors and actresses can be blacklisted for their views. Religious views that align with humanists are quite welcome in public schools. They qualify as tolerant and, as long as the words used are politically correct, all is well. In a politically hyped environment, words do matter.

Some secular humanists and political activists agree that students might be triggered by any one of the previously mentioned themes for a variety of reasons. Therefore, the issues may (1) fragment and marginalize, (2) be known to be socially divisive, (3) include slanted presentation toward issue advocacy, (4) encourage political partisan, and bias, (5) be largely founded on opinions, (6) emphasize emotions, (7) encourage accusations toward those in disagreement, (8) incite side-taking that alienates students, (9) capitalize on disunity, and (10) drive wedges between people's beliefs.

EFFECTS OF RELIGIOUS HUMANISM

It should be remembered that most of the same people who sit in evangelical churches on Sundays have jobs in the secular world throughout the week. There is some concern about the efforts of sincere evangelicals limiting themselves, in terms of conversations and actions, while they are engaged in a secular environment. That is, while most evangelicals are open and willingly share their fair with those like them in a safe environment, there is greater reluctance to do the same in the not-so-welcoming environment. This now seems to be the case among a growing number of White evangelicals in the United States.[66]

According to some researchers, the downplaying of religious verbal expression focuses on the actions being taken that would impress the secular world, while leaving out the message that is not valued as important. Indiana University assistant professor Brad Fulton explains: "Despite being portrayed as hyper-religious and persistent proselytizers, my research indicates that some evangelicals actually downplay religious expression when working with religiously diverse and secular groups."[67]

Impact upon Evangelicals

Fulton provides the example that "when 26,000 evangelicals from 500 churches volunteered with Portland's Serving the City initiative, they adopted a self-imposed 'no proselytizing' policy as they helped with cleaning up parks, refurbishing schools and conducting clothing drives. . . . These evangelicals simply want to serve their neighbors."[68] One very significant observation from the study is that the fieldwork performed extended to "politically centrist and conservative evangelical organizations—not just a politically liberal subset of evangelicals, from whom a secular approach might be more expected."[69]

The study extends to analyzing four modes of public religion, which are categorized as "secularist, generalist pluralist, particularist pluralist, and exclusivist."[70] What is quite interesting from this study is that evangelicals acted more like secular religious people in their work that extended outside the walls of the church. They self-imposed restrictions, so as not to discuss the reasons behind why they were helping.

Thus, the term "evangelical" became acceptable and associated with any other secular organization performing work in the community. This represents a point of intersection between the sacred and the secular—the likes of which was initiated by the sacred, or in this case evangelical Christians. As a result, "ethnographic research on white evangelicals participating in multi-faith initiatives in Los Angeles, Portland, Boston, and Atlanta indicates they prefer the secularist mode that uses faith-specific language rather than the generalist mode that invokes interfaith language."[71]

New York University professor Marcia Pally observes that modern evangelicals are not monolithic and that they seek to cross religious divides to seek the common good for America.[72] This could be the result of the liberalization of evangelicals, or the term being applied to groups once reserved for the title mainline denominations. Evangelicals whose actions speak louder than words, but whose words are only found in their actions seem to have redefined the term by which they so enthusiastically applied in the past. Is American culture now on the verge of another definition with which to contend—the *secular humanist evangelical*?

Traditional emphases on evangelism and doctrine are two reasons younger people feel less welcome in churches today. They are comfortable, however, with good works, but they shun any language or even the implication of judgmentalism. In the words of Stacia Datskovska, after not hearing what she wanted to hear from the pulpit one Sunday, she writes: "I suddenly understood why so many of my friends were making promises to leave their respective denominations. Like I did that day at church, they likely felt alienated from attending a service that is supposed to instill hope."[73]

Datskovska's advice to the church, as a post-Christian young person, is that "the Christian church experience needs to start transcending the traditional and adapting to the times."[74] She, and so many others, have become disillusioned with the social judging, traditional doctrine, and resulting hypocrisy they view from parishioners.

According to a 2018 Barna Research Group study, nearly one-fourth of teenagers blamed adult hypocrisy as the reason they avoid traditional worship, and that atheism has nearly doubled that of the American adult population, among Generation Z, making those born between 1999 and 2015 the "first truly post-Christian generation."[75]

As this chapter comes to a close, we return to the words of Rousas Rushdoony and Kenneth Hansen. Rushdoony concludes, "Not only is education a new religion, but it rests on a specifically anti-Christian doctrine of man."[76] Hansen agrees that education is not founded on a sinful human nature, as found in Christian orthodoxy. Education is based on children's "natural human goodness and almost infinite improvability."[77] Thus, according to Hansen, education has a full-fledged soteriological, sin-forgiving nature, which is demonstrated by those who place their "faith in the power of education."[78]

Evangelicals are slowly moving over into the religious humanist camp. For many years, public or "state schools have thus been inescapably religious."[79] While still in denial, their common faith that is placed in America's public-learning institutions has been "described as made up elements provided by Rousseau, Jefferson, August Comte, and John Dewey."[80] As it stands, "Civil religion is an apt designation for this faith."[81]

NOTES

1. Mary Eberstadt. *Primal screams: How the sexual revolution created identity politics*. 2019. West Conshohocken, PA: Templeton Press, p. 58.
2. Peter Kreeft. *I burned for your peace: Augustine's confessions unpacked*. 2016. San Francisco, CA: Ignatius Press, pp. 94–95.
3. "Religion." *Dictionary.com*. Retrieved June 14, 2020, from https://www.dictionary.com/browse/religion.
4. "Education." *Cambridge Dictionary*. Retrieved August 16, 2020, from https://dictionary.cambridge.org/us/dictionary/english/education.
5. Ephesians 4:11, *New American Standard Bible*.
6. Eberstadt. *Primal screams: How the sexual revolution created identity politics*, p. 59.
7. Rousas J. Rushdoony. *The messianic character of American education*. 1976. Nutley, NJ: The Craig Press, p. 18.
8. Ibid., p. 20.
9. Ibid., p. 21.
10. Ibid., p. 29.
11. Ibid., p. 29.
12. Ibid., p. 23.
13. Richard Kirk. "How the sexual revolution created identity politics." *American Thinker*. January 12, 2020. Retrieved January 23, 2020, from https://www.americanthinker.com/articles/2020/01/how_the_sexual_revolution_created_identity_politics.html.
14. Eberstadt. *Primal screams: How the sexual revolution created identity politics*, p. 61.
15. Kirk. "How the sexual revolution created identity politics." *American Thinker*.
16. Paul Kurtz. "Affirmations of humanism: A statement of principles." *Free inquiry*. 2019. Retrieved December 27, 2019, from https://secularhumanism.org/what-is-secular-humanism/affirmations-of-humanism/.

17. Ibid.
18. Rousas J. Rushdoony. *The messianic character of American education*. 1976. Nutley, NJ: The Craig Press, p. 31.
19. Rushdoony. *The messianic character of American education*, p. 32.
20. Ibid., p. 18.
21. Ibid., p. 155.
22. John Dewey. *Problems of men*. 1946. New York, NY: Philosophical Library, p. 59.
23. Hillary Rodham Clinton. *It takes a village*. 2016 (1996). New York, NY: Simon & Schuster.
24. Rushdoony. *The messianic character of American education*, p. 256.
25. Ibid.
26. Ibid., p. 309.
27. Board of Directors. "Humanist Manifesto I." *American Humanist Association*. 1973 (1933). Retrieved December 27, 2019, from https://americanhumanist.org/what-is-humanism/manifesto1/. Humanist Manifest III (2003) supersedes Humanist Manifest I.
28. Rushdoony. *The messianic character of American education*, p. 122.
29. Nicholas Murray Butler. *The meaning of education: Contributions to a philosophy of education*. 1917. New York, NY: Scribner's, p. 184.
30. Board of Directors. "Humanist Manifesto I." *American Humanist Association*.
31. Leo Pfeffer. "The 'religion' of secular humanism." *Journal of Church and State*. October 1, 1987. 29 (3): 495–507. Retrieved December 26, 2019, from https://doi.org/10.1093/jcs/29.3.495.
32. Phil Zuckerman. "Why education corrodes religion." *Psychology Today*. November 3, 2014. Retrieved December 26, 2019, from https://www.psychologytoday.com/us/blog/the-secular-life/201411/why-education-corrodes-religious-faith.
33. Rushdoony. *The messianic character of American education*, p. 315.
34. Alfred North Whitehead. *The aims of education*. 1952. New York, NY: Mentor Books, p. 26.
35. Aaron J. Ghiloni. "Interreligious education: What would Dewey do?" 2011. *Religious Education*. 106 (5): 476–93. Retrieved December 26, 2019, from DOI: 10.1080/00344087.2011.613345.
36. John Corrigan. "Introduction: The study of religion and emotion." *The Oxford Handbook of Religion and Emotion*. September 2009. Retrieved December 26, 2019, from DOI: 10.1093/oxfordhb/9780195170214.003.0001.
37. Andrew Sullivan. "A humanist Jesus." *The Atlantic: Daily Dish Archives*. February 17, 2007. Retrieved December 27, 2019, from https://www.theatlantic.com/daily-dish/archive/2007/02/a-humanist-jesus/230790/.
38. Rushdoony. *The messianic character of American education*, p. xii.
39. Aaron Ames. "Why Christian children don't belong in public schools." *The Federalist*. May 2, 2019. Retrieved December 26, 2019, from https://thefederalist.com/2019/05/02/christian-children-dont-belong-public-schools/.
40. Rushdoony. *The messianic character of American education*, p. 23.

41. Ernest J. Zarra III. *The entitled generation: Helping teacher teach and reach the minds and hearts of Generation Z.* 2017. Lanham, MD: Rowman & Littlefield Publishers.

42. Carmine Gallo. "You are not the center of the universe: Admit it and you'll be more confident than ever, according to science." *Inc.* July 31, 2019. Retrieved December 26, 2019, from https://www.inc.com/carmine-gallo/you-are-not-center-of-universe-admit-it-youll-be-more-confident-than-ever-according-to-science.html.

43. Nicholas Kristof. "A confession of liberal intolerance." *New York Times.* May 7, 2016. Retrieved December 28, 2019, from https://www.nytimes.com/2016/05/08/opinion/sunday/a-confession-of-liberal-intolerance.html.

44. "Monergism," *Theopedia.* Retrieved December 28, 2019, from https://www.theopedia.com/monergism.

45. John McCarthy. "Student-centered learning: It starts with the teacher." *Edutopia.* September 9, 2015. Retrieved December 27, 2019, from https://www.edutopia.org/blog/student-centered-learning-starts-with-teacher-john-mccarthy.

46. Ernest J. Zarra III. *The Age of teacher shortages: Reasons, responsibilities, reactions.* 2019. Lanham, MD: Rowman & Littlefield Publishers.

47. Ernest J. Zarra III. *Detoxing American Schools: From social agency to academic urgency.* 2020. Lanham, MD: Rowman & Littlefield Publishers.

48. Alex Nitzberg. "Far left courses at American colleges." *Accuracy in Academia.* December 16, 2016. Retrieved August 30, 2020, from https://www.academia.org/far-left-courses-at-american-colleges/.

49. Greg Lukianoff and Jonathan Haidt. "The coddling of the American mind." *The Atlantic.* September 2015. Retrieved June 9, 2020, from https://www.theatlantic.com/magazine/archive/2015/09/the-coddling-of-the-american-mind/399356/.

50. Ernest J. Zarra III. *America's sex culture: Its impact on teacher-student relationships today.* 2020. Lanham, MD: Rowman & Littlefield Publishers.

51. Kurt Smith. "Love is a choice more than a feeling." *Psych Central.* July 8, 2018. Retrieved January 22, 2020, from https://psychcentral.com/blog/love-is-a-choice-more-than-a-feeling/.

52. Jennifer Kabbany. "Iowa State professor forbids students from criticizing BLM, gay marriage, abortion." *The College Fix.* August 18, 2020. Retrieved August 18, 2020, from https://www.thecollegefix.com/iowa-state-professor-forbids-students-from-criticizing-blm-gay-marriage-abortion/.

53. Micaiah Bilger. "College professor threatens to dismiss pro-life students from her class. *LifeNews.* August 17, 2020. Retrieved August 18, 2020, from https://www.lifenews.com/2020/08/17/college-professor-threatens-to-dismiss-from-pro-life-students-from-her-class/?fbclid=IwAR0GR8ptp7fvma1ECDp9xwcGfxcLVp3J0_FFDQU2FQnX7ARB_VrXhqgF5NM.

54. Ibid.

55. Joel Thiessen. "Kids, you make the choice: Religious and Secular Socialization among marginal affiliates and nonreligious individuals." *Secularism & Nonreligion.* April 29, 2016. 5(1): 6. Retrieved December 28, 2019, from https://secularismandnonreligion.org/articles/10.5334/snr.60/.

56. Ernest J. Zarra III. *Helping parents understand the minds and hearts of Generation Z*. 2017. Lanham, MD: Rowman & Littlefield Publishers.

57. Thiessen. "Kids, you make the choice: Religious and Secular Socialization among marginal affiliates and nonreligious individuals." *Secularism & Nonreligion*, p. 2. Emphasis mine.

58. Robert Jastrow. *God and the Astronomers*. 1978. New York, NY: W. W. Norton & Company, Inc., p. 116.

59. Mary Grabar. "The Zinn Education Project: Teaching Trump-hate and other dogma." *The American Spectator*. January 6, 2020. Retrieved May 11, 2020, from https://spectator.org/the-zinn-education-project-teaching-trump-hate-and-other-dogma/.

60. Tom Mackaman and David North. "The New York Times and Nikole Hannah-Jones abandon key claims of the 1619 Project." *International Committee of the Fourth International (ICFI)*. September 22, 2020. Retrieved September 22, 2020, from https://www.wsws.org/en/articles/2020/09/22/1619-s22.html.

61. Ibid.

62. Wilfred McClay. "A radical pseudo-historian meets his match." *The James G. Martin Center for Academic Renewal*. April 15, 2020. Retrieved April 15, 2020, from https://www.jamesgmartin.center/2020/04/a-radical-pseudo-historian-meets-his-match/.

63. Ibid.

64. Ibid.

65. Hugh Hewitt. "Podcast: 1619 project founder admits it is not historical: Larry Elder with Bob Woodson." *Townhall Review*. July 29, 2020. Retrieved August 19, 2020, from http://townhallreview.com/2020/07/1619-project-founder-admits-it-is-not-historical-larry-elder-with-bob-woodson/.

66. Brad R. Fulton. "Evangelicals downplay religious expression when working with secular groups." *The Conversation*. March 3, 2020. Retrieved May 4, 2020, from https://theconversation.com/evangelicals-downplay-religious-expression-when-working-with-secular-groups-131821.

67. Ibid.

68. Ibid.

69. Ibid.

70. Wes Markofski, Brad Fulton, and Richard L. Wood. "Secular evangelicals: Faith-based organizing and four modes of public religion." *Sociology of Religion*. Summer 2020. 81 (2): 158–84. Retrieved May 4, 2020, from https://doi.org/10.1093/socrel/srz045.

71. Ibid.

72. Marci Pally. *America's New Evangelicals: Expanding the vision of the common good*. 2011. Grand Rapids, MI: Wm. B. Eerdmans Publishing Company, pp. 53, 220–21.

73. Stacia Datskovska. "Churches could win back more teens like me if they were more welcoming and less judgmental." *USA Today*. August 18, 2019. Retrieved May 4, 2020, from https://www.usatoday.com/story/opinion/voices/2019/08/18/churches-need-less-tradition-more-flexibility-welcome-teens-column/2011731001/.

74. Ibid.

75. Staff. "Atheism doubles among Generation Z." *Barna Research Group*. January 24, 2018. Retrieved May 4, 2020, from https://www.barna.com/research/atheism-doubles-among-generation-z/.

76. Rushdoony. *The messianic character of American education*, p. 316.

77. Kenneth H. Hansen. *Public education in American society*. 1956. Englewood Cliffs, NJ: Prentice-Hall, p. 9.

78. Ibid.

79. Rushdoony. *The messianic character of American education*, p. 316.

80. George Huntston Williams. *The church, the democratic state, and the crisis in religious education: An opening session address*. 1948–1949. Cambridge, MA: Harvard Divinity School Bulletin, p. 41.

81. Ibid.

Chapter 3

The God of Self

> *It's not hard to imagine why students arriving on campus today might be more desirous of protection and more hostile toward ideological opponents than in generations past. This hostility, and the self-righteousness fueled by strong partisan emotions, can be expected to add force to any moral crusade.*[1]

> *So we have the prophetic word made more sure, to which you do well to pay attention as to a lamp shining in a dark place, until the day dawns and the morning star arises in your hearts. But know this first of all, that no prophecy of Scripture is a matter of one's own interpretation, for no prophecy was ever made by an act of human will.*[2]

The goal of education for most parents is the placement of their children into schools and education programs that are meant to lift them up academically and prepare them for life. At least, this was the goal until recently. Such a goal is difficult to accomplish when school is canceled or students are required to take their studies exclusively online. With many parents home during the pandemic of 2020, the crafting of student learning underwent a transformation. These changes in schooling caused more than a few parents to sit up and take notice, in terms of what their children were actually learning.

RESHAPING MINDS THROUGH EMOTIONS

One of the ways schools are reshaping the minds of students is teaching them to reason with their emotions. The phrase *emotional reasoning*[3] comes with its own interesting connotations. In fact, on its own, it comes across as a contradiction at first glance. Parents sometimes use this type of reasoning when their teenage child has violated a home rule of conduct. Nevertheless, whether it is a politician, news media anchor, or a teacher, reasoning by emotions can lead people into *feeling* something that is not based on reality or truth.

When feelings guide a person's reasoning, there is greater liability when it comes to what is true and right. Yet schools are tapping into emotions to guide students in the development of their moral compass. This is the essence that underlies the social-emotional programs through which American students are taken. In its mature version, it appears as sanctuary cities, empathy toward repeat criminal offenders, and a feeling of hatred that is stoked against law enforcement.

It is not by accident that Millennials and Gen Z young adults are referred to as the "therapy generation."[4] Public-learning institutions have had a hand in the *neediness* of today's younger generations through them focusing on emotions. Along with being needy and feeling their ways through decisions, there is another dynamic in play: the development of a narcissistic generation.[5]

The focus on self has not provided the best groundwork for mental health and student wellness. When the world around young people is uncooperative to the ends desired, these same people are uncertain of how to handle the unscheduled moments of serendipity.

The Gospel of Goleman

Schools that refer to an educational program have to be careful the way they frame it. An educational program that refers to the term social-emotional health of the children comes with less of a trigger, when parents hear it. Educators are told that all students possess emotional intelligence,[6] and school is a natural environment in which to build this intelligence.

Displays of certain traits, such as empathy, joy, and others, are demonstrated by children as their emotional intelligence grows. Along with these traits as such, understanding peer-relationships, tolerance, and being open to change are also markers for maturity. Restorative discipline strategies as a means of correction are sometimes employed as extensions of social and emotional learning. Students become programmed on how to respond to certain stimuli. This intake occurs as students are instructed to reconsider many of their personal, familial, religious, and sexual ideas, and constructs they experience. But then the tables turn.

Through a well-designed emotional gospel, students are sometimes told there are really no significant differences between boys and girls. They are asked to believe that genetics, biology, and birth do not define humans and that their inner feelings are their true identities. Social-emotional learning leans in here and impacts students' feelings about such statements and provides strategies on dealing with these and more.[7]

Adding further challenges to students' social and emotional learning is the fact that current public school culture has bought into the philosophy that individual feelings are as fluid as a person's *conversion* from one sexual or gender identity to another. As a result, judging one's emotions as *wrong* belies the notion that emotions were valid as truth for the moment they were expressed. When these realizations are expressed, the gospel of Goleman has taken root.

Sometimes conflict arises when children come home and inform their parents that they are not who or what they have been told they are and that their biology cannot define them. Likewise, similar conflict may occur as children question whether there are any differences between the sexes. When these things occurs, the *re-crafting* of students' minds and beliefs has already begun. This is a first step toward wholesale conversion of thought and belief. What could be more religiously humanistic, or at least cultic?

James Comer observes the conflict amidst social-emotional learning and the common sense that most students possess. Comer asserts:

> Strong evidence now shows that social, emotional, and academic learning is greatly influenced by good environment-brain interactions, by the mediators of those interactions, and by resultant child experiences. Schools that have created cultures that make this dynamic possible have demonstrated that, with the help of parents and educators, poor children and children of color can develop well and be academically successful and prepared for most life tasks. However, the blame game, political and economic opportunism, and harmful race-class-gender relationships, among other issues, have prevented our society from acting on what is almost common sense.[8]

Therefore, the idea is that social-emotional learning and brain development are sequenced. This should be a plus for students. But a person's emotions can override reality. In other words, is it possible for a human being to create out of his or her emotions a new being, or new person? Are emotions enough for a person to claim a new identity? If so, what emotional reasoning does a person actually follow to relinquish a previously claimed emotional identity, in order to claim emotional ownership over a new one?

Moral Reprogramming

There are few things more intimate than a person's sexuality. The pressure upon students facing sexual decisions often results in confusion for them. For example, many American sex education programs are occupying more curriculum space and time in public schools. Yet, the average seven-year-olds are more than a little perplexed about what they hear and how to process it, especially if the message is contradictory to what they hear at home.

If the first time the students learn about the details of human sexuality is from school, they will come away with a skewed understanding. This then establishes a benchmark, or beginning point for the schema of sexuality for children. As a result, some sex education programs are programming students.

Traditional morality is being impressed by humanistic ideas about sexuality in the minds of our nation's students. Included in this new programming are new ideas about race, gender, sexuality, marriage, and family relationships. This leads to some very unsettled minds and ideas that probably would have occurred at a later time. This also leads to some unfinished academic business.

Unsettled Minds and Ideation

Once questions are generated about traditional families in America, the challenge to heteronormative Euro-centric thinking is planted in the minds of students. People are now able to select their gender and sexuality from a menu of thirty-one genders. However, this challenge is made to appear as a scientific fact. But this is not the case. Students' minds and emotions are being manipulated. The fact that heteronormativity is called into question enables heterosexual students to question their own identity.

Sex education curriculum has become advertising practices that until recently were viewed as taboo in mainstream America. Students derive their sense of empowerment through their choices. They begin to believe that they can create a newly discovered personage ex nihilo. It is as if the discovery of one's true gender and sexual identity is the paramount spiritual zenith in life. Essentially, students grow into positions and progress quite early to the status of demi-God quite early in life. Later they take ownership of their inner deity by their self-sufficient sex and gender choices.

Americans are now told that such personal and emotional choices are to be celebrated—especially when it occurs outside the heteronormative construct. This construct is currently defined as intolerant, harmful, and even downright evil in western society.[9] It is believed to be so, just because professors in the Ivory Towers say that it is the case.

When children are unsettled about their identities, and choose to accept new ones, many claim they feel as if they had been born-again.[10] The feelings of release and newness are said to parallel what it feels like to undergo a rebirth. If someone refers to a student by a name they no longer recognize, the child simply says, that's my dead name.[11] Interestingly, the term *born-again* is the same language used by others with similar religious-type experiences. In a sense, there is a newness that is felt in a person's soul, at least for a time.

A similar experience is claimed when children come to faith in Jesus Christ.[12] They profess to be new creatures in Christ.[13] Emotions are escalated and when things somehow begin to make sense for the first time, something inside appears to have awakened. There is a similar experience with the gospel message of Jesus Christ, but the experience is vastly different.

Back in the decades of the 1970s–1990s, the "I Found It" movements, the Jesus stadium movements, and the Promise Keepers movement were prominent. Add to this the Billy Graham Evangelistic outreaches where many young people gave their hearts, minds, and emotions—and their souls—to Jesus Christ.

But psychologists dare not celebrate this particular conversion of identity. This spiritual identity does not have its sole origin in emotions. Christian conversions that are just emotional are like any other conversion based on emotions. There is no lasting life-change. Many have gone out of their religion the way they came in: by emotions.

In terms of the Christian conversion, there is the claim of a new creature that is created, and not merely a new identity. Rather than their own identity, Christians who are converted believe their identities are in Christ. Conversely, those who convert by emotions have a new identity in themselves.

In Christian conversions nothing is lost, but in the process there is something new added, which is a new nature that replaces the old. The person is not elevated to a lofty position in self, but in Christ. He is the newness in their lives. Contrast this with a new sexual or gender identity and, although there are similarities in both, the conclusions and results are vastly different.

Those claiming a humanistic, religious-type experience in discovering a new sexual identity, and those walking away from their chosen religious identity into a new spiritual identity, share something in common. The commonality is that the decision to make both is motivated by elevating the self to a position of absolute authority over changes to their personhood and humanity. Realistically, one change originates from within, while the other point of origin comes from without. Conversions are tricky business. Only longevity of a changed life, and subsequent peace and joy, are true indicators of changed lives.

A very real question remains. Can a person be his or her own god, practice the worship of self, and survive in the real world? There are serious issues among those who are trying to do just that. Suicide rates and addictions are way up, indicating that not all is well in the realm of the younger generations' godhood identity.[14]

LOSING ONESELF TO FIND ONESELF

As a result of the inroads made in schools by political and social identitarians, children today are encouraged through the curriculum, such as language arts, to question their identity and explore all the options, in order to find it.[15] Parents are told not to impress any social constructs upon their children. Yet, teachers and educational experts are doing exactly that. They are presenting a construct that states there is no construct. The result of this is generational confusion.

Parents a greatly concerned when their children disregard and rebel against the established fabric of their families. Parents are also concerned when children question the facts of science and biology. The persuasive presentations coming from activist groups are tempting children to think about themselves differently. In some cases, children attempting to find themselves may become lost to themselves and lost to their families. No teacher should ever become involved in causing such outcomes,[16] regardless of political correctness or personal biases.

The philosophy of losing oneself to find oneself[17] is a principle, derived loosely from a reinterpretation from one line of teachings of Jesus in Luke 9:24. Luke records Jesus' words, "For whoever wishes to save his life will lose it, but whoever loses his life for My sake, he is the one who will save it." This type of principle harvesting, or cherry-picking by humanists, is a tactical approach to emphasize oneself.

As a result, followers are encouraged to reflect on who they are and even to consider alternate identities from which to experiment.[18] Recent decades are replete with examples of this type of mind-shaping. Shaping the mind bends the will and allows doubt to fill a void psychologically. Then to validate reality, an experience or two that feels good then enters the emotions. This type of practice is retraining by indoctrination and is unfortunately occurring in many westernized nations.[19]

A growing number of students have adapted to the idea of the *fluidity of the self*. Students that make their own claims expect that their proclamations are to be accepted across the populace without exception. Yet, they are coming up unhappy even in their new identities.[20] One's attempts at authenticity are not to be questioned, even when serious confusion abounds. However, according to Mary Eberstadt, the "liberal-progressive side has missed something. . . . Identity politics is not so much politics as a primal scream. It's the result of the Great Scattering—our species' unprecedented collective retreat from our very selves."[21]

WORSHIP OF THE SELF

American educational institutions have been labeled everything from places for atheistic indoctrination, satellites of socialism, to being assigned the title of messianic hope of the future.[22] Each passing decade brought with it nuances in educational philosophies. One of these nuances resulted in focusing only on the positive, and that failure was not an option.

Educators were duped into thinking that telling students they were wrong was hurtful and not in line with a movement to build students' self-esteem. Some educational theorists were wrong. Providing for every need and most desires of children, without teaching them that sometimes they are in error, or morally wrong, yielded material and emotional expectancies exacted from the rest of society.

Values such as hard work and sacrifice are lost on many young people in America today. Life is more of a game to be played in the streets with cell phones than it is overcoming a set of unpredictable challenges. After taking a good, hard look at our nation, few can conclude that our nation has not produced a generation of narcissists and that this reality is not problematic in schools and in American society.

Worship of the self has a long and storied history. It begins, if you will, in the Book of Genesis. Sometimes in the course of history, we see figures larger than life that appear on the world's stage, bearing the title of god, or goddess, and being worshiped by people within their empire, or by their nation. This can be seen from the emperors of Rome, to the monarchs of Asia and Europe, and on into the western world during the Renaissance. The twentieth century with the empires and nations of Japan, Germany, Soviet Union, and North Korea are also good examples.

There is one thing that all leaders of the past and present have in common. They demanded cult-like obedience and loyalty from followers. Withholding either could result in severe punishment or even death. During the administrations of Presidents Obama and Trump, America had experienced rapid growth of the cult of personality, exacerbated by a certain level of narcissism. The media were there and chronicled the growth as advocates on the one hand, and destroyers on the other hand.

It is in this sense, that "twenty-first-century education is evolving and has many of the earmarks of a new type of cult. Instead of becoming a disciple of a guru or a mystic leader, *woke folk* choose their own personal and social awareness."[23] Instead of continuing the paradigm of the recent past, which focused on heaping worshipful sentiments upon political leaders, the younger generations have now adopted their own personalized claim of worship.

Students now worship themselves in many ways. Truly, "self-worship has become their ultimate expression of sacrifice on the altar of emotional identity and feelings."[24] Eberstadt reveals reasons for the current immature behaviors and attention-getting devices of younger adults. She writes:

> One thing that seems to happen is some people, deprived of recognition in the traditional ways, will regress to a state in which their demand for recognition becomes ever more insistent and childlike. This brings us to one of the most revealing features of identity politics: its infantilized expression and vernacular. . . . What critics of identity politics have missed is that the manifest panic

behind cries of cultural appropriation is real—as real as the tantrum of a toddler. It's as real as the developmental regression seen in the retreat to safe spaces on campus, those tiny ersatz treehouses stuffed with candy, coloring books, and Care Bears. It's as suggestive as the pacifiers that were all the rage as campus accoutrement in the 1990s.[25]

The Practice of Exclusivity

American culture has become far too tribal and, along with this, far too worshipful of exclusive numeric minorities. Exclusion is not a unifier. Exclusion is an enabler of empowerment which feeds the continuing rise of the cult of personality. This phenomenon has been growing and the expressions of religious devotion toward people have been prominent in America for decades.[26]

Within such religious expressions toward humans there is the rise of one of the traits that eventually brings down even the best of groups. The trait is *pride*. Pride has brought down many, ranging from politics to religion, and from athletics to entertainment. Pride is now an incorporated character trait of self-worship, expressed within tribal groups. By nature the emphasis placed on *self* over others is exclusive, and not unifying. Narcissists naturally worship themselves before celebrating others.[27]

When pride and empowerment are enjoined, even the smallest of groups tend to rise to levels of authority. For example, as an effort to incorporate pride and power, there now exists the tribal acronym LGBTTQQIAAP.[28] Ancient wisdom captures the ultimate outcome of pride: "Pride goes before destruction and a haughty spirit before stumbling."[29] Eventually, the flawed self usually catches up with us all—new identity or not.

Without mentors, or a connection to previous generations by family, the young adults among us are subject to some bad actors. They are easily manipulated to join groups and factionalize into tribes. For example, the riots of the summer of 2020 revealed just how manipulated and tribal young people can be.

TRIBALISM AND WORSHIP

Tribalism is generally described as people being organized by groups, according to values, behaviors, attitudes, and even race and ethnicity. Tribalism has taken on extra-special meaning during times of struggle over racial, gender, and ethnic tensions. Members in support of a tribe tend to vilify those that are unsupportive of them.

Andrew Sullivan addresses the essence of *tribalism* in America.

> Healthy tribalism endures in civil society in benign and overlapping ways. We find a sense of belonging, of unconditional pride, in our neighborhood and community; in our ethnic and social identities and their rituals; among our fellow enthusiasts. There are hip-hop and country-music tribes; bros; nerds; Wasps; Dead Heads and Packers fans; Facebook groups. (Yes, technology upends some tribes and enables new ones.) And then, most critically, there is the *Über*-tribe that constitutes the nation-state, a mega tribe that unites a country around shared national rituals, symbols, music, history, mythology, and events, that forms the core unit of belonging that makes a national democracy possible.[30]

Sullivan does not see a problem with tribalism. However, he misses the larger context and original warnings by the framers of the Constitution and the Federalist Papers. Others disagree with Sullivan and consider tribalism as destabilizing democracy "when it calcifies into something bigger and more intense."[31]

Sullivan admits this, once politics are involved in tribalism. He adds, "The most significant fact about American tribalism today is that all three of these characteristics now apply to our political parties, corrupting and even threatening our system of government."[32] Such reasoning could not be more poignant at this juncture in American history.

Twenty-first-century tribalism is elevated by technology and social media. A good example of this was the response to the tragic death of George Floyd. Protests and riots had swarmed American cities. Most of these protest groups paired off over time into their tribes and mixed messages emerged, even leading to violence and chaos.

What was missing from the equation was the complete story. The media played directly to tribal instincts. Unfortunately, such incidents of media incitement are not exceptions. The rest of the Floyd story shaped a more comprehensive narrative.

One example is the *group-utopian* collection of revolutionaries who proclaimed an autonomous state in Seattle. Even in the midst of coming together over ideology and values, the expression and practice of their revolutionary socialism became contentious. People in the same tribe began to view their differences of utopian expression with greater and greater differences.

Race became a point of division and, without clear leadership and discipline, problems arose in the very place established without any law and order. Rapes and murders began to occur and, shortly after, the small tribal society broke down into chaos.[33] Without leadership and common rule enforcement, even the smallest of tribes stands little chance of successful identity.

Politics is tribal, and that tribalism is responsible for the factionalizing, marginalizing, and race-mongering that besets so very much of the nation.[34] Taken to its extremes, even those not nativists to a *tribe* can ultimately make the claim that their identity is whatever and whomever they would chose to be. There are some very recognizable personalities who have done just that. Examples of this range from Elizabeth Warren[35] to Rachel Dolezal,[36] and on to many others who came out during various stages of their lives to proclaim an identity other than that which has been their norm, or their biology.

In the case of Warren, she claimed to be descended from a Cherokee tribe, which late proven a spurious claim.[37] Dolezal claimed to be Black,[38] served time in prison for welfare fraud, changed her name to Nkechi Diallo, and after several years also came out as bisexual.[39]

The subjective claims of well-known people are sometimes so powerful that their emotions are unable to be separated from their present reality. They develop such a following that their new identity forges a construct, ultimately reinforced by recognition from others. In the case of Warren, efforts to apologize fell on deaf ears, due to her transparent political motives. The result was the call by Native Americans for her to retract her ancestry claims.[40]

The insidious part of tribalism is not in the thoughts. It is in the actions. Tribalism is the wrong direction for America. Yet, those with renewed inner purpose and woke identities cannot be thwarted, or convinced otherwise. Common sense and law enforcement are no longer persuasive, and force only emboldens. American society is taking sides in declaring factional, tribal group identification. But inside all of this there is an irony.

One cannot find his or her identity in chaos without the social disorder eventually destroying itself. It happens sooner or later to each radical tribal group bent on anarchy and destruction. History is chock full of governmental and political identity movements eventually failing. From Rome, the Ottoman Empire, to the Nazis, fascists, and communists and yes, this will eventually be true for the cults of fascist Antifa and Marxist Black Lives Matter groups.

All movements, whether geo-political, governmental, or social, reach a zenith and then they either dissipate or implode over time.[41]

IDENTITY WITHOUT UNITY

The rise of multicultural education has done very little to unite the various cultures in America. Some actually expected that the top-down academic and forced social programs would result in unity. Others expected a societal fissure to develop. In some ways, all of the above occurred.

The Multicultural movement was not an organic movement. Like many programs that are controversial multiculturalism was generated by state-level bureaucrats and then forced top-down upon public-learning institutions. The race and gender activists are making every effort to force acceptance of their agenda as well. Government and public school districts caused greater rifts between certain cultures by requiring programs that isolated one or two groups for attention.

Israel Zangwill's 1908 Broadway play gave birth to the phrase *melting pot*. The play by the same title was a reference to those immigrants who had come to America legally and assimilated around the turn of the twentieth century.

The idea of such a culture where individuals were not more discernible than the group to which they belonged was a fanciful philosophical notion. The melting pot was much more like a crucible than a cauldron, later producing its own potion of truth and individualized cultures. The crucible produced even more marked tribal distinctions in cities and suburbs.

American culture of the twenty-first century has less unity and more personal and tribal identity. This is certainly not what Zangwill envisioned. There are very few values held over from the mid-twentieth century. So much about American culture has now been politicized and where there is political power there is exclusivity.

All too often, where there is exclusivity, there is also punishment of detractors. This is quite obvious today within both the grievance and cancel cultures, and the outlandish provocations of racial tub-thumpers.

In the midst of this culture sits America's children. These children are being trained in schools according to the philosophical ideologies that are prevalent among adult tribes.

Identitarianism is "now is the heart and soul of politics itself for many people, not only in America but elsewhere."[42] There is no better place for case studies in identitarianism than on American college campuses.

Emotions are the foundation for sensing what is right and wrong among tribal identitarianists. Yet, replacing truth is like aging, minus the maturing. Without maturity, a group's purpose can be lost in short order. A very basic premise of identitarianist groups is found in "the idea that the tradition formed by Athens and Jerusalem, Christianity and Western philosophy, was the designated enemy of diversity in the eyes of multiculturalism's defenders."[43]

Religious usurpation usually gives status quo a run for its money. Incorporating religious values into emerging cultures is equivalent to a victory for religious secularism. This is certainly the case with the elites of the nation. They clamor for worship of self from the echo chambers of their souls, while screaming louder to gain attention to their own self-proclaimed divinity.

CRITICAL RACE THEORY AND WHITE FRAGILITY

American culture has drifted leftward, and the psychology behind this drift became prominent during the Obama Administration. Whites are now marginalized and given labels as haters and bigots if they hold biblical and theological views on social practices. Christians are now even blamed by Ivory Tower elites for their "White Christian Privilege"[44] being responsible for causing "slavery and genocide."[45]

Some students are being told from multiple directions today that within them is a fragileness and character flaw because of their birth. In today's racially charged culture, this fragility is isolated to one race of people. To combat what is called *Critical Race Theory* (*CRT*), President Trump signed an executive order banning all such racial indoctrination programs within federal programs and federal agencies. Some federal agencies ignored the order and this set up another level of struggles within the fight against anti-racism.[46]

Essentially, CRT is "a framework that offers researchers, practitioners, and policy-makers a race-conscious approach to understanding educational inequality and structural racism to find solutions that lead to greater justice. Placing race at the center of analysis, Critical Race Theory scholars interrogate policies and practices that are taken for granted to uncover the overt and covert ways that racist ideologies, structures, and institutions create and maintain racial inequality."[47]

White Fragility

According to pop-author, and associate professor of Education at the University of Washington, Seattle, Robin DiAngelo, of all the races, it is Whites who are fragile. They are fragile because they are supposedly fearful of losing their majority status, their material wealth, and subsequent political and economic powers, as a direct result of the empowerment of Latinos, Hispanics, and Black African Americans.[48]

In general, DiAngelo's theory states that as White students grow, fragility manifests itself in many ways. These manifestations come as a result of birth and skin color, family rearing, and fear. The term White Fragility, coined by DiAngelo, is used as a pejorative as it describes the fear that Whites have toward people of other demographics, especially Blacks. But John McWhorter contends that DiAngelo's book aims to combat racism but in the process talks down to Blacks.[49] Could this be because DiAngelo is White and is unknowingly the prime example of her own White Fragility?

The influence of the accusations of racial fragility is not going unnoticed in America. In fact, DiAngelo is paid upwards of $20,000 to hold seminars on this topic at corporations and businesses. Psychologist Jean Twenge, in her 2010 book with W. Keith Campbell, observed that negative personality traits were rising parallel to other concerns, among the nation's college students.

In the book *The Narcissism Epidemic*, Twenge observed that among college women the rate of narcissism has risen especially fast, irrespective of race, when compared to just a few years earlier. With narcissism comes a thin skin and a serious inability to take criticism.

The inability to take criticism is manifested in the fragile nature of reactions in being offended—and it is not just applicable to White students. Often offenses are not offensive and there is a misinterpretation of a word or comment, which is lumped into preconceived assumptions which some are taught to believe is true. When people use emotional reasoning, they feel what they think.

There is a self-esteem movement among Black youth, to a degree that has never been seen before. The empowerment and support is astronomical, which could be a reason there is criticism and categorization of Whites as racists. Narcissism that results in a group of people as lower than another, based solely on race, is always immoral. These actions represent insecurities that are covered by extroversion and self-acclaim.

Some researchers claim this combination has led to a culture of "vindictive protectiveness."[50] In other words, how dare anyone judge one's work, attitude, words, or actions![51] It is declared mean-spirited. Offering any judgment of value or worth to anything or anyone in today's narcissistic and vindictively protective culture brings outcry. The psychology of revenge is alive and well among today's younger generations. It has become another tactic to shield the self-gods that are claimed to reside within, from being attacked and ultimately tarnished.[52] Apparently, in order to feel greater love for oneself, others must be shamed and thereby lowered in status.

One of the reasons these actions may are prevalent among today's youth is explained by Lukianoff and Haidt, when they stress the new era of protectiveness "may be teaching students to think pathologically."[53] This reaction is, of course, a result of certain insecurities that had develop over time when one is not critiqued in school. Narcissism is not wedded to one race or ethnicity.

WHEN RACE BECOMES A GOD[54]

There are so many people taken in by Black Lives Matter that it is both interesting and frightening, in terms of the future of our national psyche. Discussing race honestly and openly is of greater value than killing and violence in the name of something as murky as social justice. But BLM is not merely a movement to protest police brutality. The group is now an admitted, full-fledged Marxist-social-justice revolutionary organization.

What is not murky are tactics taken by BLM toward those expressing disagreement and dismay at the organization. People are being fired, placed on suspension, having to resign from corporate positions, while being doxed online. They have also had their own lives threatened by violence. Homeowners' private properties and businesses, small and large, are being invaded and some destroyed.

The reality is that any criticism expressed toward BLM brings the response that the critic is part of the problem. Today's all-purpose default term is *racist*, and it is used to cause immediate shame and racial marginalization.

BLM and the Practice of Shaming

The pressure for corporations to comply with social justice mantras is great. More and more, people are being let go if they are implicated in stating or posting anything critical about BLM. Departments are established in some human resources departments by employees to ferret out critical social media posts of protesters by employees. If George Orwell was alive today, he might be shocked to realize how prophetic his 1984 story has become. Those once under the thumb of power eventually take power and exercise their own tyranny.

Athletes are shamed for supporting the police. People are being ridiculed for their support of America's national symbols. Such support and honor are said to be racist and disrespectful of the *cult* of BLM. What is now part of American culture is the shaming of people with whom there are mere disagreements. The fallout from this practice is not lost on America's children.

How do children see it, and how does this translate to classroom disagreement and overall schoolwide demeanor? Children in homes are taught how to hate and distrust based on skin color, and this is horrible. They are also taught to distrust authority, including law enforcement.

Teaching a child to distrust and hate others based on skin color is child abuse.[55] Children are not born haters, and neither are they born with racism lurking within their DNA, just because of skin color.[56] This must end or schools will become little more than places of heightened emotions and disunity—and a tinderbox waiting to ignite.

Philosopher Rene Descartes, is credited with the phrase, "I think, therefore I am." If Descartes's statement was reworked for today, it might sound something like, "I emote, therefore I act." Emotional reasoning is now the standard for being on someone's side. Logic is ridiculed as some sort of White Supremacy. The thought that 2+2=4 is criticized as a logic of White Supremacy and is racist is absurd.[57] But this is just one area in which the nation is fractured. Such fractious thinking means that students of color are somehow withheld any substantive mathematics education.[58] Certainly academe is in trouble.

Seemingly, each time society takes a few positive steps up the steep hill of race relations in this nation, there is a Sisyphus whose weaknesses in the climb either cause retreat or some groups' actions incentivize sabotage of efforts of advancement. On an economic note, does anyone really and truly think all the owners of professional athletic teams, CEOs of these teams, the members of corporate business boards, and others are really now **woke** to BLM and its goals? Are these people somehow now *born-again* emotionally to perceive police brutality and systemic racism?

Is White Privilege now all forgiven and forgotten since White-owned entities are giving BLM what they want? Or are those caving to demands while playing their own version of the Devil and Daniel Webster—just to get whatever a person can in the short term, keep their jobs and stockholders happy, and deal with the cost for it all down the road?

GODS IN THE PEWS: THE RELIGIOUS BECOMES SECULAR

Churches are moving away from their traditional messages and welcoming secularism. Denominations, such as the Presbyterian Church of the United States, United Methodist Churches, Lutheran churches (except the Missouri Synod), and formerly evangelical Baptists and other churches have followed the forces of secular culture, in liberalizing their beliefs.[59] Although the term "evangelical" covers a large group, they are most often defined as churches which hold fast to orthodox teachings of the Bible and Jesus Christ, and have not succumbed to the secular culture, particularly in matters biblical authority concerning social issues such as truth, marriage, life, sexuality, and gender.

But what is taking place today in the United States, even among the most evangelical of churches, is a movement to the left socially and politically. These institutions are taking positions on cultural issues that are usually reserved for those in liberal politics. But this makes sense. The more secular and liberal the people become during the week, the less religious these same people are in the congregations on weekends. For example, evidence of this appeared in the recent article titled, "How Sunday schools are raising the next generation of secular humanists."[60]

The author found that "parents who take discipleship of their kids seriously are typically disappointed by the quality of their kids' Sunday school program,"[61] because there is an apparent lack of depth to what the kids are learning. What has been going on in schools for years has now found its way into church denominations. A dumbed-down generation in faith and academics, but heightened in self-acclaim and emotions, presents to leaders a willingness to follow rather than to question.[62]

As a result, there are concerns in some churches that Sunday school teachings are more in line with humanism than with biblical wisdom.

Some of these concerns are represented by the fact that humanists tend to worship earth, nature, self, material goods, as well as pleasure. Such tendencies lead to challenges because of their seepage into houses of worship. Some of these challenges are illustrated by the following five questions:

- Why are young people leaving traditional religious beliefs behind or walking away from their faith?
- What competing messages are the church and secular society sharing that are not resonating with the newer generations, and why do these messages fall short of relevance?
- What issues mean the most to Millennials and Generation Z, and where do religious humanists and the church stand on these issues?
- Why is humanism viewed as a viable truth alternative?
- How can the church reclaim those who believe that religious truth answers fewer questions than secular experts?

A book could be written to answer each of these questions. Another good case of an identity challenge in American culture is *feminism*. There are claims by certain feminists in the United States that promote the equality of men and women, and this equality is meant to be taken as literal.

Gender and sexual differences are blurred so much today that some men and women are uncertain as to their gender. Moreover, these same people express uncertainty as to their places in the world, yet they come to church on Sundays and hear a validating post-Christian view of women.

For example, non-binary claims are confusing to many people. The advent of *girlish boys*, and *boyish girls* has some people wondering which of the two they are.[63] So, in their confusion, they claim neither of the two as their identity.[64] What does this confusion do to males and females?

There has taken place a psychological revolution that has falsely claimed women can become men and men can become women. Children seeing this confusion do not know how to handle this confusion they see in adults. They especially are uncertain what to do if they are told their confusion can become their own personal clarity.

Specifically, in terms of men in society, Suzanne Fenker writes that they have lost their mojo and "40 years of feminism has eroded male power to such a degree men no longer recognize their disempowerment, which starts in their very own homes."[65] Fenker continues:

> Today, almost a quarter of U.S. Children live in single-parent homes. In the vast majority of these homes, the single parent is the mother. This is detrimental to both sons and daughters, but is particularly devastating for boys. After all, girls still have their same sex parent as a model for womanhood, but boys have no such model for manhood. Instead, they're being raised primarily by women—not just at home but at school, where the majority of their teachers are women. The dearth of fathers and of male leadership, combined with a relentless war on men and masculinity, has emasculated our men. They have dispensed with their masculine attributes (or never developed them) and are now feminized. . . . By suggesting that men and women are essentially the same, we set them up to fail. We ignore biological reality at our own peril. . . . What men and women look for in a relationship and what they need from each other within that relationship is not the same. Being malleable with gender roles is great, but ignoring biology is not.[66]

Teaching children how to make changes in culture, or change behaviors of others are, as John Marriott calls them exercises of "deconversion."[67] Marriott asserts culture is defined as "a comprehensive shared set of largely subconscious assumptions and values of a group that are the product of both history and institutions, and which constitutes for them a social reality. It is the space in which we live and move and have our being. As such, it has incredible power to shape the kind of people we are and what we accept as reasonable and moral."[68]

As a counter to humanistic teachings, there are four particular areas upon which churches need to focus. According to Natasha Crain and others, "Sunday schools are doing very little to offer a strong response to counter the culture narrative, and what they are doing is actively contributing to kids walking away to secular humanism."[69] These four areas are summarized and expanded to include:

(1) *Lessons focus on character development without thoughtful ties to theism.* In doing so, questions such as If there was no God, who would get to

decide right and wrong, good and evil? How could evil even be defined? Why should people ever agree to a common good, if there was no framework or basis for goodness?

(2) *Who is Jesus, did He exist, and is He God?* Contrast this to the secular view where self is a god and identity the expression of self-worship. What were Jesus's claims about Himself and what did others think about Him at the time he was on the earth? Because Jesus made the overt claim that He is God does not mean His followers are also gods.

There is a teaching among hyper-faith churches that Jesus's followers are gods. This same teaching appears in the Mormon religion and is taken from a couple of out-of-context passages of the Bible: (1) "You are gods, and all of you are sons of the Most High," (Psalm 82:6), and (2) where Jesus referred to the psalm with the words "Has it not been written in your Law, 'I said, you are gods'"? (John 10:34) Is there a difference between being a good, moral teacher and God in the flesh? Did Jesus actually rise from the dead? If so, then in what ways should this change His followers?

(3) *Bible teaching is limited to what's in the Bible, and rarely addresses questions about the Bible.* How the sixty-six books were selected for inclusion into the Bible is left largely unaddressed. Also left unaddressed is any discussion on what some see as apparent contradictions in biblical passages, and how these align with the biblical, historical, and archaeological evidences.

(4) *Churches aren't supporting parents enough in discipleship, so parents end up focusing on raising nice kids.* Raising nice kids is a complementary goal. But how to deal with life in the world outside the church can be a real challenge. Even parents with years in the Christian faith are often unaware of how to equip their own children to stand firm against the onslaught that is pervasive and infiltrates their minds.

Parents who allow their children to become just good people to fit into the culture have a lot in common with the humanists who cherish such values. They share the perspective that humans can become good by themselves and need no outside assistance from an Almighty God. In fact, eventually, according to Crain, these kinds of children "eventually discard Christianity in favor of simply being good without God."[70]

Throughout the years of their schooling, from K–12, and on into college, students are used to getting their way. From the time they step into the real world, where they have to compete, young adults are less recognized for their self-perception and often have difficulty adjusting.

WHAT HAS BEEN WROUGHT?

What has American secular culture and its humanistic philosophy wrought for the students in the nation? In terms of our disappearing sexual and gender differences, teachers are telling our nation's boys to act differently than what they would act naturally as males, and employ more empathy and emotional sensitivity. "Masculinity and men are also objects of new denigration, as the popular phrase toxic masculinity, among other signpost reveals."[71]

In the beginning, the term toxic masculinity was "an expression once relegated to women's studies classrooms that suddenly seems to be everywhere."[72] What begins in the Ivory Towers slowly makes its way across the cultural landscape like *The Blob*,[73] engulfing all that dare to stand in its way.

America has the religion of humanism to thank for this form of gender denigration, while empowering the confused child and young adult as gods over their lives. Males have been emasculated. Whites have been castigated, traditional beliefs are being repudiated, and evangelical Christians are excoriated.

Society in general has been seriously affected by ideologies that redefine all constructs that do not fit radical narratives. All things considered, the nation is at a tipping point. If there is a call for return to the principles that beckoned the less fortunate to our shores, one wonders whether these principles would even be discernible over the din of protests and the obfuscation of the land of the free, by placards and banners.

NOTES

1. Greg Lukianoff and Jonathan Haidt. "The coddling of the American mind." *The Atlantic*. September 2015. Retrieved June 9, 2020, from https://www.theatlantic.com/magazine/archive/2015/09/the-coddling-of-the-american-mind/399356/.
2. 2 Peter 1:19–21. *New American Standard Bible*.
3. David Burns. *Feeling good: The new mood therapy*. 1980. New York, NY: William Morrow & Company, Inc. Cf. David Burns. *Feeling great: The revolutionary*

new treatment for depression and anxiety. 2020. Eau Claire, WI: PESI Publishing & Media.

4. Peggy Drexler. "Millennials are the therapy generation." *The Wall Street Journal*. March 1, 2019. Retrieved October 10, 2019, from https://www.wsj.com/articles/millennials-are-the-therapy-generation-11551452286.

5. Ernest J. Zarra III. *The entitled generation: Helping teachers teach and reach the minds and hearts of Generation Z*. 2017. Lanham, MD: Rowman & Littlefield Publishers.

6. Robert Goleman. *Emotional intelligence: Why it can matter more than IQ*. 2006. New York, NY: Random House Publishers.

7. Joseph A. Durlak, Celene E. Domitrovich, Roger P. Weissberg, and Thomas P. Gullotta. *Handbook of social and emotional learning*. 2015. New York, NY: The Guilford Press.

8. James P. Comer. "Making SEL work for all children: Afterword." In Joseph A. Durlak, Celene E. Domitrovich, Roger P. Weissberg, and Thomas P. Gullotta, Editors. *Handbook of social and emotional learning*. 2015. New York, NY: The Guilford Press, p. 590.

9. Chris Tompkins. "Why heteronormativity is harmful." *Tolerance*. July 18, 2017. Retrieved April 29, 2020, from https://www.tolerance.org/magazine/why-heteronormativity-is-harmful.

10. Meredith Talusan. "Celebrate your kid's transition. Don't grieve it." *New York Times*. October 18, 2019. Retrieved December 28, 2019, from https://www.nytimes.com/2019/10/18/opinion/sunday/gender-transition-death-grief.html.

11. Ryan Roschke. "What it means to 'dead-name' a transgender person, and why you should stop." *Pop Sugar*. June 18, 2018. Retrieved September 23, 2020, from https://www.popsugar.com/news/What-Dead-Naming-Transgender-Person-43923268.

12. Larry Fowler. "Introducing your child to God." *Focus on the Family*. July 24, 2019. Retrieved December 28, 2019, from https://www.focusonthefamily.com/parenting/leading-your-child-to-christ/.

13. 2 Corinthians 5:17. *The New American Standard Bible*.

14. Jean M. Twenge, A. Bell Cooper, Sarah G. Binau, et al. "Age, period, and cohort trends in mood disorder indicators and suicide-related outcome in a nationally representative Dataset, 2005–2017." *Journal of Abnormal Psychology*. 2019. 128(3):185–99. Retrieved August 19, 2020, from https://www.apa.org/pubs/journals/releases/abn-abn0000410.pdf. Cf. Markham Heid. "Depression and suicide rates are rising sharply in young Americans, new report says. This may be one reason why." *Davos 2020 Mental Health*. Retrieved August 19, 2020, from https://time.com/collection/davos-2020-mental-health/5550803/depression-suicide-rates-youth/.

15. Staff. "Discovering my identity: Grade levels 3-5." *Teaching Tolerance*. 2020. Retrieved August 19, 2020, from https://www.tolerance.org/classroom-resources/tolerance-lessons/discovering-my-identity.

16. Tim Fitzsimons. "Teacher reinstated after parents complained about Black Lives Matter, LGBTQ posters." *NBC News*. August 27, 2020. Retrieved August 28,

2020, from https://www.nbcnews.com/feature/nbc-out/teacher-reinstated-after-parents-complained-about-black-lives-matter-lgbtq-n1238498.

17. Kasia Jamroz. "To find yourself you need to lose yourself." *The Huffington Post*. August 31, 2017. Retrieved August 19, 2020, from https://www.huffpost.com/entry/to-find-yourself-you-need-to-lose-yourself_b_59999870e4b033e0fbdec524.

18. Diane Benscoter. "How cults rewire the brain." *TED Talk*. February 2009. Retrieved December 28, 2009, from https://www.ted.com/talks/diane_benscoter_how_cults_rewire_the_brain.

19. Stephen Adams. "Our 13-year-old boy was brainwashed into thinking she's transgender: Parents accuse school of secretly radicalizing mentoring sessions that convinced her that she was really a boy." *Daily Mail*. March 14, 2020. Retrieved August 19, 2020, from https://www.dailymail.co.uk/news/article-8112841/Our-13-year-old-brainwashed-thinking-shes-transgender.html.

20. Staff. "Teen depression study: Understanding depression in teens." *National Institute of Mental Health*. 2018. Retrieved August 19, 2020, from https://www.nimh.nih.gov/health/publications/teen-depression/teendepression_20-mh-8089_150205.pdf.

21. Mary Eberstadt. *Primal screams: How the sexual revolution created identity politics*. 2019. West Conshohocken, PA: Templeton Press, p. 109.

22. Rousas John Rushdoony. 1995 (1963). *The messianic character of American education*. Vallecito, CA: Ross House Books.

23. Ernest J. Zarra III. *Detoxing American schools: From social agency to academic urgency*. 2020. Lanham, MD: Rowman & Littlefield Publishers, p. 5.

24. Ibid.

25. Mary Eberstadt. *Primal screams: How the sexual revolution created identity politics*, pp. 64, 66. Cf. Vida Roberts. "BABY BAUBLE pacifiers as accessories are the latest trend on fashion front." *The Baltimore Sun*. November 23, 1992. Retrieved June 12, 2020, from https://www.baltimoresun.com/news/bs-xpm-1992-11-23-1992328203-story.html.

26. Paul C. Vitz. *Psychology as religion: The cult of self-worship*. 1995. Grand Rapids, MI: Wm. B. Eerdmans Publishing Company, pp. 126 ff. and 166 ff.

27. Leon F. Seltzer. "The gullibility of the narcissist: What you need to know." *Psychology Today*. August 13, 2018. Retrieved September 23, 2020, from https://www.psychologytoday.com/us/blog/evolution-the-self/201808/the-gullibility-the-narcissist-what-you-need-know.

28. Chelsea Ritschel. "What so all the letters in LGBTQIA+ stand for?" *Independent*. June 22, 2020. Retrieved August 28, 2020, from https://www.independent.co.uk/life-style/lgbtqia-meaning-full-version-stand-plus-lgbt-pride-month-acronym-a9574351.html.

29. Proverbs 16:18. *New American Standard Bible*.

30. Andrew Sullivan. "America wasn't built for humans." *New York Magazine*. September 18, 2017. Retrieved June 12, 2020, from https://nymag.com/intelligencer/2017/09/can-democracy-survive-tribalism.html.

31. Ibid.

32. Ibid.

33. Staff. "Enough is enough. 44 protesters arrested as Seattle police clear CHOP area." *KOMO News*. July 1, 2020. Retrieved August 20, 2020, from https://komonews.com/news/local/seattle-police-clearing-chop-area-after-durkan-issues-executive-order.

34. Steve Kornacki. *The red and the blue: The 1990s and the birth of political tribalism*. 2018. New York, NY: HarperCollins Publishers.

35. Astead W. Herndon. "Elizabeth Warren apologizes to Cherokee Nation for DNA test." *New York Times*. February 1, 2019. Retrieved June 12, 2020, from https://www.nytimes.com/2019/02/01/us/politics/elizabeth-warren-cherokee-dna.html.

36. Kirk Johnson, Richard Perez-Pena, and John Eligon. "Rachel Dolezal, in Center of Storm is defiant: 'I identify as Black.'" *New York Times*. June 16, 2015. Retrieved June 12, 2020, from https://www.nytimes.com/2015/06/17/us/rachel-dolezal-nbc-today-show.html.

37. Astead W. Herndon. "Elizabeth Warren apologizes to Cherokee Nation for DNA test." *New York Times*. February 1, 2019. Retrieved June 12, 2020, from https://www.nytimes.com/2019/02/01/us/politics/elizabeth-warren-cherokee-dna.html.

38. Decca Aitkenhead. Rachel Dolezal: "I'm not going to stoop and apologise [*sic*] and grovel." *The Guardian*. February 25, 2017. Retrieved June 12, 2020, from https://www.theguardian.com/us-news/2017/feb/25/rachel-dolezal-not-going-stoop-apologise-grovel.

39. Joshua Bote. "Rachel Dolezal reveals that she's bisexual in the middle of pride month." *USA Today*. June 17, 2019. Retrieved June 12, 2020, from https://www.usatoday.com/story/news/nation/2019/06/17/rachel-dolezal-shares-shes-bisexual-during-pride-month/1478536001/.

40. Jacob Knutson. "More than 200 native-Americans urge Elizabeth Warren to fully retract ancestry claims." *Axios*. February 26, 2020. Retrieved August 19, 2020, from https://www.axios.com/elizabeth-warren-native-american-ancestry-apology-8b8f1d1d-b2da-4d08-8ab9-2a547498e212.html.

41. Jason Whitlock. "NBA players trapped in BLM cult need your love, not a boycott." *Outkick*. August 17, 2020. Retrieved August 28, 2020, from https://www.outkick.com/if-you-want-to-empower-the-blm-cult-boycott-the-nba-bubble/.

42. Eberstadt. *Primal screams: How the sexual revolution created identity politics*, p. 26.

43. Ibid., p. 21.

44. Matt Lamb. "Professor blames 'white Christian privilege' for slavery and genocide." *The College Fix*. September 11, 2020. Retrieved September 12, 2020, from https://www.thecollegefix.com/professor-blames-white-christian-privilege-for-slavery-genocide/?fbclid=IwAR1lwknge2o9DDV_Hl6OcrQba08fNsbeDnZDd-4GLD1t0NOLNVaY15nlXFU.

45. Ibid.

46. Christopher F. Rufo. "Even after Trump ordered and end, federal agencies still push insane 'critical race theory." *New York Post*. September 15, 2020. Retrieved September 19, 2020, from https://nypost.com/2020/09/15/federal-agencies-still-pushing-insane-critical-race-theory/.

47. Paula Groves Price. "Critical race theory." *Oxford Research Encyclopedia.* 2020. Retrieved September 19, 2020, from https://oxfordre.com/education/view/10.1093/acrefore/9780190264093.001.0001/acrefore-9780190264093-e-1.

48. Robin DiAngelo. *White fragility.* 2018. Boston, MA: Beacon Press.

49. John McWhorter. "The dehumanizing condescension of White fragility." *The Atlantic.* July 15, 2020. Retrieved August 20, 2020, from https://www.theatlantic.com/ideas/archive/2020/07/dehumanizing-condescension-white-fragility/614146/.

50. Greg Lukianoff and Jonathan Haidt. "The coddling of the American mind." *The Atlantic.* September 2015. Retrieved June 9, 2020, from https://www.theatlantic.com/magazine/archive/2015/09/the-coddling-of-the-american-mind/399356/.

51. Ibid.

52. Peg Streep. "The psychology of revenge and vengeful people." *Psychology Today.* June 19, 2017. Retrieved August 20, 2020, from https://www.psychologytoday.com/us/blog/tech-support/201707/the-psychology-revenge-and-vengeful-people.

53. Lukianoff and Haidt. "The coddling of the American mind." *The Atlantic.*

54. Dr. Ernie Zarra. "BLM: The newest bully on the block?" *Personal Blog, Dr. Ernie Zarra.* June 16, 2020. Retrieved June 27, 2020, from https://drerniezarra.com/dr-zarras-blog/f/blm-the-newest-bully-on-the-block.

55. Tarra Bates-Duford. "Teaching a child to hate: 10 Consequences of hate." *Psych Central.* August 1, 2016. Retrieved September 23, 2020, from https://blogs.psychcentral.com/relationship-corner/2016/08/teaching-a-child-to-hate-10-consequences-of-hate/.

56. Marie Hartwell-Walker. "We can teach children not to hate." *Psych Central.* 2020. Retrieved August 30, 2020, from https://psychcentral.com/blog/we-can-teah-children-not-to-hate/. Cf. Brooke Emery. "The upbringing of a creature: The scope of a parent's right to teach children to hate." *The Modern American.* Fall, 2008. 4(2): 60–71.

57. Emma Colton. "Math professor claims equation 2+2=4 reeks of white supremacy patriarchy." *Washington Examiner.* August 10, 2020. Retrieved August 21, 2020, from https://www.washingtonexaminer.com/news/math-professor-claims-equation-2-2-4-reeks-of-white-supremacist-patriarchy.

58. Lee Ohanian. "Seattle schools propose to teach that math education is racist—Will California be far behind?" *Stanford University Hoover Institution.* October 29, 2019. Retrieved August 21, 2020, from https://www.hoover.org/research/seattle-schools-propose-teach-math-education-racist-will-california-be-far-behindseattle.

59. Derek Thompson. "Three decades ago, America lost its religion. Why?" *The Atlantic.* September 26, 2019. Retrieved August 30, 2020, from https://www.theatlantic.com/ideas/archive/2019/09/atheism-fastest-growing-religion-us/598843/.

60. Natasha Crain. "How Sunday schools are raising the next generation of secular humanists." *Christian Mom Thoughts.* January 20, 2020. Retrieved June 2, 2020, from https://christianmomthoughts.com/how-sunday-schools-are-raising-the-next-generation-of-secular-humanists/.

61. Ibid.

62. Ernest J. Zarra III. "Ernie Zarra: Eventually we're going to leave a dumbed-down generation behind." *The Bakersfield Californian.* September 13, 2016. Retrieved

August 30, 2020, from https://www.bakersfield.com/opinion/ernie-zarra-eventually-were-going-to-leave-a-dumbed-down-generation-behind/article_a93412a6-c762-5e4b-95ce-e5fa11ace395.html.

63. Gwen Aviles. "Grey's anatomy star Sara Ramirez comes out as nonbinary." *NBC News*. August 28, 2020. Retrieved September 12, 2020, from https://www.nbcnews.com/feature/nbc-out/grey-s-anatomy-star-sara-ramirez-comes-out-nonbinary-n1238692.

64. Ibid.

65. Suzanne Fenker. "How America's woman-dominant sexual dynamic is destroying marriages and families." *The Federalist*. January 20, 2020. Retrieved May 6, 2020, from https://thefederalist.com/2020/01/20/how-americas-woman-dominant-sexual-dynamic-is-destroying-marriages-and-families/.

66. Ibid.

67. John Marriott. *A recipe for disaster: Four ways churches and parents prepare individuals to lose their faith and how they can instill a faith that endures*. 2018. Eugene, OR: Wipf and Stock Publishers, pp. 29–40.

68. Crain. "How Sunday schools are raising the next generation of secular humanists." *Christian Mom Thoughts*.

69. Ibid.

70. Ibid.

71. Eberstadt. *Primal screams: How the sexual revolution created identity politics*, p. 86.

72. Maya Salam. "What is toxic masculinity?" *New York Times*. January 22, 2019. Retrieved June 15, 2020, from https://www.nytimes.com/2019/01/22/us/toxic-masculinity.html.

73. Lang Thompson. "The Blob: TCM Film Article." *Turner Classic Movies (TCM)*. 2020 (1958). Retrieved September 23, 2020, from http://www.tcm.com/this-month/article/31590%7C0/The-Blob.html.

Chapter 4

Cracks in the Ivory Towers

The crisis of Western Civilization lies in the steady decay of truth in the symbols of order rooted in the philosophic and spiritual traditions.[1]

For the time will come when they will not endure sound doctrine, but wanting to have their ears tickled, they will accumulate for themselves teachers in accordance to their own desires; and will turn away their ears from the truth, and will turn aside to myths.[2]

Pressure has been building up inside America's academic institutions of higher education for some time. There are ever-deepening cracks fracturing the Ivory Towers of the universities. Inside the bubbles that house America's so-called academic elites are the echo chambers, which reverberate narratives that spark emotional unrest and agitate the young. With each reverberation the gap between everyday Americans and those in higher education grows.[3]

Some of the research that comes out of America's universities runs the gamut. From the arcane and bizarre, to the fictitious and ridiculous, professors seem enchanted by the sounds of their echoes. One of the more recent bizarre propositions to emerge from the Ivory Towers is the idea that a *fear of fatness*, or as some refer to it as *obesophobia*, stems from being anti-Black. Another is that cutting one's lawn might be racist.[4]

According to Sabrina Strings, a Black sociology professor at the University of California, Irvine, the indexing of the measure of body mass, known as the BMI of a person, is a racist measure. She adds, "We cannot deny the fact that fat-phobia is rooted in anti-Blackness. This is simply an historical fact."[5] Many of these propositions are addressed in the best-selling book *Cynical Theories: How Activist Scholarship Made Everything about Race, Gender, and Identity—and why this harms everybody*,[6] by Helen Pluckrose and James Lindsay.

Higher education has transitioned into a place of social and political ideation. For example, Harvard University law professor, Elizabeth Bartholet shared a concern about parents and homeschooling. Her position includes contentions that pose questions such as, "Do we think that parents should have 24/7, essentially authoritarian control over their children from ages zero to 18? I think that's dangerous. . . . I think it's always dangerous to put powerful people in charge of the powerless, and give the powerful one's total authority."[7]

The Ivory Towers are becoming places of liberal moral unrest, and this unrest is relentless in radical ideas that are released into mainstream America. The towers once revered for their intellectual prowess and reason, are now diminishing in correlation to rising political activism, extreme theories, biased and bogus history, and racist and gender tropes. That is not to say that all of academe is tarnished, as such.

American education continues to diminish as elitists in academe manufacture myths into the psyches of young adults and to spur political activism. This trend is dangerous to traditional America, and we have seen its dangers play out in many cities in 2020.

IVORY TOWER ACTIVISM

Emotions seem to have replaced reason, and students are the reflections of this change. Today, higher education is generally less concerned about truth and students' academic preparation. They complain about the lack of quality of students' work, yet advance theories meant to work against intellect and spark emotions. Higher education is now a place for secular battles to originate. Even the suggestion to add Judeo-Christian ideas to the marketplace of ideas is ridiculed by academe and triggers many to label even the request as hate language.[8]

Perhaps, Nancy Pearcey best illustrates this antagonism to America's religious heritage when she writes that overcoming the padlock on the doors of academe means first finding ways past the gatekeepers of facts and values,[9] whose philosophies are antagonistic to Christianity.

The contrast is stark between Christianity and humanism, which is one reason why the former is increasingly disallowed in the towers of academe. In recognizing the differences in worldviews that lead to activism, Mohler adds, "Christians must realize that the more enduring contest is . . . between worldviews. A clash of worldviews reveals all the fault lines of a society, from education and economics, to arts and entertainment. Eventually, everything is at stake. Over time, every culture conforms in general terms to one worldview, not to more than one. One morality, one fundamental picture of the world, one vision of humanity prevails."[10] The fault lines are shifting below the foundations of the Ivory Towers, but no one should expect a collapse any time soon.

Some professors in undergraduate programs are not shy about pushing their political and moral views on their students. Instead of teaching, these professors are proselytizing with the intent of creating an incentivized, purpose-driven motivational buzz, resulting in student action. There are few things more fulfilling than knowing students are taking the words of professors and acting on them. John Ellis agrees: "advocacy has now replaced analysis as the central concern of the campuses. And not just advocacy, or spirited advocacy. Campus political advocacy is more than passionate. It is ferocious."[11]

Tenure is often the protection that serves as the umbrella of professional and professorial untouchability. Tenure is now a cover for hateful language, disparaging remarks, and vitriolic retorts. The religion of Christianity and its supposed restrictive theology has now given way to a religious replacement, which should bear the label of hate language.

Tenure even covers threatening words and the provocation of violence, as well as the cancellations of people's views that do not fit those of academic privilege. Conservatives Ben Shapiro, Ann Coulter, David Horowitz, and others understand this well, as they have been shouted down on college campuses for their positions as conservatives.[12] Professors have said little about these restrictions of free speech, but would scream to the heavens from the pinnacles of their towers if their own speech was restricted.[13]

FREE SPEECH ME FOR ME, BUT NOT FOR THEE

The cases involving Milo Yiannopoulos at UC Berkeley, Charles Murray and Alison Stanger at Middlebury College, Heather McDonald at UCLA,

Christina Hoff Sommers at Lewis and Clark College, and Professor Brett Weinstein at Evergreen College are evidence of the growing trend among college students to use violence and cancel tactics the keep people from campus—especially conservative voices.[14]

The fact that faculty in certain academic departments do not call out violence demonstrates at least a silent affirmation of the violence. It also demonstrates a fear that they could be next if they speak out against what many refer to as tribal bullying. Apparently, in some humanities departments at some colleges, there is obviously among most of the faculty "no objection to beating up people with whom you have intellectual disagreements."[15]

More and more students are becoming hardened in their political and social positions, and enforcing these positions by bullying detractors. Their minds are being ruled by their emotions and emotionally solicited to act on behalf of the elite professoriate and well-educated radicals. Today's students "must have gotten those resolutely closed minds from somewhere, and it's not hard to figure out the most likely source: their teachers."[16]

Along with their closed-mindedness to views other than their own, the students' colleges and universities grant protections and explicitly empower race and gender activists. They do so over academics and critical inquiry. For example, rather than analyzing the Gross Domestic Product (GDP) of the United States in a macro-economics class, and comparing GDPs to those of other nations, colleges might go a different direction. In another example, students may be required to examine racist underpinnings in White economic theory, and its effects upon urban settings. Students then are required to volunteer their time in underserved urban neighborhoods.

This type of project bodes well for the activist professor and her research for publication, but students wonder why they feel depressed when the real work world does not recognize their emotions and racial emphases as criteria for employment. There is still a place for reason, logic, and common sense. One New York University professor is criticizing higher education for more than its price of a degree.

Scott Galloway of NYU's Stern School of Business calls out colleges for what he describes as "being drunk on exclusivity"[17] and creating a clear and definitive "caste system."[18] Professors are able to exploit this exclusivity and also enchant their reactionary demographic with additional *entitlement-splaining*. Entitlement-splaining is the rationale used to impress students' affects in order to justify and exacerbate growing feelings of discord. This helps to secure the students' psyches and confidence and then build additional radicalized views. However, this accomplishes little-to-nothing toward help students access careers and build toward their futures.

Biases, Trash-Talk, and Radicals, Oh My!

Advocates of the divisive modern critical race and gender theories allow no room for discourse. The proponents are adamant about disallowing arguments against their positions. To disagree with the modern voices echoing from the towers of academe is to compete on the merits of theories. But, any competition is rejected and is treated as intolerable to the theorists. Shunning and ridiculing are often the results of questioning the theoretical positions.

The actions of shaming others are best seen on social media where tenured professors find safe spaces to vent their true feelings. Many professors do not realize that the volumes of their voices have caused deepening cracks in the integrity of the very towers from which they proclaim their positions. These cracks have widened all the way to the very moral foundation of education itself.[19] Yet, still these towers stand.

There are several examples of professors openly showing political biases, possibly spurred on as a result of the recent 2020 presidential election and the COVID-19 pandemic faced by the nation. The results are becoming more and more concerning. Some professors use their classrooms to agitate-by-day but try to balance their work in contrast to their social-media-voices-by-night. But this line is more often blurred today.

To make matters worse, socialist and progressive student activists are stalking select conservative professors' social media posts and keeping record of the numbers, comments, and likes attributed to the professors. Their aim in tracking these professors is to threaten them and to get them fired from their teaching posts. The liberals of the Ivory Towers have little to say about this phenomenon, until one of their own becomes the target.

There are several reasons why students are acting this way. The students have become more liberal in actions. As liberals, they are generally more rude and vile in the ways they treat dissent and they tend to feed others' emotions, as well.

The celebration of violence among leftists is reinterpreted by left-wing news organizations as something other than what reality demonstrates. The

Ivory Towers are replete with liberal-minded scholars who believe their ideas are to be accepted without question. It is as if their words are dictum, ex cathedra, and are associated as *Verbum Dei*.

Tim Groseclose, in his book *Left Turn: How the Liberal Media Distorts the American Mind*, illustrates the point that "liberals have worse manners; they go to church less; they more often live in aggressive, urban environments; they shout people down at public speeches; and they use more vulgarity when they talk . . . bias really does affect people's views . . . the media are even further away from the natural, non-distorted position of the average voter. That is, not only are the media biased, they're even more biased than people realize."[20] In addition, according to Larry Greenfield, "a fellow at the Claremont Institute . . . they [liberals] worship the god of Equality."[21]

This worship is subsumed in actions of physical force and violent confrontations.

Attorney General under President Donald Trump, Bill Barr, has stated, "The left wants power because that is essentially their state of grace, their **secular religion**, they want to run people's lives, so they can design utopia for all of us, and that's what turns them on, and it's the lust for power, and they weren't expecting Trump's victory and it outraged them."[22]

Tenure and Free Speech

To illustrate the growing phenomenon, Professor Brittany Cooper, a tenured professor at Rutgers University in the Department of Women's, Gender, and Sexuality Studies, used Twitter against conservatives defending President Trump's actions in handling the coronavirus. Cooper tweeted vile language and her profane hatred of Donald Trump, in response to tweets supporting the president. Her words of hatred extended to those that voted for Trump.[23]

In another example, Cooper, who also authored the *Eloquent Rage: A Black Feminist Discovers Her Superpower*, referred to an economic recovery after the pandemic, by claiming "that most black people did not want the country to reopen and understood to do so would mean more death of black bodies."[24] She was seemingly pinning President Trump for future casualties.

People who favor free speech and open and deep conversations are being censored on some social media platforms. But Cooper bragged she could curse and tweet and she cannot be fired for either. Conservatives are not treated with the same consideration on social media platforms such as

Facebook and Twitter. So, to find places where they can post as freely as radicals and racists, some people are leaving behind Twitter and Facebook, and heading to Parler and Reddit.[25]

Cooper further illustrates how certain demographics are able to find support by social media platforms, as she writes:

> The majority of black voters overwhelmingly did not vote for Trump. The highest demographic that did was Black men at just a measly 15 per cent. They are literally willing to die from this clusterf****d COVID response rather than admit that absolutely anybody other than him would have been a better president. And when whiteness has a death wish, we are all in for a serious problem. No Black person deserves this and Black women knew would be absolutely awful for him to be president. And now we all live in daily fear F**k each and every Trump supporter. You all absolutely did this. You are to blame.[26]

Cooper bragged she could not be fired because she has tenure.[27] One has to wonder whether a person from another demographic had said similar things about a previous president, whether the result would have been the same, or whether tenure would make no difference in today's protected class academic environment.

Cooper's rants on Twitter shows both her bias and an arrogance that accompanies the empowerment associated with protected race status and protected academic tenure. When the politically correct message is supported by the media platform on which it is posted, all the world seems right. But posting something contrary to the left-leaning status quo, and an orchestrated gas-lighting or doxing, comes along an onslaught of shaming of the poster. In fact, organized groups might even visit the house of someone labeled as a dissenter of the group's messaging. BLM and Antifa have already resorted to this many times.[28] Bullying by the left seems an acceptable form of free speech.

No college wants to be referred to in the media as racist for firing a Black professor, especially when the professor maintains that systemic racism already exists at the college and it is just looking for a reason to act out. Is academe undergoing a fundamental split in its tower structure? Are there now both coexisting Ebony and Ivory Towers?

Another example of using tenure to one's advantage is the case involving Professor Eric Rasmussen, from Indiana University, Bloomington. Rasmussen posted a quote on Twitter from an article written for the *Unz Review*. The title of the article was "Are women destroying Academia? Probably."[29]

A colleague, Maggie Hopkins, who had worked alongside Rasmussen on the faculty council was offended by the tweet.[30] She replied by stating, "This article suggests there should be far fewer women at universities. I am deeply offended by this Tweet, and my ability to feel that offense does not diminish my intellect."[31] The quote in question from the *Unz* article includes the following: "Geniuses are overwhelming male because they combine outlier high IQ with moderately low Agreeableness and moderately low Conscientiousness."[32]

Rasmussen replied to Hopkin's tweet the following day with the reply, "You saying how offended you are is an anti-intellectual argument, if one can indeed call it an argument. I am not responsible for your difficulty in listening to opposing views. What do you think about Agreeability, Conscientiousness, and Genius?"[33]

Rasmussen was not fired from his job as a tenured professor, but pressure had been placed on him because of his views. Taking to social media to vent political, racial, or gender viewpoints hurts the relationships between colleagues back at work. Yet, under the guise of academic freedom, professors can impact a generation of minds with their own personal viewpoints, right from inside their classrooms and online through social media platforms—and a growing number do just that.

One needs only to read the writings of many of today's college professors in the social sciences, humanities, and many political science undergraduate courses at universities and colleges to see the overwhelming support of socialist and other radical groups in the United States. The oldest Antifa group in the United States is in Portland, Oregon. The stated goal of Antifa was to bring down the Trump Administration and to establish communism.

According to Mark Bray, the author of *Antifa: The Anti-Fascist Handbook*, and an ardent supporter of the far left, he refers to Antifa's actions as "revolutionary self-defense."[34] He writes, "Once freed of the values of free speech and democratic values, violence becomes merely politics by other means."[35] Antifa are a well-organized twenty-first-century resurrection of guerilla warfare. In one sense, they are a newer revolutionary group.

On the other hand, depending on who does the research, the groups mimics Nazism, with the tactics of the Bolsheviks, and fights against twentieth-century western values.[36] Are academics condemning the actions of this warfare on America's own soil? Jonathan Turley criticizes these academics by asserting, "These are scholars who have embraced the anti-thesis of the life and values of academia."[37]

ORWELL REVISITED

Many question the reasons for identity politics coming of age at this time in history. College campuses in the west "have become proscenia for the enactment of identity panic, complete with safe spaces, trigger warnings, appropriation conflicts, and other intriguing linguistic innovations."[38] Senior Research Fellow at the *Faith and Reason Institute*, Mary Eberstadt writes, "As everyone knows, sexual identity, racial identity, ethnic identity, and the rest of the pack have become essential to leftist politics—so much so that imagining today's progressivism without these group identities or their agendas is an exercise in futility."[39]

Colleges have ramped up their human resources departments and hired social justice lookouts whose sole jobs are to target those who merely criticize partisan identitarianism. The truth is these human resources departments "now operate in part as weaponized hall monitors, patrolling . . . social media accounts for transgressions."[40]

There should no longer be any wonder as to why some people are suddenly ousted from their places of employment or when coaches and athletes are shamed and bullied into knee-taking compliance—or even fired. Human resource departments employ accountability activists whose role is to oust people over their adverse political or social positions contrary to the status quo.

In terms of those seeking employment, human resource departments can even be highly discriminatory in seeking candidates that they sometimes resort to Internet searches, possibly even violating privacy laws of the applicant.[41] As an employee, however, what a person posts online now comes under greater scrutiny and can lead to discipline.

Disagreement with the status quo on sensitive cultural topics can often lead to dismissal and public shame. John Ellis explains, "It's a sign of weakness, not strength, when faculty radicals banish from campus anything that might compete with their cherished beliefs. . . . Critics of today's campuses talk of students as snowflakes, but the real snowflakes here are the ideas of the campus radicals: too fragile to survive unrestricted debate. The safe spaces that radicals really want to create are safe spaces for their ideas."[42]

As a result, radical faculty and staffers protect their own and celebrate the people with whom they agree as heroic, while diminishing disagreement and seeking ways to remove those with whom they disagree. For anyone seeking the basic reason as to why colleges and universities are unwilling to allow open and honest debate about differing faculty viewpoints, the answer is simple.

Far too many colleges hire liberal and Marxist leftist professors to shield their entrenched departments from debate.[43] It's the same kind of conclusion that can be drawn from examination of cult leaders and their strategies for pushing their doctrinal ideas.

Acceptance or Cancellation?

In academe, professors either choose to buy into the philosophy of groupthink, or they risk being silenced. The pressure is great to conform, or be canceled. Faculties in the humanities "are systemically emptying the classrooms of all but one political doctrine, that of the radical left."[44] As a result of their efforts and, along with colleges replacing retiring professors with more leftist hires, "radical faculty are making sure that students hear one side only and pressing them to accept it without hearing the other. This alone constitutes a stunning collapse of the quality and integrity of higher education."[45]

As Ellis explains, too often a professor is "too much the captive of his unshakable belief system,"[46] and that his or her "political activism will always undermine and corrupt academic thought."[47] This is one reason there are recommendations by radical professors to disestablish departments in academic disciplines that are not advocates of social justice.[48] Not favoring the social justice ideology can result in being canceled and this is a result supported by a vast number of professors nationwide.[49]

For example, any group that is afforded special protections on college campuses and files a formal complaint about supposed offensive rhetoric, that language can then be elevated to harassment or hate speech.[50] Over the last few years, Republicans were usually the first ones accused of hate speech. However, there are deep concerns also about Democrats embracing their own versions of hate speech and their use of it against their opponents.[51] Far too often, the hate speech of the left is justified by some strangely applied rationale.[52]

The goal of modern public education is looking more and more like its outcome to be measured in the number of disciples it counts as activists.[53] Students are graduating from institutions of higher learning with changed values. One of these forces focuses squarely on White students and the lobbying to end gifted education for them.[54] In the minds of secular progressives, whiteness is equivalent to racism, and giftedness programs have been far too White for far too long.[55]

In California, Democrats passed legislation requiring an ethnic studies course that students must take for graduation from state colleges. A similar course is already required for the state's high school students. The ethnic studies course states that it "urges students to become 'agents of change' and mandates that all students complete an 'engagement/action project'. . . the course guide suggests only one project to meet this requirement: promoting 'voting rights for undocumented immigrant residents' in local elections."[56] The curriculum "tars white students—by dint of their whiteness—as oppressors. 'Whiteness' is defined as 'more than a racial identity marker, it separates those that are privileged from those that are not.' White kids will have to endure this harassment to graduate."[57]

When the cure for a problem is to require others to be wounded, then the number counted among the injured increases. Such injury is harmful and no doubt provokes greater racial disharmony. Orwell's depiction of the transfer of porcine power seems highly resonant within the towers of academe today.

RACIAL DIVISION AND COMMON SENSE

For the sake of argument, imagine there are racial differences between work ethics of those of various races, and these are principles that are in-born, latent, and implicit. Imagine also that these differences have been observed since the days of the races' forefathers, and still exist in people today. Now, the challenge is to insert any race into the imagination and consider the outcome.

Anyone seeking a heated argument should entertain a conversation with a person about privilege and fragility. While so engaged, mention there is a difference in work ethic and insist that it is innate because of skin color and history and then watch the reaction. One group might argue because of slavery it has been kept at bay without the opportunities to get ahead. They could state the main reason holding them back is systemic institutional racism.

But another group could reply that slavery ended a long, long time ago and the ancestors of freed slaves have had a lot of time to improve their lot? A third group could point to overcoming obstacles and finding success, and a fourth group might express joy at the opportunity to live outside a communist or socialist nation. There are no winning arguments with race when ad hominem pejoratives are injected to cast a pall over an entire race.

Heather McDonald, a fellow at the Manhattan Institute, discovered an interesting phenomenon. She found whenever she questioned others about the existence of what has come to be known as *systemic racism*, there were few replies. When she asked for others to define the term, and to point out where it is found—and the extent to which it could be found—there were even fewer replies. In today's climate of politically correct easy-triggers, the mere challenge to "the belief of undiminished, systemic racism"[58] means that McDonald is immediately saddled with the label of "proven racist, and must be silenced."[59]

In contrast, a genuine conversation could be had about the government providing $14 trillion to fight poverty and the improvements made since President Lyndon Johnson's War on Poverty in America in the 1960s. Even with this, students are behind educationally and economically. The answer to having meaningful conversations about difficult topics is the building of genuine relationships.

These can be accomplished by leaving buzz phrases and assumptions behind. People should work *to gather* each other to the same mission because we are all human. If unity is the aim, then this is what has to happen in order for *together-ness* to be achieved. The nation needs more of this and less of one-sided, shout down activism.

What about White Privilege?

In all candor, if there is such a thing as privilege set up for Whites, then successful Blacks have figured out that they can access the same privilege and achieve wonderful things despite calling America a racist nation. As an example, President Barack Obama received very large percentages of the White vote for both of his presidential elections. Also, there is more wealth in the Black communities than ever before.

Where Black communities are not doing well, the result is as much as the political machinery that has run those communities for decades, as it is culture, or anything else. Few want to address a systemic cultural problems in Black communities and are intent on casting blame, rather than work for solutions.

The reality in America today is that privileges go way beyond race and into opportunity. If this was not the case, and accessing the American Dream was not possible for anyone but Whites, then only Whites would be successful in America. People from other nations would not want to come here to live and work. Common sense and economic indicators demonstrate this is definitely not the case as gains and improvements are noted in the Congressional Joint Committee report on *The Economic State of Black Americans in 2020.*[60]

What some people call privilege, most in the United States calls *opportunity*. However, seeing skin color as a privilege and opportunity is a barrier to the person and to his or her success. The reality is that if people want to work hard, regardless of their skin color, background, or struggles in life, there are opportunities for all people to gain educationally and economically. In fact, Black students' graduation rates from high schools are at all-time high, and this data includes charter, private, and public K–12 institutions.[61]

Joe Biden, as candidate for president in 2020, struggled mightily, overcame personal tragedies, and became successful in life. After securing the nomination for president for the Democratic Party, not once did anyone claim Joe Biden was the product of White Privilege—even after his running mate Senator Kamala Harris called him a racist during the primary debate cycle. Is this because Whites on the left are not considered racists, even after they are branded as such by their running mates?

Political opportunism is vastly different than economic opportunism. For example, Ben Carson, the former Trump Administration's Secretary of Housing and Urban Development (HUD), and South Carolina Senator Tim Scott focused intently on housing and business programs under President Trump's leadership. They specifically targeted their attention to over 8,000 areas defined as "Opportunity Zones."[62] These were established to help build up urban communities and provide investments in those communities. But there is always more work to do, and as long as conversations about race are difficult to have, progress will remain slow.

The positive news is there are more wealthy Blacks at or near the top economically in America than ever before. If there is implicit bias and latent systemic discrimination, how has so-called White Supremacy and subsequent privilege with its stranglehold on America even permitted such success for non-Whites?

Colleges are now making certain that students come to terms with their White Privilege. As an example of requirements at a community college in Idaho, students are required to list examples of their own White male privilege. If they cannot think of any, says the professor, then "that in itself represents a privilege."[63] Realistically, it is just as easy today to conclude there is Black Privilege,[64] and female privilege, as much as there is White Privilege. But isn't that the point?

The privilege is there for all? Opportunities for success abound in the United States regardless of one's beginning, their upbringing, or one's present condition. This message does not resonate from the towers of academe because it will not inflame people. It is not part of the rhetoric of social justice and the agenda into which students have been indoctrinated. Indoctrination does not yield a balanced education.

America is not a perfect nation, and some of our national stains are kept alive in society on purpose. The reality is that the nation is *becoming* a more perfect union over time. Furthermore, in this pursuit, having frank discussions on race do not make a person racist. Such discussions may trigger some to default to their emotions, but that is to be expected because of their own training, political affiliations, and expectations placed upon them by fellow identitarianists. The racial and social identity activists do not like open discourse. However, to achieve any semblance of a beginning of racial harmony, the rhetoric of separation has to end.

What could be a root cause of this inability of identitarians to accept being challenged? Eberstadt contends: "To say that post-1960s level of fatherlessness, divorce, shrinking families, and abortion, among other trends, have become major impediments to the understanding of self is not to say these things are the only phenomena propelling identity politics. This brings us to a critical moral stipulation: that real crimes and injustices have been committed against real sexual and racial and other minorities—wrongs that have naturally driven many people to group identities in the hopes of preventing more wounds."[65]

There are societal wounds that transcend even race, yet many of these are left invisible because one's vision of problems may be skewed by an external that has its foundation in one immovable viewpoint.

UNIVERSITIES' HARD LEFT TURNS

As mentioned several times throughout this book, humanism is the religion of the left and its places of worship are today's public-learning institutions. From K–16, America's schools are teeming with Marxist and leftist ideologies. These ideologies are coupled with historical ignorance as they point in the directions of other failed socialist states.

Why would America's schools be the point of focus for spreading such secular political ideologies? The short answer is because it is the result of the moral and ethical vacuums that exist in schools, all of which have left no American learning institution unaffected.

Universities as Replacements for Churches

Twenty-first-century universities and colleges are secular replacements for churches and houses of worship. Institutions of learning, whether K–12 or higher education, all have their pulpits, doctrines, and sacred writ that is handed down from the spires. Some of the radicals that occupy the academic towers practice religious humanism. Their goal is to remain unchallenged and grow in power.

Colleges are more than safe places for radicals' religious teachings. They are also places where strong influences occur and places where students emerge with radicalized viewpoints just as strong. For example:

- Judging people by their age, race, and sex is wrong. We wish you privileged, old White men would get that.
- *All Whites are racists* declarations are made, as a person of color stands next to his or her White spouse and children.
- Assuming that people do not care about Black lives if they support the fact that all lives matter.
- White students proclaiming the evils of White privilege and systemic racism, as they attend elite Ivy League universities, other private colleges, or the University of California education system.

The following passage from an article titled *The University and Social Change* was written by the Students for a Democratic Society (SDS), whose inception dates back to the early 1960s with Tom Hayden as its first president

(1962–1963).⁶⁶ The SDS was considered very far left during the turbulent 1960s.

Today, it would be considered mainstream on America's college campuses. There are eerie similarities to the SDS' ideas and some of today's Marxist, radical left-wing university professors, particularly in their goals stated for seizing power and spreading of their radical ideas.

The article states: "the university is located in a permanent position of social influence. Its educational function makes it indispensable and automatically makes it a crucial institution in the formation of social attitudes." Ellis addresses this statement and concludes "there is a rather unkind word for this: indoctrination."

Todd Gitlin, former president of the SDS (1963–1964), explains five points of focus of the SDS at its inception and beyond.⁶⁷ It is worth noting that Gitlin now is a professor of journalism and sociology at Columbia University, demonstrating the point that Marxists do move on in life but take their philosophies and ideologies with them.

> The organization favored direct action to oppose "white supremacy" and "imperial war," and to achieve civil rights and the radical reconstruction of economic life (i.e., the redistribution of money into the hands of African-Americans in order to fight racism). SDS was increasingly suspicious of established authorities and looked askance at corporate power. But there was no single political doctrine; for most of its existence (1962–69), SDS was an amalgam of left-liberal, socialist, anarchist and increasingly Marxist currents and tendencies.⁶⁸

Frankly, the SDS was a forerunner to what the nation is dealing with in public schools, with history content revisionism, via the works of Howard Zinn and the 1619 Project. The Black Lives Matter radicals seem to have taken a page from the SDS. Their website has a similar gathering of ever-changing, loose-ended progressive goals and presses some of the same SDS ideologies upon schools and American businesses.

There is no surprise that both SDS and BLM leaned heavily on Marxism to establish their groups.⁶⁹ In Ellis' words, "Rightly or wrongly, the pervasive campus mood of this particular historical moment was much closer than usual to the habitual mindset of the radical left, which always tended to see conspiracies of the rich and powerful against ordinary people."⁷⁰

Four additional major events flavored and cemented the protests of twentieth-century radicals. These eventually paved the way for additional protest movements of the 1960s. These events included the (1) Vietnam War, (2) Civil Rights struggles of the 1950s–1960s, (3) Civil Rights Act of 1964, and (4) Voting Rights Act of 1965.[71]

It is true that "the greater the concentration of any political group, the more extreme it will become. Thus, the political left on campus has grown more radical over time."[72] But there is a small, but growing campus movement afoot, which is focusing on recapturing America's history from the revisionists.[73]

Cultural Sins: Triggers and Micro-aggressions

Converts to religious humanism feel strongly about the severity of micro-aggressions and the importance of trigger warnings.[74] They are less concerned about freedom of speech that comes from critics than they are their own freedom.[75] The small words, actions, jests, looks, smiles, and various other gestures can be determined to be micro-aggressions by an aggrieved person or a group.

Confused feelings, resulting from subjectively offensive words, are all that are needed for micro-aggressions to have occurred. Micro-aggression watchdogs tell others that micro-aggressions are the same as causing violence, even if it is in the mind. A stated or felt personal offense—even if interpreted incorrectly—is a harm done and results in victimization. Examples of micro-aggressions range from asking where people were born, or about their favorite foods, their ages or genders.

To the humanist, such questions are probative and a harmful motive is ascribed to the person asking the questions. To make matters worse, so-called progressives at many public-learning institutions are making every effort to spot gestures they could report as discriminatory against one or more politically protected groups.

Trigger warnings are stated cautions. These are cautions to students that there might be something flagrant, offensive, emotional, or even surprising about to arrive in their presence. The emotional maturity of some college-aged students is low. As a result, some might possess a high emotional reactionary response to a very small stimulus. In some cases, there are serious past experiences that may haunt a student and a trigger[76] warning might worsen student distress, due to some form of Post-Traumatic Stress Disorder (PTSD). For example, mentioning a lesson title, or teaching a lesson on physical or sexual abuse, could trigger past trauma on the part of someone victimized in the past. In fact, just jesting about something could be described as a micro-aggression, or even classified as harassment on K–12 campuses and at college.

Similarly, a person who is offended secondarily or vicariously could also flag an instructor for not providing ample warning or disclaimer about a topic. These cultural sins, and more, are now institutionalized and strike fear into the hearts and minds of advocates of free speech.[77] How long will it take before actually warning about *triggers* comes with its own micro-aggression label?

FROM THE TOWERS TO THE PULPITS

Places of higher education are not the only institutions with Ivory Tower reputations. Throughout history, many churches in America have also occupied lofty positions in American culture. A good example is Black churches, which served as the foundation of the Civil Rights Movement under Rev. Dr. Martin Luther King, Jr. in the mid-twentieth century. Both higher education and a growing number of churches have in common progressive liberal ideologies.

The political and religious liberalization of the American church is not a recent phenomenon. J. Gresham Machen illustrates this reality with the early twentieth-century warning: "If the liberal party, therefore, really obtains control of the Church, evangelical Christians must be prepared to withdraw no matter what it costs."[78] Evangelical warnings like these were in no short supply in the twentieth century. They appear even less today because of apathy and a fear of offending people.

Mainline denominations that have veered left and have adopted political agenda for their churches have also redefined marriage and family. Changed ideas in roles for women in churches, as well as alternate sexual orientations and previously questionable relationships, are now mainstays in churches' doctrinal statements. The culture has changed, and liberal churches have secularized what was once sacred in their denominations and church doctrinal statements.

Historically, the separatists in churches "realized that before the Great Depression, when the opponents of the gospel are almost in control of . . . churches, the slightest avoidance of the defence [sic] of the gospel is just sheer unfaithfulness to the Lord."[79] Over the years, churches have adopted more of a secular institutional character, incorporating it into their religious platforms and statements of faith. This was evident also during Machen's time. He describes that nature of ongoing challenges to the church, at the time.

> We have today the entrance of paganism into the Church in the name of Christianity. But in the second century a similar battle was fought and won. From another point of view, modern liberalism is like the legislation of the middle ages, with its dependence upon the merit of man. And another Reformation in God's good time will come. . . . It is possible that the existing churches may be given over altogether to naturalism, that men may then see that the fundamental needs of the soul are to be satisfied not inside but outside of the existing churches, and that thus new Christian groups may be formed.[80]

Here in the twenty-first century a new Christian culture has been formed. This culture has produced the mega-church phenomenon and it has spread out across America. Along with this culture came humanism, which is rampant in churches whose doctrines are becoming increasingly more progressive, focused on prosperity, human choices, and which have become social-gospel institutions.

RELIGIOUS HUMANISM AND CHOICE

Few issues among Americans stir emotions as does the abortion issue. The phrases pro-choice and pro-life are the hallmarks of side-taking and categorize whether a person is viewed as a murderer of babies or a hater of women's health choices over their own bodies. For the vast majority of American voters, there is no middle ground.

An interesting point to consider is the number of pro-life advocates with very liberal social policies, and the number of pro-choice advocates in the churches, who hold conservative views on issues regarding other women's rights. There are very few in the Ivory Towers that will admit to a pro-life philosophical, theological, or even practical position.[81] It is virtually non-existent.

The always controversial Ann Coulter, a conservative firebrand, brings to light a very considerable point. She asks, "If women are so pro-abortion, why are virtually all abortionists men? If ever there was a need for a Take Our Daughters' to Work Day, it's at the abortion mills."[82]

Coulter goes on to include a 1982 quote attributed to quote Edward Eichner, who was the director of a Cleveland abortion clinic at the time. When asked about women abortionists, Eichner replied that women were not in favor of performing "abortions over and over for moral reasons." Likewise, if a pregnant physician showed up to perform abortions, this might upset the patients. In the words of Eichner, "if a woman is carrying a baby, she doesn't like to abort someone else's." These ideas are not welcome on college campuses, and invitations for Coulter to speak have either been rescinded, or she has been personally threatened and accosted to keep her from speaking. Whatever happened to *choice*?

Choice has become one of the central tenets of religious humanism and its protection for women is as enshrined in culture, just as any other right interpreted by the Supreme Court. A woman's choice for abortion is not found as a right by all constitutional scholars in the United States. In fact, the court said it was not perceptible but interpolated from within the penumbras of the First, Third, Fourth, and Ninth Amendments to the Constitution.

Giving someone the opportunity to choose to own human life as property smacks of another period in American history where the same right was granted. One would think that (1) any church offering the view that God is all right with abortion, and (2) that the Almighty desires humans to possess other human life as their property, that (3) such an institution has adopted a political platform and cast aside an orthodox biblical tenet.

Any person arguing a pro-abortion stance from a religious perspective should also stop to consider this fact. Some people in churches in the south, years ago, also said that they could choose human life as their property.

Religious Humanism and God

Writing about evolution, Coulter states, "Liberals' creation myth is Charles Darwin's theory of evolution, which is about one notch above Scientology in scientific rigor. It's a make-believe story, based on a theory that is a tautology, with no proof in the scientist's laboratory or the fossil record—and that's after 150 years of very determined looking. We wouldn't still be talking about it but for the fact that liberals think evolution disproved God."[83] She adds, "Although God believers don't need evolution to be false, atheists need evolution to be true."[84]

The majority of humanists, religious or not, have little problem with ending human life through abortion, especially since evolution passes on no intrinsic valuation of life. Some would even argue that ending human life could occur at any stage along the way—even if newborn.

The religious humanist might object to infanticide. Nevertheless, humanists in general "tend to converge on [the] liberal, pro-choice stance. Humanists value happiness and personal choice."[85] Those that hold to a survival-of-the-fittest ethic, and seek to apply it to neo-natal medicine, the ultimate outcome would be Peter Singer's eugenics. Singer says "parents should have the right to kill newborn babies with birth defects, such as Down syndrome and hemophilia, because killing a disabled child . . . 'is not morally equivalent to killing a person.'"[86]

Ronald Bailey describes Singer's views: "As such, he believes animals have rights because the relevant moral consideration is not whether a being can reason or talk but whether it can suffer. . . . Singer distinguishes . . . between persons and non-persons. Persons are beings that feel, reason, have self-awareness, and look forward to a future. Thus, fetuses and some very impaired human beings are not persons in his view and have a lesser moral status than, say, adult gorillas and chimpanzees."[87]

This is the same Princeton professor at the *Center for Human Values* who argues that there is "nothing morally wrong with parents conceiving children in order to harvest them for spare parts for an older child—or even for society to breed children on a massive scale for spare parts."[88] Singer's views debase human life to the level of property and not unlike those of the Nazis, and their experiments with the Jews. Again, the choice associated with ownership of human life as property rears its ugly head.

The Ivory Towers house some of the major culture shapers in American society today. The professors in the towers bear the responsibility for the beliefs of many young adults and the subsequent actions that emerge from their beliefs. Some of these professors are responsible for the accusations that America is (1) race-fragile, (2) endemically and systemically racist throughout all of its institutions of business and economics, (3) propping up failing schools, (4) favoring Whites in CEO, coaching, and corporate athletic positions, (5) empowering injustice within law enforcement, (6), biased in politics, and so on.

Some self-proclaimed leftist professors are also responsible for students adhering to Marxist mantras and student willingness to overthrow the oppressive current democratic system of the United States and remove its capitalistic moorings.

The most concerning and odious doctrine for which the radical American professors are responsible—and by which the towers they occupy will eventually collapse—is saddling and sentencing of an entire race of children and young adults as hopelessly and latently biased and racist because of the color of their skin. There was a time in America's past when this was the case. The nation should question why the application of a past wrongdoing should be allowed in twenty-first-century American society.

NOTES

1. Montgomery C. Erfourth. "The Voegelin enigma." *The American Interest*. December 10, 2014. 10(3): 4. Retrieved May 19, 2020, from https://www.the-american-interest.com/2014/12/10/the-voegelin-enigma/.

2. 1 Timothy 4:3–4. *New American Standard Bible*.

3. Howard Gold. "Opinion: At America's most woke colleges, extreme liberal politics fails students and free speech." *Market Watch*. January 27, 2020. Retrieved September 12, 2020, from https://www.marketwatch.com/story/at-americas-most-woke-colleges-extreme-liberal-politics-fails-students-and-free-speech-2020-01-27.

4. Mike Miller. "Mowing your yard just might be racist, America; Yep, it might be time to 'decolonize your lawn.'" *Red State*. September 18, 2020. Retrieved September 19, 2020, from https://www.redstate.com/mike_miller/2020/09/18/mowing-your-yard-just-might-be-racist-america-yep-it-might-be-time-to-decolonize-your-lawn/?fbclid=IwAR0pbh111Q1VzSE5cyFyo4OCe-l_yUa4jORqmayH5Cu0pHQZash3BLBac-Y.

5. Matt Lamb. "Sociology professor: Fat-phobia is rooted in anti-Blackness." *The College Fix*. August 21, 2020. Retrieved August 30, 2020, from https://www.thecollegefix.com/sociology-professor-fat-phobia-is-rooted-in-anti-blackness/. Cf. Maddie Sofia. "Fat phobia and its racist past and present: An interview with Sabrina Strings." *NPR*. July 21, 2020. Retrieved August 30, 2020, from https://www.npr.org/transcripts/893006538.

6. Helen Pluckrose and James Lindsay. *Cynical theories: How activist scholarship made everything about race, gender, and identity—and why this harms everybody*. 2020. Durham, NC: Pitchstone Publishing.

7. Selim Algar. "Harvard professor wants to ban homeschooling because it's 'authoritarian.'" *New York Post*. April 23, 2020. Retrieved September 2, 2020, from

https://nypost.com/2020/04/23/harvard-professor-wants-to-ban-authoritarian-home-schooling/. Cf. Patrick J. Wolf, Matthew H. Lee, and Angela R Watson. "Harvard law professor's attack on homeschooling is a flawed failure and terribly timed, too." *Education Next*. May 5, 2020. Retrieved September 24, 2020, from https://www.educationnext.org/the-journal/.

  8. James Loeffler. "The Problem with the 'Judeo-Christian tradition.'" *The Atlantic*. August 1, 2020. Retrieved September 23, 2020, from https://www.theatlantic.com/ideas/archive/2020/08/the-judeo-christian-tradition-is-over/614812/.

  9. Nancy Pearcey. *Total truth: Liberating Christianity from its cultural captivity*. 2005. Wheaton, IL: Good news Publishers.

  10. R. Albert Mohler, Jr. *The gathering storm*. 2020. Nashville, TN: HarperCollins Christian Publishing, p. 190.

  11. John M. Ellis. *The breakdown of higher education: How it happened, the damage it does, and what can be done*. 2020. New York, NY: Encounter for Culture and Education, Inc., p. 4.

  12. Ibid., p. 17.

  13. Raymond M. Berger. "Why do liberals shut down free speech and conservatives don't?" *The Times of Israel*. August 12, 2020. Retrieved September 23, 2020, from https://blogs.timesofisrael.com/why-do-liberals-shut-down-free-speech-and-conservatives-dont/.

  14. Ellis. *The breakdown of higher education: How it happened, the damage it does, and what can be done*, pp. 2–3.

  15. Ibid., p. 14.

  16. Ibid., p. 5.

  17. Julia La Roche. "NYU professor rips colleges for being 'drunk on exclusivity,' says coronavirus will force change." *Yahoo Finance*. April 20, 2020. Retrieved April 21, 2020, from https://finance.yahoo.com/news/nyu-marketing-pro-expects-tremendous-price-pressure-on-us-colleges-after-coronavirus-201541903.html.

  18. Ibid.

  19. Jason Brennan and Phillip Magness. *Cracks in the Ivory Tower. The moral mess of higher education*. 2019. Oxford, England: Oxford University Press.

  20. Tim Groseclose. *Left turn: How the liberal media distorts the American mind*. 2011. New York, NY: St. Martin's Press, pp. 5–6.

  21. Ibid., p. 5. Brackets mine.

  22. Mark Levin. "Antifa is a new form of urban guerilla warfare: An interview with Attorney General Bill Barr." *Life, Liberty, and Levin*. August 9, 2020. Retrieved August 10, 2020, from https://www.foxnews.com/shows/life-liberty-levin. Emphasis mine.

  23. Matthew Wright. "Rutgers professor blames Trump's clusterf****d COVID response and his supporters for welcoming a mass winnowing of Black folks as African Americans make up 30 per cent of all US cases of the virus." *Daily Mail*. April 30, 2020. Retrieved May 8, 2020, from https://www.dailymail.co.uk/news/article-8273377/Rutgers-professor-says-Trump-supporters-welcome-mass-winnowing-Black-folks-amid-Covid-19-deaths.html.

  24. Ibid.

25. Abraham Brown. "Parler's founder explains why he built Trump's new favorite social media app." *Forbes*. June 27, 2020. Retrieved June 28, 2020, from https://www.forbes.com/sites/abrambrown/2020/06/27/parlers-founder-explains-why-he-built-trumps-new-favorite-social-media-app/#12b60c285016. Adam Smith. "Parler: What is the app that MPS and right-wing celebrities are joining?" *Independent*. June 24, 2020. Retrieved June 28, 2020, from https://www.independent.co.uk/life-style/gadgets-and-tech/news/parler-app-mps-right-wing-twitter-katie-hopkins-a9579241.html.

26. Wright. "Rutgers professor blames Trump's clusterf****d COVID response and his supporters for welcoming a mass winnowing of Black folks as African Americans make up 30 per cent of all US cases of the virus." *Daily Mail*.

27. Ibid.

28. Penny Starr. "Antifa and Black Lives Matter activists harassed people on sidewalks in Washington, DC, on Saturday and clashed with police leading to the arrest of at least four individuals." *Breitbart*. August 30, 2020. Retrieved September 15, 2020, from https://www.breitbart.com/politics/2020/08/30/dc-antifa-black-lives-matter-activists-threaten-diners-clash-police/. Cf. Joshua Rhett Miller. "Seattle BLM protesters demand White people 'give up' their homes." *New York Post*. August 14, 2020. Retrieved August 16, 2020, from https://nypost.com/2020/08/14/seattle-blm-protesters-demand-white-people-give-up-their-homes/.

29. Lance Welton. "Are women destroying academia? Probably." *The Unz Review*. November 2, 2019. Retrieved May 8, 2020, from https://www.unz.com/article/are-women-destroying-academia-probably/.

30. Michael Brice-Saddler and Deanna Paul. "University says a professor's views are racist, sexist, and homophobic—but it can't fire him." *The Washington Post*. November 22, 2019. Retrieved May 8, 2020, from https://www.washingtonpost.com/education/2019/11/20/university-says-professors-views-are-racist-sexist-homophobic-they-cant-fire-him/.

31. Ibid.

32. Lance Welton. "Are women destroying academia? Probably." *The Unz Review*. November 2, 2019. Retrieved May 8, 2020, from https://www.unz.com/article/are-women-destroying-academia-probably/.

33. Brice-Saddler and Paul. "University says a professor's views are racist, sexist, and homophobic—but it can't fire him." *The Washington Post*.

34. Jonathan Turley. "Opinion: The hypocrisy of Antifa." *The Hill*. August 29, 2017. Retrieved September 13, 2020, from https://thehill.com/blogs/pundits-blog/civil-rights/348389-opinion-antifa-threatens-to-turn-america-into-an.

35. Ibid.

36. Nikita Vladimirov. "Antifa's heritage of oppression." *Washington Examiner*. September 13, 2017. Retrieved September 19, 2020, from https://www.washingtonexaminer.com/red-alert-politics/antifas-heritage-oppression.

37. Turley. "Opinion: The hypocrisy of Antifa." *The Hill*.

38. Mary Eberstadt. *Primal screams: How the sexual revolution created identity politics*. 2019. West Conshohocken, PA: Templeton Press, p. 6.

39. Ibid.

40. Ibid., p. 7.

41. Jonathan A. Segal. "Social media use in hiring: Assessing the risks." September, 2014. *Society for Human Resource Management.* September 2014. Retrieved August 21, 2020, from https://www.shrm.org/hr-today/news/hr-magazine/pages/0914-social-media-hiring.aspx.

42. Ellis. *The breakdown of higher education: How it happened, the damage it does, and what can be done*, p. 17.

43. Jon A. Shields. "The disappearing conservative professor." *National Affairs.* Fall 2018. Retrieved September 12, 2020, from https://nationalaffairs.com/publications/detail/the-disappearing-conservative-professor.

44. Ellis. *The breakdown of higher education: How it happened, the damage it does, and what can be done*, p. 42.

45. Ibid., p. 42.

46. Ibid., p. 39.

47. Ibid., p. 39.

48. Ibid., p. 40.

49. Scott Jaschik. "Professors and politics: What the research says." *Inside Higher Ed.* February 27, 2017. Retrieved September 12, 2020, from https://www.insidehighered.com/news/2017/02/27/research-confirms-professors-lean-left-questions-assumptions-about-what-means.

50. Jonathan Turley. "No, the U.S. does not need European-style hate speech laws. *USA Today.* November 8, 2019. Retrieved September 12, 2020, from https://www.usatoday.com/story/opinion/2019/11/08/no-us-not-need-european-style-hate-speech-laws-column/4157833002/. Cf.

51. Corey Lewandowski. "Why do so many Democrats embrace hate speech"? *The Hill.* March 24, 2019. Retrieved September 12, 2020, from https://thehill.com/opinion/white-house/435477-why-do-so-many-democrats-embrace-hate-speech.

52. Arthur Milikh. "The left encourages hate speech—for some." *Real Clear Policy.* June 2, 2020. Retrieved September 3, 2020, from https://www.realclearpolicy.com/articles/2020/06/02/the_left_encourages_hate_speech__for_some_494926.html.

53. Jennifer Gonzalez. "How ordinary teachers become activists." *Cult of Pedagogy.* May 10, 2015. Retrieved April 29, 2020, from https://www.cultofpedagogy.com/teacher-activism-education-reform/.

54. Kari Donovan. "School activists want to end gifted classes for White students." *National File.* November 3, 2019. Retrieved April 29, 2020, from https://nationalfile.com/school-activists-want-to-end-gifted-classes-for-white-students/.

55. Ann Dornfield. "Too White? A criticism of Seattle Public Schools gifted programs for decades." *KUOW News.* November 14, 2020. Retrieved September 19, 2020, from https://www.kuow.org/stories/cold-war-anxiety-and-affirmative-action-the-dawn-of-gifted-education-in-seattle-schools.

56. Betsy McCaughey. "Left-wing activists trying to hijack kids' minds with 'ethnic studies.'" *New York Post.* August 22, 2019. Retrieved January 15, 2020, from https://nypost.com/2019/08/22/left-wing-activists-trying-to-hijack-kids-minds-with-ethnic-studies/.

57. Ibid.

58. Ellis. *The breakdown of higher education: How it happened, the damage it does, and what can be done*, p. 15.

59. Ibid., p. 15.

60. Congressman Don Beyer. "The economic state of Black America in 2020." *Joint Economic Committee*. 2020. Retrieved September 12, 2020, from https://www.jec.senate.gov/public/_cache/files/ccf4dbe2-810a-44f8-b3e7-14f7e5143ba6/economic-state-of-black-america-2020.pdf.

61. Jennifer Cheeseman Day. "88% of Blacks have a high school diploma, 26% a bachelor's degree." *United States Census Bureau*. June 18, 2020. Retrieved September 23, 2020, from https://www.census.gov/library/stories/2020/06/black-high-school-attainment-nearly-on-par-with-national-average.html.

62. Ayesha Rascoe. "White House looks to opportunity zone extension in wake of COVID-19." *NPR*. May 22, 2020. Retrieved September 12, 2020, from https://www.npr.org/2020/05/22/859697610/white-house-looks-at-opportunity-zone-extension-in-wake-of-covid-19.

63. Henry Kokkeler. "Mandatory class at Idaho college tells students to list examples of white and male privilege." *College Fix*. September 25, 2020. Retrieved September 26, 2020, from https://www.thecollegefix.com/mandatory-class-at-idaho-college-tells-students-to-list-examples-of-white-and-male-privilege/.

64. John Blake. "It's time to talk about Black privilege." *CNN*. March 31, 2016. Retrieved August 21, 2020, from https://www.cnn.com/2016/03/30/us/black-privilege/index.html.

65. Eberstadt. *Primal screams: How the sexual revolution created identity politics*, p. 13.

66. Staff. "Who are the SDS?" *Newsweek Magazine*. May 20, 2968. pp. 62–63.

67. Todd Gitlin. "What was the protest group Students for a Democratic Society? Five questions answered." *Smithsonian Magazine*. May 4, 2017. Retrieved July 15, 2020, from https://www.smithsonianmag.com/history/what-was-protest-group-students-democratic-society-five-questions-answered-180963138/.

68. Ibid.

69. Jeff Gordon. "SDS: An analysis." *Progressive Labor*. October, 1968. 6(5). Retrieved August 21, 2020, from https://www.marxists.org/history/erol/1960-1970/pl-sds.htm. Cf. Yaron Steinbuch. "Black Lives Matter co-founder described herself as trained Marxist." *New York Post*. June 25, 2020. Retrieved August 21, 2020, from https://nypost.com/2020/06/25/blm-co-founder-describes-herself-as-trained-marxist/.

70. Ellis. *The breakdown of higher education: How it happened, the damage it does, and what can be done*, p. 51.

71. Ibid., pp. 54–55.

72. Ibid., p. 54.

73. Anthony Jones. "My generation is being raised to hate America—it's time to stand up for our history." *USA Today*. September 23, 2020. Retrieved September 24, 2020, from, https://www.yahoo.com/news/generation-being-raised-hate-america-110031647.html.

74. Greg Lukianoff and Jonathan Haidt. "The coddling of the American mind." *The Atlantic*. September 2015. Retrieved June 9, 2020, from https://www.theatlantic.com/magazine/archive/2015/09/the-coddling-of-the-american-mind/399356/.

75. John O. McGinnis. "Liberals versus political speech: The Left wants to put people behind bars for expressing opinion that it doesn't like." *Manhattan Institute of Public Policy Research City Journal*. Spring 2016. Retrieved September 24, 2020, from https://www.city-journal.org/html/liberals-versus-political-speech-14330.html.

76. Staff. "On trigger warnings." *American Association of University Professors*. August 2014. Retrieved June 6, 2020, from https://www.aaup.org/report/trigger-warnings.

77. Lukianoff and Haidt. "The coddling of the American mind." *The Atlantic*.

78. J. Gresham Machen. *Christianity and liberalism*. 1983 (1923). Grand Rapids, MI: Wm. B. Eerdmans Publishing Company, p. 166.

79. Ibid., p. 174.

80. Ibid., p. 178.

81. John J. Conley. "Can a prolife scholar survive in academia?" *American Magazine*. October 16, 2018. Retrieved September 12, 2020, from https://www.americamagazine.org/faith/2018/10/16/can-pro-life-scholar-survive-academia.

82. Ann Coulter. Godless: *The church of liberalism*. 2006. New York, NY: Crown Publishing Group, p. 84.

83. Ibid., p. 198.

84. Ibid., p. 201. Cf. James Tunstead Burtchaell. *Rachel weeping and other essays about abortion*. 1982. Kansas City, MO: Andrews McMeel, p. 43.

85. Staff. "A humanist discussion on abortion." *Humanists UK*. 2020. Retrieved August 30, 2020, from https://humanism.org.uk/humanism/humanism-today/humanists-talking/humanist-discussion-on-abortion/. Cf. Sarah Henry. "Abortion access is a religious freedom issue, say humanists." *American Humanist*. October 4, 2019. Retrieved August 30, 2020, from https://americanhumanist.org/press-releases/abortion-access-is-a-religious-freedom-issue-say-humanists/.

86. Coulter. Godless: *The church of liberalism*, p. 274.

87. Ronald Bailey. "The pursuit of happiness: Controversial philosopher Peter Singer argues for animal rights, utilitarian ethics, and a Darwinian left." *Reason*. December 2000. Retrieved May 13, 2020, from https://reason.com/2000/12/01/the-pursuit-of-happiness-peter/.

88. Marvin Olasky. "Blue-state philosopher." *World Magazine*. November 27, 2004. Retrieved May 13, 2020, from https://world.wng.org/2004/11/blue_state_philosopher.

Chapter 5

Seeking Converts

> *Secularization . . . cannot and will not tolerate the biblical worldview on any matter or issue. Indeed, the secular storm not only threatens issues of public policy like religious liberty, abortion access, and marital laws, but also levies a full broadside into private homes. . . . If parents object to secularization, then they must be removed from the equation.*[1]

In twenty-first-century America, there is no shortage of information. The abundance of media sources provides an inundating surplus of knowledge. Some of this information is accurate and some of it is not. One thing certain in this information abundance is that America continues to change right before our eyes. The media are certainly one source responsible for this change.

Other sources are the schools that America's children attend. The adoptions of ever-changing educational philosophies are causing rapid advancement in the ways teaching and learning occur across the education spectrum. State departments of education are complicit with teachers' unions and local associations in their support of the newest of philosophical narratives.

Then there are the social activists and influencers that affect cultural opinions in society, including K–16 educational institutions. One of the ideas presently finding large-scale acceptance in the United States is the secularizing of religion. What is the attraction for secularists when it comes to religion and culture these days?

RELIGIOUS HUMANISM AND ITS ATTRACTION

Throughout this chapter, the term *secular* will be used interchangeably with the term *humanism*. Humanism has become its own religion and is a good example of the definition of an old belief in the form of a newer religious cultic paradigm. This author is not the first to make this claim.[2]

A cult has been defined as "a gathering of people who owe allegiance to one . . . who ostensibly represents truth. The truth which catalyzes a religion requires its followers to believe, rather than understand or have proven to them, a view of the universe."[3] The definition relates to cults of personality and groups, and blind faith is the mission and leadership's expectations associated with them.

Would anyone be surprised to learn that schools and colleges are actively recruiting students to a secular religion and that it is being proffered by slick presentations on campuses? The fact is, younger generations are falling prey to secularist cult leaders whose messages have all the trappings of religion encased in their recruiting approach. The concern today is that certain cult leaders have cultivated a growing population of willing followers right on college campuses and have gained a foothold to advance their cause to the masses, especially including those in K–12 schools.

Many of these students being recruited seek their own sense of belonging and purpose, which provides a fertile environment for cult recruiters. Generation Z is unique in that respect.[4] However, it is ironic that these young adults have been placed under the umbrella term "The Therapy Generation"[5] by the *Wall Street Journal*.

The Messaging and Impact

In terms of the messaging of religious secularists, "The dogma of the cult is the same as the dogma of any church. It is a group of prejudices which may or may not be related to reality. . . . These prejudices are the truths of the cult, what members believe [and] their reason for being."[6] An excellent example of this is Black Lives Matter, a cult that is based on religious secularism and uses race to advance its agenda. BLM is increasingly finding support from churches of all denominations and its message is hidden behind a secular Marxist-anarchist philosophy.

BLM has now impacted professional athletics, and has become part of the nation's political rhetoric, pressuring businesses into compliance with their message. BLM has made inroads into all of American education, and there are no signs it will stop there.[7] In the realm of politics, Cori Bush, the first BLM member, ran for U.S. Congress and won her Democratic primary against ten-term incumbent, Lacy Clay.[8] BLM's efforts to lead a Marxist-style revolution among students is not lost to anyone who would read their original website.[9] The overarching goal is the dismantling of America as we know it and the shattering of all of its institutions that are supposedly systemically racist.

BLM intends to accomplish this radical change under the guise of social justice, which they have religionized for secular purposes. The purpose is to make converts, particularly among younger teachers who see their mission as activists and evangelists for grander purposes. In many ways, today's educators are being used in the process of "recruiting people and assisting them to become born again."[10] The urban colloquialism assigned to such an experience among today's followers of the BLM cult is the term *wokeness*.

Who Are the Followers?

There are characteristics associated with those who fall prey more easily to ideological charlatans. Recruits that discover a message that comes across as exclusive to them are more inclined and willing to give their time and finances to advance a cause as followers. Leaders encourage actions by followers, and most often these calls-to-action are to be carried out through peaceable and means exclusive to the group in question. However, sometimes leaders stimulate followers to act more violently and destructively. Why is this the case? Why do followers willingly travel such a revolutionary path?

First, there is a dearth of history knowledge among the younger generations. What history they do know has been largely revised. Past major conflicts are often not in the memories of the young. Neither are the young taught the actual history of America in many schools and colleges. For all they know, the followers are blazing a new path in history.

Second, there are millions of teenagers and young adults just searching amidst the moral vacuum that is found in American education, and in society in general. Their sense of purposeless was compounded by the COVID-19 pandemic and inflamed political discourse associated with a presidential election year. *Third*, there is a deep desire in the souls of many students to be part of something larger than themselves and, with smart technology, they are more impressionable toward impulses that involve emotions.

The reality is that students want to enjoy affiliation and desire a hero figure to lead them. "They want answers and affection. They will join just about anything if approached properly since they are truly people without purpose."[11] Recruits for today's secular and religious cults fit a generalized composite profile.

> The most ignorant, confused, and suggestible potential recruit is the college sophomore or junior. They have been exposed to a year or two of nihilistic drivel that has served to erode their values and their understanding of the universe. In class after class, they have been repetitiously exposed to superfluous attempts to describe attributes of problems, rather than learning how to do anything. Their confused professors are distinguished only by their ignorance as they preach that there is no right or wrong, merely shades of gray. Such an ironically bizarre exposure to the world of learning can only confuse youth further and heighten their hunger to know. Academic induced frustration is converted into a need for knowledge that can be exploited by any organization than claims to know truth.[12]

The Attraction

Messaging and tapping into the psyches of people are important to all groups seeking a following. Also, the addition of critical phrases helps to increase the energy in a group. One such term is *systemic racism*. Such terms generalize specific issues. When this generalization occurs, it becomes easy to cast aspersions. Any so-called revelations of new terms that are passed on as truth proclamations are not to be questioned by followers. Truth that is applicable to a chosen group is often most attractive because of its claim of exclusivity.

There is no one objective truth to those who claim all truth is subjective, which is one reason the changes in rhetoric are so exciting. Yet, from a leader there is the expectation of exclusive truth statements. This is a contrast from the positions of younger recruits that deplore the static nature of their parents' understanding of the world.

Recruitment is simplified in the following model.

- A group claims a truth for itself.
- The group establishes a narrative based on its claim.

- Supporters are recruited based on the narrative.
- Members of the media and politicians are enjoined in the narrative.
- The narrative is often repeated until it becomes an untouchable moral truth.
- Recruits become followers to recruit other members.
- Smart technology is used throughout the process of recruitment.

A good example of this model is the claim that all Whites are racists and they are fragile. It fits the narrative that America is based on White Supremacy and male patriarchy—and that both are institutional. Another example is the claim that gender is fluid. The narratives are established as subjectively and emotionally true. Sources are then found for both by cherry-picking and claiming authoritative sources, and then off it goes to others to repeat. This is why no one really has any examples of something institutional or systemic. Most of these narratives emerge from universities and colleges and their ivory towers, and are taught to students as if the revelations are exclusively meant as truth for the generation in question.

The details about cult recruits could easily apply to today's college and university students in large numbers. There should be no shock in learning the passage quoted above dates back to 1980. In each era, there are leaders who find it within their power to sway millions into error. History is replete with examples. History often repeats itself with new packaging.

In order to perpetuate the messaging of radicalism, the philosophies presented on campuses must appeal to some emotional aspects of students' lives. Accordingly, the ideas find their ways from college texts to the K–12 institutions and their curricula.

RELIGIOUS HUMANISM AND RELIGIOUS CULTS

The following list is not exhaustive but does provide a snapshot of most cults.[13] The reader is encouraged to reflect on the recent racial, sexual, and anti-political cult groups that have risen recently within American culture. In addition, readers should dutifully research and examine the teachings of these groups. Each has a growing impact upon K–12 schooling, higher education, entertainment, athletics, and the business world.

As the reader examines each of the following, close attention should be paid to two focal points: (1) the tactics and methods used to ensure their followers maintain allegiance to the narratives defined for them, and (2) the strategies employed to spread their teachings into America's unsuspecting communities.

A snapshot of characteristics of cults includes:

- The claim of a newly inspired message, or revelation for all followers
- The emphasis on only one way to show dedication, and it is the way prescribed by a leader or a group of leaders
- Exclusive message defending intolerance of outsiders and criticism
- Revision of the past and how it offered less hope than the current message of futuristic utopia
- There are one or more leader figures that have arisen for such a time as this in history, often claiming status of overcoming difficulties and hardships as proof of legitimacy of message, and also to attract empathy
- The teachings of the group are the result of a special gnosis of the leader and his or her ability to be in touch to a realm above the rest of the group; channeling of spirits and occultic new age-ism practices may be shared
- There is a special claim to followers that finding the reality of the message discovered by leaders will awaken them multi-dimensionally, including spiritually and emotionally
- There is a messianic element in the organization itself and for the workers of the causes laid out by the organization; in some cases, there are warnings of wars, impending apocalypses, or civil unrest if these causes are ignored
- Unbelievers are said to be blinded by the truth because of implicit issues in areas like race because of other religions, an ignorance, or lack of education
- Detractors or dissenters of the group or its message are demonized, labeled, and shamed
- There are cherry-picked, out-of-context quotes, and/or religious phrases and scriptural verses to prop up broad support for its organizational purposes
- Denouncement of outsiders as unbelievers and enemies
- Contrasting failures of unbelievers with promises to replace failed states with new programs and policies of fairness
- Financial exploitation occurs, which is directed at communities, businesses, and politicians
- There are also disruptions of systems and promises of violence, as well as use of the legal system, against those who will not go along with the stated beliefs

- Organization seeks to make itself at home within broad swaths of culture, including schools, often using rhetoric that appeals to fractures in society, as it attempts to mainstream its messaging
- The message of the cult finds a home in the public-learning institutions of America through placing its members into key positions on school boards, as professors at colleges, and elected to office

EXPOSURE COMES IN MANY FORMS

Those seeking converts to their humanist ideology definitely do have an agenda. Leaders often convince union leaders, and state bureaucrats, of their intentions and positions, by pressuring them. Support ripples down from the top and finds its way to the general masses. For example, this is the way it is for sex, race, and gender groups that have pressured politicians and education policy-makers. What follows is one example of sex education that comes with LGBTQ+ support.

After succumbing to the political pressure, the groups supporting sex education in many states support the narrative that students (1) "should have sexual pleasure at all ages,"[14] and that includes (2) "out of wedlock sex with anyone . . . [which] is just fine at any age."[15] Are parents aware this agenda is moving rapidly into lower grades with each passing year? There is a concerted effort to expose children to a line of thinking that, by most standards, is contrary to the values of most American parents.

In addition to parents, teachers are the frontlines of cultural change for many children. Some of these cultural changes have become worrisome to teachers and unions, especially during the pandemic of 2020 with both hybrid and online distance learning. Parents are equally concerned. It seems that outcry arose when teachers became worried that parents might hear and see what they were teaching their students.[16]

Some districts are even going so far as to make parents sign agreements not to monitor their child's virtual classes. The claim is that what a child shares might be of a private nature and is not intended for parents' ears.[17] But then there are Zoom-bombers, sexually harassing teachers. According to anecdotes shared with this author, bombers are causing disruptions to online classes, posting pornographic videos, and even masturbating on camera. Apparently, sexual exposure and harassment now come in many forms.

Sexual Activism in Schools

Contrast the previous actions with this author's recollection of an encounter with a very outspoken lesbian teacher-in-training. When asked what is the reason she wanted to be a teacher, she replied, "So I can become a proud vocal activist for children who are emerging LGBTQ+ or who are curious." When challenged about what sixty-or-so parents might say about her goal, she replied, "Who cares. They need to deal with their bigotry and homophobia."

Along with race and gender, sex is being pushed consciously by some into the psyches of today's younger students. Some would argue, "Students are going to find out anyway." Is current sex education curriculum a reason why teachers are pressing for parents to sign agreements not to watch what goes on in their children's online classes? Regardless, parents should request to view the materials in advance. If they are not allowed, then that should present caution.

Teachers are instructed by the *National Education Association*, and through the support of LGBTQ+ groups, that children as young as ten should learn how to put on condoms. Such activities are within the practice sections that come along with the newer sexual education programs, which are supported by groups whose aims are to expose children to a variety of sexual choices,[18] and which American sex culture has enabled to become part of a new sexual normal.[19]

THE SACRIFICE OF INNOCENCE

Our children are being sacrificed sexually and exposed to materials that are not age or emotionally appropriate. An example of this is the exposure of younger children to genitalia by way of handing out lifelike models of erect penises for children to fondle. Some teachers, along with concerned parent groups, are caught unwittingly by the inclusion of adult-like tactical exposure to sex toys and the cavalier approach to sexuality. In fact, a growing number of teachers, as well as parents, are highly disturbed by this sexualization of children.[20]

As a result of teacher discomfort, outside groups are scheduled to come into schools and teach our nation's children about sexual practices, ways to experience it pleasurably and safely, and even being open to having sex with students of the same biological gender. With these propositions in mind, it is obvious why parents are often not allowed to attend these sex education meetings with their own children.

The Cult of Sex

In terms of sex education curriculum used by California, there is no allowance for any outside speakers whose scientific research or medical opinions differ from those acceptable to the state department of education and its guidelines. Such speakers are not allowed access to students in any official way. Allowing any other message is to ensure competing ideas and most cults cannot abide by these conflicts. Here is a sample of what the state of California has mandated.

> All instruction and materials in grades K–12 must be inclusive of LGBTQ students. Instruction shall *affirmatively recognize* that people have different sexual orientations and, when discussing or providing examples of relationships and couples, must be *inclusive of same-sex relationships.* [EC § 51933(d)(5)]. It must also teach students about gender, gender expression, gender identity, and explore the harm of negative gender stereotypes. [EC § 51933(d)(6)]. This means *that schools must teach about all sexual orientations* and what being LGBTQ means. The California Healthy Youth Act requires that sexual health education be appropriate for use with students of all genders and sexual orientations (EC § 51933(d)) and clearly states that part of the intent of the law is "to provide pupils with the knowledge and skills they need to develop healthy attitudes concerning adolescent growth and development, body image, gender, sexual orientation, relationships, marriage, and family." [EC § 51933(d)(2)]. The California Healthy Youth Act also prohibits sexual health education classes from promoting bias against anyone on the basis of any category protected by Education Code §220, which includes actual or perceived gender and sexual orientation.[21]

When a cult group gains power at the state level, the result is usually not one with which most parents would agree. Imagine such a group having similar power at the federal level? One has to question why exposure to sexuality is so important to bureaucrats, and who is lobbying them for this exposure.

These types of sex education programs mandated by states such as California leave little room for focusing on abstinence, and certainly elevates alternate sex and gender expressions over heterosexual relationships in importance. The fact is, the more options students think they have at their disposal, the greater the opportunity for sexual experimentation and encounters. This is not information; this is indoctrination.

The new sexual revolution among children will lead to more curiosity about sexual pleasure with members of the same and opposite sex. As children reach the teenage years, and then young adulthood, there will be an "overabundance of available sexual partners"[22] which will then pressure relationships by making it more difficult "to hold the attention of any one of them."[23] Certainly, childhood innocence is in the crosshairs as a target for early sexual exposure.

The Cult of Gender

At the federal level, the Equality Act of the 116th Congress addressed issues of discrimination against anyone belonging to the LGBTQ+ faction. A quick review of the new 2019 H.R.5 legislation reveals that about 85 percent of the Act is geared toward making certain people are held accountable if there is any form of discrimination against any member of the LGBTQ+ communities. It also lays out very clearly what comprises discrimination against members of the faction. The Act includes language that inserts the following into Section 3 of the Civil Rights Act of 1964, Paragraph 3, of Section 3, regarding Public Accommodations:

(a) PROHIBITION ON DISCRIMINATION OR SEGREGATION IN PUBLIC ACCOMMODATIONS—SECTION 201 OF THE Civil Rights Act of 1964 (42 U.S.C. 2000a)[24] is amended—

(1) in subsection (a), by inserting "sex (including sexual orientation and gender identity)," before "or national origin"; and . . .

(C) by inserting after paragraph (3) the following:

(4) any establishment that provides a good, service, or program, including a store, shopping center, online retailer or service provider, salon, bank, gas station, food bank, service or care center, shelter, travel agency, or funeral parlor, or establishment that provides health care, accounting, or legal services;

(5) any train service, bus service, car service, taxi service, airline service, station, depot, or other place of or establishment that provides transportation service.[25]

The average reader might well overlook the obvious in this Act. In the words of the president of *The Southern Baptist Seminary*, R. Albert Mohler, "the Equality Act explicitly codifies the Christian worldview as hatred, bigotry, and no longer valid as seen by the legal system."[26] The Equality Act is in the hands of the Senate, but that has not stopped the highest court in the land from issue decisions on other cases pertaining to LGBTQ+ rights.[27]

The Supreme Court recently decided a case involving Title VII of the *Civil Rights Act of 1964*. At issue was whether the term *sex* includes sexual orientation and gender identity. On June 15, 2020, the Supreme Court held that the term did extend to the factions in question.

Critics argue that essentially the court stepped out of its role as interpreter of the Constitution and decided to make up a new direction for lawmakers to appease their LGBTQ+ lobbyists who pressured them. Supporters cheered the 6-3 decision. The concerns for religious practitioners are the effects the Supreme Court's decision will have upon the church and the application of the free exercise clause of the First Amendment to the Constitution, over and against the pressure of gender groups. Both sex and gender cult groups seem to have had an effect on most institutions in American society. Schools are no exception.

The California sex education framework informs teachers that students in kindergarten can identify themselves as transgender and offers tips for how to talk about that, adding "the goal is not to cause confusion about the gender of the child but to develop an awareness that other expressions exist."[28] Adults who think other adults cannot claim their own child's gender and sexual identity are exercising the same authority they claim birth parents are violating. Despite the goal of self-autonomy, it comes far too early in the lives of children. Children do not think like adults, and they should not be expected to reach conclusions, as such.

Such expectations only confuse children. But this is what a cult is expected to do. Pressing followers toward acceptance of another person's understanding of what is right and best is the optimum goal of the culturally woke crowd. This pertains to race, sex, or gender. Such pressure is direct manipulation upon minds and hearts and is tantamount to deception by confusion. The confused should not be allowed in schools to cause confusion in others, especially among the younger students.

The California framework also advises teachers that the real issue is to force people to see the LGBTQ+ community issues as civil rights issues. Attaching the message to a civil rights era is a bait-and-switch method used to lull citizens into thinking what people experienced based on sexuality and gender are somewhat equivalent to the hundreds of years of slavery and Jim Crow cultural racism and restrictions experienced by Black Americans. This is a false equivalency, which is also another tactic used by cults.

In a warning offered by the late Joseph Nicolosi, he writes, "The psychological profession now relies on surface appearance and self-report, and is bowing to the new, cultural conviction that 'I can self-create.' Instead, my profession should return to penetrating the real reasons why a psychological phenomenon exists."[29] It is comments like these, as well as and his therapeutic work with dysphoria, that Nicolosi's books have been banned from being sold on Amazon.

In the words of Stephanie Gregson, director of the *Curriculum Frameworks and Instructional Resources Division* at the *California Department of Education*, "I think that people hear the word 'transgender' or 'gender identity' in guidance for kindergarten through grade three and they think the worst ... It's really about civil rights issues."[30] But who will ever argue about issues regarding civil rights and risk being called phobic or a racist?

Parents are justified in their concerns. "The framework gives tips for discussing masturbation with middle-schoolers, including telling them it is not physically harmful, and for discussing puberty with transgender teens that creates 'an environment that is inclusive and challenges binary concepts about gender.'"[31] The nation must end the glorifying of sex and gender among our children.

America is sexualizing its children earlier and earlier. Each passing year brings with it new liberal humanistic pieces of legislation. The latest entertainment exploitation is found in the Netflix feature titled *Cuties*, for which there may be charges of violating child exploitation laws.[32] There is a serious effort under way to shape the minds of American children, and it is coming by ways of social, racial, and gender activists, humanistic teachers, and organizations that believe children should be sexualized earlier. Add to this the onslaught of social media and the battle for the minds of America's children is a siege unparalleled in the nation's history.[33]

The Battle for Minds

The battle for the minds and wills of children is fought daily in America's public-learning institutions. The essence of this battle has, at its core, the challenge to what it means to be male and female. An example of this battle is found in the book recommended for high school students' sex education. The book is titled *S.E.X.: The All-You-Need-to-Know Sexuality Guide to Get You Through Your Teens and Twenties*, and is brimming "with descriptions of anal sex, bondage and other sexual activity."[34]

In addition to major conflicts with science, there is continued jamming of secular sexuality and popular gender ideologies into the minds of students of all ages. In an age of science and data and detailed genetics, teachers and parents are allowing emotions and psychological theory to drive so much of understanding.[35]

Another battle for the minds of children is with children as young as four. They are being told that their parents did not know their gender when they were born, "so they assigned"[36] them genders and the children are encouraged to figure themselves out over time. Gender cultists have recruited teachers and their influence on children is a tool to cause children to question their gender and sexual beliefs right at school. So, is it any small wonder that a child becomes confused about his or her place and role in the family, relationships, the school, and in society at large?

Could early sexual experimentation and the confusion about gender and sexuality be contributing factors to the skyrocketing rate of suicides and attempted suicides among teenagers? The evidence indicates the answer is yes.[37] All is not lost in the battle against cultic teachings on sex and gender that are confusing our children. But the onslaught on the minds and hearts of children is a very real cultural struggle. One of the elements of the battle is the pressure placed on teachers.

According to Rebecca Friedrichs, "America's . . . teachers have been silenced and bullied by the very organization that is pushing the sexualization of children: That is, labor unions." This sexualization is supported by the *National Education Association* (NEA), which works in partnership with the *Southern Poverty Law Center* (SPLC), the *National Association for the Advancement of Colored People* (NAAACP), the *American Civil Liberties Union* (ACLU), the *Gay, Lesbian, and Straight Education Network* (GLSEN; formerly called Gay and Lesbian Independent School Teachers Network), and the National Center for Trans-Equality, Human Rights Campaign (NCTEHRC), among others.[38]

These groups compile hate lists, which are overseen by the SPLC, and which is comprised of institutions and individuals not supportive of the progressive racial, gender, and sexual agenda. Teachers that are vocal in not accepting the unions' pushes for acceptance of the organizations' philosophies and practices are targeted.

Innocence and Victimization

Children's sexuality is the last phase of human innocence. To sacrifice this innocence on some humanistic, philosophical altar constructed by adults is wrong. Some teachers' own universes are scarred by their own personal sexual confusion, and in some cases they are victims of child sexual abuse themselves. Gaining entrance to the doorways of the minds of children eventually affects the emotions and plants the curiosity of adult pleasures.

The trauma experienced by some teachers should not be relived at the expense of children and their exploitation. The door to early victimization of generations of children becomes an even greater possibility. The fact is exposing children to early sexual knowledge is, for pedophiles, pederasts, and korephiles, their dream scenario.

There are some encouraging signs. Recently a "veteran California teacher explained that most teachers are disturbed by the decades-long push to indoctrinate and oversexualize school children by teachers' unions dedicated to far-left cultural and political causes and not the well-being of kids."[39] The voices from the towers and halls of state governments are not listening. Anyone arguing that early sexual exposure makes kids safer, and the more knowledge the better, is demonstrating that the sacrifice of the last bastion of childhood innocence is best accomplished in tandem with schools and sexual and gender groups, many of which may be comprised of victims of sexual abuse themselves.[40]

NEW FAMILY PARADIGM

The question of family definition and composition is important for both secularists and sacralists. If marriage is less important today, and the result is more cohabitating as the new arrangement, then the traditional family is no longer fashionable. Such arrangements seem to play into the desires of men and diminish certain aspects of commitment.

Eberstadt takes it further with her position that "feminism is a case study linking identity politics with the biased familial landscape. Many women are now exactly what feminist identitarians say they are: victims—only not in the way that feminism understands. They are captives behind enemy lines, but the enemy is nothing as abstract as the binary, or patriarchy, or gender norming."[41] Has humanism played out well for the staunch feminist?

Mohler points out, "Secularism sets out to redefine humanity."[42] Politicians that support the margins of culture sometimes forget that the mainstream voter is their electorate. What exactly happens when a fringe element of American society gets to exercise power of hundreds of millions of other people? They run the risk of experiencing tyranny of the majority by the factions. Some states are controlled by one-party governments. In terms of political and progressive humanistic forces, there is a tyranny marshalling forces "against the family unit because the future disciples of the new worldview are our children."[43]

Similarly, religious humanists are seeking converts that reject thousands of years of history. Progressives are much more hostile to traditions of American history, including the nuclear family, and the *dreaded concept* of traditional biblical marriage.[44] For progressives to succeed, they "must eradicate any semblance or scent of a pre-modern or biblical worldview in the upbringing of the future generation."[45] Essentially, humanism—both secular and religious—must be made acceptable as a replacement to the institution of faith in tradition, including the sacredness of marriage.[46]

IS RELIGIOUS HUMANISM REPLACING CHRISTIANITY?

Marcia Pally, in her book *The New Evangelicals*, addresses the changes in perception that are occurring among evangelicals toward secularization of churches in doctrine and practice. Aligned with this secularization, there is an acceptance by a growing number of twenty-first-century evangelicals who embrace more humanistic and liberal governmental policies and practices.

According to Pally, the "new evangelical embrace of liberal, democratic government does not suggest agreement with other political actors on all church-state issues—on the rights of churches and the rights of the state . . . disagreement between new evangelicals and government has to date been navigated in political negotiation and in courts, where standards are constitutional."[47]

Mohler warns churches that if they are not extra careful, they "will look less and less like churches and more and more like the secular world around them,"[48] and that "passive pressures of secularization, therefore, inevitably undermine the ecclesial structures established by Christ in the New Testament."[49] America is experiencing the exodus of those previously holding to a traditional Christian mission and, in the process, watching this great transition of a generation from its religious traditions to religiously humanistic ones. Why is this occurring?

The Waning Appeal of the American Church

The more specific question is why are evangelical churches losing their appeal with younger Americans? The reason is that a secular message has become their substitute religious message of the faith. Christian organizations are trying to ameliorate the losses by investing in greater efforts of stewardship over Generation Z and Millennial issues, such as nature and climate change. The *Evangelical Environmental Network* (EEN) is an example of this. Its mission is "caring for all of God's creation by stopping and preventing activities that are harmful (e.g. air and water pollution, species extinction) . . . creation-care fills us with the joy that only comes from doing the will of God."[50]

When humanistic purposes intersect with religious purposes, today's young gravitate toward the more popular of the two. The fact is that humanism is more secular and more appealing to the *self* and *human independence*. These are not as important in the teachings of evangelical Christianity, for example. The younger generation seeks a sense of purpose whereby they can make an immediate and self-gratifying difference. As a result, many college students today cling to some aspects of their upbringing, but tend to yield to a humanistic form of religiosity. Refer to chapter one for a full discussion.

In other words, creating a secular idol or cause to be worshiped provides a tangible, action-oriented opportunity to please themselves. These actions fulfill a sense of purpose—one to which evangelical churches need to pay attention. Whether it is the environment, animals, water, or energy, the issue of stewardship of the earth and its resources is a very important topic for young adults. Taken together, these constitute humanistic religious tenets for the religious humanists among us.

If the environment is god-like, and is worthy of worship, then efforts to clean it up are met with more than social applause and validation from fellow-worshipers. An excellent example of this is the Jesus' Third Way. In this teaching, young people find elements of socialism, Marxism, communism, and Christianity, blended together, in sort a repackaging of liberation theology.[51] As stated earlier, it provides young people with the assurance of enough belief nostalgia and combines it with social activism that—one that might even exceed the social-gospel movement of late nineteenth and early twentieth centuries.[52]

Secular Actions Become Sacred

These types of actions demonstrate how the secular can become the sacred. It can happen in any institution. In fact, "the secularization of most educational institutions is an accomplished fact . . . many college and university campuses are deeply antagonistic to Christian truth claims and the beliefs held by millions of students and their families."[53]

Christian Smith and Melina Lundquist Denton, in their book *Soul Searching: The Religious and Spiritual Lives of American Teenagers*, identified the trend of youth to forego their parents' faith but hold onto a looser version of their family's belief system. For example, rather than a conservative evangelical set of beliefs, a majority of the youth describe their belief system as more humanistic, and thereby secular. Some of the main beliefs of such a belief system are that God is not relationally involved in people's lives, that good people will go to heaven when they die, and that feeling good about oneself and having a good life is important, among others. Such descriptors are dripping with religious humanism, which is why this belief system earned the label *Moralistic Therapeutic Deism* (MTD).[54]

Akin to the belief system of some of America's founders, and taken from European political philosophers and deist ministers, a *Moralistic Therapeutic Deistic* belief system is like William Paley's Watchmaker illustration. Basically, there is a deity who made the world, wound it up, and stepped back to watch it run, while leaving the watch behind as evidence of an intelligent designer. The goal of this deity is to bring happiness and niceness to the world, and the deity is called upon to shape some circumstances in such ways that young people will get what they desire.

Smith and Denton reported that a growing number of teenagers in the United States are not interested in mimicking the faith traditions of their upbringing. They include a point which should grab the attention of all parents. The authors explain, "Because adolescence represents a crucial developmental transition from childhood to adulthood, research on teens can disclose important knowledge about religious socialization and change in the life course.

Adolescents comprise a population that many religious organizations, both congregations and parachurch ministries, target to exert influence in their lives. Adolescence and young adulthood are also life stages when religious conversion is likely to take place."[55] If teens are not committing to church, then to what else could they be committing?

THE CULT OF RACE

In addition to sex and gender, racial identity is one of the latest trends to capture a generation. However, there are significant problems with this. One of the main concerns is that elevating race might take the nation back seventy-five years. So, political correctness allows only for Blacks to elevate their race. The exclusive nature of groups like BLM are attractive to young supporters of all races. Even before the ink has dried on the organizations first placards, the group is able to mobilize hundreds and thousands for protest.

The bait for young people is they have somehow been convinced that law enforcement all over America is targeting the Black community and its young men for unjust treatment. The Black Lives Matter group has successfully quieted dissenters by violence and shame. But they have marginalized many of their own racial demographic, particularly in the urban areas.

Most Americans are certain that Black Lives Matter, and no one would ever dispute this. To do so would bring ruination to a career, and hate groups would unleash their converts to descend upon the dissenters. Agreeing with the statement on the protest placard is one thing. If a person wants a voice in the organization, one has to be Black enough, as ESPN's Sage Steele discovered recently.[56]

Steele was not allowed to be part of a "network special on race and social justice claiming she isn't Black enough."[57] She was not considered authentic enough as a Black person, since she has a White mother and a Black father. Steele writes, "Trying to define who is and isn't Black enough goes against everything we are fighting for in this country, and only creates more of a divide."[58] By that criteria, one also needs to cancel Senator Kamala Harris and former President Barack Obama, as well as the children of these politicians from anything relating to the all-Black grouping. Cult groups do these things, and followers merely go along without seeing the lack of logic.

Leaders of the cult of race wield power. The group leaders seem to have more sway over people's decisions than do most churches and their leaders. Based on the number of young people that took to the streets in 2020, the leftist gospel of BLM, based on a Marxist philosophy, appears more life-changing to the younger generations than the Gospel of Jesus Christ. At least it seems more edgy and exciting and allows human nature to act without great restraint. The religious experience on the streets is apparently better than the one in the pews. Is this feeling not the essence of humanism?

Converts to the cult of racial ideology are convinced that (1) schools are pipelines to prison for young people of color, that (2) law enforcement is exterminating people of color, and (3) Whites are privileged and continue to exercise racism. Young people hear these things in schools. Some families also teach their children harmful rhetoric at home, connecting emotions to cognitive confusion. The result of the repetition of information such as this triggers expected reactions.

The racial cult leaders inform people that every White person has a virus of racism in their brains and cannot help the blindness to their own racist actions.[59] This amounts to a form of cancellation. Therefore, what exists today in such groups are attempts at reversals of perceived supremacy and dominance, incorporating the application of pointed guilt and shame—the very standard tactics used by cults to keep members in line.[60]

Conversion and the Power of Persuasion

There are so many people and organizations signing on with Black Lives Matter, that it is both interesting and frightening in terms of our national identity. The group capitalized on a horrible death and within weeks they and others had no mention of the tragedy that caused their initial reactions. As an example of the cultic response to a cultural issue, BLM and its followers went on the attack. Social media and bulk texting through apps caused hundred-to-thousands to show up in flash mobs for weeks, and the rest is history.

BLM demonstrates public outrage when a White police officer is accused of excessive force involving a Black man. There is always a rush to judgment and this foments anger. Matters become worsened when there is the release of selected and edited media clips to the public. However, in contrast, the thousands of Black-on-Black killings in America receive little-to-no attention from the media or BLM.[61] See chapter 6 for a critique of Black Lives Matter.

Race Consciousness

Chief Equity and Inclusion Officer for an Indiana K–12 school district, Erica Buchanan-Rivera, reflects back to her childhood in a non-racially diverse public school. She writes of her childhood that her "pathway into education was not ignited by what teachers *did for me*, but rather by what those who were responsible for my growth and learning *did not do* and the lack of intentionality to create an identity-affirming environment."[62] Notice, the motivation for entering education was to provide for others what was not provided her, while a student. She speaks of education in general terms and it makes one wonder why her parents placed her in a school that was not affirming her identity?

Buchanan-Rivera admits that she attended an "elementary school that lacked racial diversity."[63] She adds, "There was not a space for dialogues about humanity in ways that would foster global consciousness."[64] In addition, she points out a flaw in her elementary school, in that her "school's educators failed to understand how identity validation and inclusive environments are catalysts to student's success."[65]

It is difficult to imagine how an elementary school student realized all of these shortcomings so early in school. The obvious answer is that once she became an adult and delved into the identity movement and through the racial and political structures by which she later identified, the past became extremely clear to her. In other words, she became *woke*. What is also interesting is that there are more students from mixed racial families today than ever before.

Buchanan-Rivera's student-centered universe now consists of a blend of culturally relevant ideologies. In other words, a form of Marxism has been revised and repurposed and made user-friendly to an uninformed generation. The addition of race to the philosophy helps to secure the images of past oppression in the present and then false equivalences can be drawn together for followers.

New Marxists can now easily "coax the masses into adopting its worldview and morality."[66] It is from this Marxist foundation that Buchanan-Rivera writes, "When students of racially and ethnically diverse backgrounds are not able to learn about their history, they are forced to function within an oppressive environment absent of multiple perspectives."[67] She takes it even further and assumes that educators, administrators, and community members must come to terms with an understanding of equity.

During the riots and protests of spring and summer of 2020, people were holding rallies and crusades. Leaders rallied people against claims of systemic police injustice and brutality. Activist leaders asked groups of Whites to raise their hands and repeat words of support for the messages decrying racism and White Privilege. They also were led in a confession and asked for forgiveness for simply being White. While confessing their guilt, Whites promised Black audiences they would do better to understand their own White corruption and make changes.[68]

This is a prime example of a secular social justice concern being elevated to a religious moment, complete with a public confession of sins. Aside from this, the majority of younger Whites see BLM as a radical group, but are more likely to join such a group because of emotions and a self-sense of distorted patriotism and purpose, albeit each morally humanistic and relative.[69]

Many Blacks see BLM as standing against systemic racism and racial injustice.[70] As with the #MeToo movement that has now morphed beyond its original goals, the BLM movement is following the same path. All cults usually do. Its focus is now a convoluted amalgamation of purposes, trying to be all things to all other radical groups in order to undertake a national rebellion.

The group will eventually fracture as a result of its internal double standards. What happens eventually to groups like these is they cannibalize themselves and implode,[71] forming splinter groupings. Once the double standards become so egregious and affect those that self-exempted from these effects, the organizational aspects, contradictory tenets, and practical applications usually fray at the organizational seams of these types of groups.

RELIGION BECOMES SECULAR

Humanism has made its mark in churches when they teach everyone to make their own happiness by their choices, human reason, and hard work. The way it comes across is that God wants everyone happy, healthy, and wealthy. In fact, they often rely on studies that report on the benefits of going to church.[72]

When church leaders speak of the positive confession, and the health and wealth message, it directly ties to the outcomes of human achievements. The fact is that the Word of Faith prosperity gospel teaching only works in the western world, where incomes are higher and the goods are nicer. In other parts of the world, providing food and daily sustenance for a family would be considered a blessing and that comes from their own soil, rather than from the store. People unwilling to wait for God's blessing in God's time begin to act as their own god, commanding things by faith until they receive what they desire. These types of proclamations are believed to be able to create reality by having faith in faith.

The religious groups in question preach that in order to get from God, one has to give more to the organization in question. This interest in physical health and material wealth is so ingrained in the minds and hearts of some religious folks that the mere mention of a negative comment, or a spiritual untruth, can undo the blessings. It also is one of the descriptors of *Moralistic Therapeutic Deism*. In other words, not having enough faith is a weakness and limits one's blessings in the material world that provides them. The responsibility of getting things from God is solely dependent on followers' abilities to demonstrate enough faith in themselves.

These types of religious teachings are humanist because of their focus on faith in self, self-improvement, self-faith, material wealth, and positive confession. But they are also religious because of their use by religious leaders. When one hears about Christian leaders, such as Creflo Dollar,[73] Joel Osteen,[74] Jesse DuPlantis,[75] or Kenneth Copeland,[76] and others, asking for millions of dollars for new jets, to travel the world and speak, one would hardly think self-sacrifice and humility.[77]

In a world of greed, where money is a pursuit of many, some church leaders have amassed multi-million dollar fortunes, while many in their congregations sacrifice each day for the cause. This is not only a secular focus on material goods but is also a cultic tactic to manipulate people to give until it hurts, so they will be blessed in return. The axiom is to *give in order to get more wealth and goods.*[78]

Whether it is the faith and prosperity teachers or BLM, the only people truly enriched are the recipients of the followers' cash.[79] It won't be long before cult's leaders feel entitled to have their own jets and millions in the bank, and justify their own carbon footprint for the cause which they are called to represent.[80]

The secular financial principles of sowing money and reaping benefits are supposed to work for all who apply them, since they are billed as laws of the universe. Charles Fillmore,[81] Emmet Fox,[82] Ernest Holmes,[83] and other proclaimed religious teachers have incorporated humanism into their attempts to make spiritual laws out of many of their teachings.

Additionally, Norman Vincent Peale, Robert Schuller, and Mark Victor Hansen[84] also played a large part in the movement that took secular principles and converted them into their religious humanism. These men assured their followers that the "law of prosperity has been proved time and time again. All men who have prospered have used the law, for there is no other way."[85]

CULTS AND VIOLENCE

Before concluding this chapter, there is the necessity to offer a few words on the rise of violence among contemporary secularists. There is a dangerous precedent being established. Specifically, domestic terrorism and property destruction are not going to improve anything in America.

The majority of Americans have much to gain by not allowing more cults to steal the consciences of the nation's children. Teachers must beware of the sides they are taking and the messages they convey to students, in the process. C. S. Lewis helps teachers to this awareness in his book *God in the Dock*. He writes,

> Of all tyrannies, a tyranny sincerely exercised for the good of its victims may be the most oppressive. It would be better to live under robber barons than under

omnipotent moral busybodies. The robber baron's cruelty may sometimes sleep, his cupidity may at some point be satiated; but those who torment us for our own good will torment us without end for they do so with the approval of their own conscience. They may be more likely to go to Heaven yet at the same time likelier to make a Hell of earth.[86]

The reality is that Americans are shunning traditional evangelicalism and converting to the attractive package of religious humanism. What is even sadder is that America "no longer values religious identity,"[87] as it once did. Conversely, radical groups are pressuring society to consider sexual, racial, or gender identities as of greater value.

With respect to the parents that see through the fog of religious humanism and the cults that affect our students with their subjective truths, maybe it's time to have a *come-to-Jesus moment*. Maybe it's also time for an old-school altar call.

NOTES

1. R. Albert Mohler, Jr. *The gathering storm.* 2020. Nashville, TN: HarperCollins Christian Publishing, p. 74.

2. Richard Wayne Lee. "Strained bedfellows: Pagans, new agers, and 'starchy humanists' in Unitarian Universalism." *UU Association.* Volume 30, No. 3. 1996. Retrieved September 20, 2020, from http://huumanists.org/publications/journal/strained-bedfellows-pagans-new-agers-and-starchy-humanists-unitarian.

3. Duke McCoy. *How to organize and manage your own religious cult: A psycho-political primer.* 1980. Mason, MI: Loompanics Unlimited, p. 4.

4. Ernest J. Zarra III. *The entitled generation: Helping teaching teach and reach the minds and hearts of Generation Z.* 2017. Lanham, MD: Rowman & Littlefield Publishers.

5. Peggy Drexler. "Millennials are the therapy generation." *The Wall Street Journal.* March 1, 2019. Retrieved October 10, 2019, from https://www.wsj.com/articles/millennials-are-the-therapy-generation-11551452286.

6. McCoy. *How to organize and manage your own religious cult: A psycho-political primer,* p. 4.

7. Staff. "Black Lives Matter: Students, campuses are central to the movement." *Association of College Unions International (ACUI).* June 11, 2020. Retrieved August 31, 2020, from https://www.acui.org/resources/bulletin/bulletin-detail/2020/06/10/black-lives-matter-students-campuses-are-central-to-the-movement.

8. Matt Winkelmeyer. "Black Lives Matter activist Cori Bush defeats corporate-backed democratic congress member. *Mother Jones.* August 5, 2020. Retrieved

August 31, 2020, from https://www.motherjones.com/2020-elections/2020/08/cori-bush-defeats-lacy-clay/.

9. *Black Lives Matter.* Retrieved August 31, 2020, from https://blacklivesmatter.com/.

10. McCoy. *How to organize and manage your own religious cult: A psycho-political primer*, p. 4.

11. Ibid., p. 24.

12. Ibid., p. 16. Cf. Walter Martin. *The kingdom of the cults.* 1981 (1965). Minneapolis, MN: Bethany House Publishers, pp. 353–60.

13. Dave Breese. *Know the marks of cults.* 1983. Wheaton, IL: SP Publications Inc.

14. Doug Mainwaring. "Most teachers quite disturbed about their unions' push for sexualization and indoctrination of school children." *Hoboken 411.* April 7, 2020. Retrieved July 18, 2020, from https://hoboken411.com/archives/137989.

15. Ibid.

16. Matt Walsh. "Walsh: Teachers openly fret that parents might hear them brainwashing children, calls parents dangerous." *Daily Wire.* August 10, 2020. Retrieved August 21, 2020, from https://www.dailywire.com/news/teachers-openly-fret-parents-might-hear-them-brainwashing-children.

17. Jeffrey Swindoll. "Tennessee school district making parents sign agreement to not monitor virtual class." *DIRSN.* August 21, 2020. Retrieved August 21, 2020, from https://disrn.com/news/tennessee-school-district-making-parents-sign-agreement-to-not-monitor-virtual-class. Cf. K. Winters. "Indoctrination? County requires parents sign forms saying that won't observe their child's virtual learning." *Law Enforcement Today.* August 22, 2020. Retrieved August 22, 2020, from https://www.lawenforcementtoday.com/county-in-tennessee-is-requiring-parents-to-not-observe-their-childs-virtual-learning/.

18. Ernest J. Zarra III. *America's Sex Culture: Its impact on teacher-student relationships today.* 2nd Edition. 2020. Lanham, MD: Rowman & Littlefield Publishers.

19. Doug Mainwaring. "Most teachers quite disturbed about their unions' push for sexualization and indoctrination of school children." *Hoboken 411.* April 7, 2020. Retrieved July 18, 2020, from https://hoboken411.com/archives/137989.

20. Cameron Sheppard. "Parents express concerns over sex education legislation." *Peninsula Daily News.* February 25, 2020. Retrieved August 22, 2020, from https://www.peninsuladailynews.com/news/parents-express-concerns-over-sex-ed-legislation/.

21. Staff. "FAQ for sexual education, HIV/AIDS, and STDs." *California Department of Education.* August 30, 2019. Retrieved January 15, 2020, from https://www.cde.ca.gov/ls/he/se/faq.asp. Emphasis mine throughout.

22. Mary Eberstadt. *Primal screams: How the sexual revolution created identity politics.* 2019. West Conshohocken, PA: Templeton Press, p. 75.

23. Eberstadt. *Primal screams: How the sexual revolution created identity politics*, p. 75.

24. Staff. "H.R.5—Equality Act." *Congress.Gov.* May 20, 2019. Retrieved June 23, 2020, from https://www.congress.gov/bill/116th-congress/house-bill/5/text.

25. Ibid.

26. Mohler, *The gathering storm*, p. 171.

27. Staff. "LBGTQ Title VII employment discrimination cases at the Supreme Court." *Family Equality*. June 16, 2020. Retrieved June 23, 2020, from https://www.familyequality.org/resources/lgbtq-title-vii-employment-discrimination-cases-supreme-court/#our-brief.

28. Staff. "California votes to overhaul sex ed guidelines for public schools to include LGBT issues." *CBS News*. May 6, 2019. Retrieved January 15, 2020, from https://www.cbsnews.com/news/california-sex-ed-curriculum-overhaul-sexual-education-guidelines-today-2019-05-08/.

29. Joseph Nicolosi. "The traumatic foundation of gender dysphoria." *Crisis Magazine*. January 6, 2020. Retrieved January 8, 2020, from https://www.crisismagazine.com/2020/the-traumatic-foundation-of-gender-dysphoria.

30. Staff. "California votes to overhaul sex ed guidelines for public schools to include LGBT issues." *CBS News*. May 6, 2019. Retrieved January 15, 2020, from https://www.cbsnews.com/news/california-sex-ed-curriculum-overhaul-sexual-education-guidelines-today-2019-05-08/.

31. Ibid.

32. Emma Nolan. "Netflix movie 'Cuties' could be investigated for violations of child exploitation laws." *Newsweek*. September 11, 2020. Retrieved September 12, 2020, from https://www.newsweek.com/netflix-movie-cuties-could-investigated-child-exploitation-laws-matt-schaefer-1531254.

33. Ken Ham. "Gone in only one generation: The battle for Kids' minds." *Christian Heritage*. April 28, 2014. Retrieved September 24, 2020, from https://christianheritagewa.org/gone-in-only-one-generation-the-battle-for-kids-minds/. Cf. Stephen Law. *The war for children's minds*. 2007. London, England: Routledge Press.

34. Staff. "California votes to overhaul sex ed guidelines for public schools to include LGBT issues." *CBS News*.

35. Paul Stevens-Fullbrook. "15 learning theories in education (a complete summary)." *Teachers of Sci*. April 18, 2019. Retrieved September 12, 2020, from https://teacherofsci.com/learning-theories-in-education/. Cf. Kim Brooks. "We have ruined childhood." *New York Times*. August 17, 2020. Retrieved September 12, 2020, from https://www.nytimes.com/2019/08/17/opinion/sunday/childhood-suicide-depression-anxiety.html.

36. Mainwaring. "Most teachers quite disturbed about their unions' push for sexualization and indoctrination of school children." *Hoboken 411*.

37. Ann P. Haas and Jack Drescher. "Impact of sexual orientation and gender identity on suicide risk: Implications for assessment and treatment." *Psychiatric Times*. December 31, 2014. Retrieved August 22, 2020, from https://www.psychiatrictimes.com/view/impact-sexual-orientation-and-gender-identity-suicide-risk-implications-assessment-and-treatment. Cf. Russell B. Toomey, Amy K. Syvertsen, and Mauro Shramko. "Transgender adolescent suicide behavior." *Pediatrics*. October, 2018. 142(4). Retrieved August 22, 2020, from https://pediatrics.aappublications.org/content/142/4/e20174218.

38. Mainwaring. "Most teachers quite disturbed about their unions' push for sexualization and indoctrination of school children." *Hoboken 411*.

39. Ibid.

40. Andrea Roberts, M. Maria Glymour, and Karestan C. Koenen. "Does maltreatment in childhood affect sexual orientation in adulthood?" *United States National Library of Medicine: Archives of Sexual Behavior.* February 2013. 42(2): 161–71. Retrieved September 24, 2020, from https://doi.org/10.1007/s10508-012-0021-9.

41. Eberstadt. *Primal screams: How the sexual revolution created identity politics,* pp. 75–76.

42. Mohler, *The gathering storm,* p. 80.

43. Ibid., p. 74.

44. Ibid., p. 111.

45. Mohler, *The gathering storm,* p. 74.

46. Dale Ahlquist. "G. K. Chesterton: It's not gay, and it's not marriage." *Crisis Magazine.* February 21, 2013. Retrieved January 8, 2020, from https://www.crisis-magazine.com/2013/g-k-chesterton-its-not-gay-and-its-not-marriage.

47. Marcia Pally. *The New Evangelicals: Expanding the vision of the common good.* 2011. Grand Rapids, MI: Wm. B. Eerdmans Publishing Company, pp. 28–29.

48. Mohler, *The gathering storm,* p. 22.

49. Ibid., p. 27.

50. Staff. "Why creation care matters." *Evangelical Environmental Network.* 2020. Retrieved September 1, 2020, from https://creationcare.org/who-we-are/beliefs.html.

51. Jocelyn A. Sideco. "Jesus third way is what I try to practice." *National Catholic Reporter.* February 16, 2017. Retrieved August 23, 2020, from https://www.ncronline.org/blogs/young-voices/jesus-third-way-what-i-try-practice. Cf. Walter Wink. *The powers that be: Theology for a new millennium.* 1998. New York, NY: Random House, Inc.

52. Staff. "Walter Rauschenbusch: Champion of the social gospel." *Christianity Today.* 2020. Retrieved August 23, 2020, from https://www.christianitytoday.com/history/people/activists/walter-rauschenbusch.html.

53. Mohler, *The gathering storm,* p. 159.

54. Christian Smith and Melina Lundquist Denton. *Soul searching: The religious and spiritual lives of American teenagers.* 2005. Oxford, England: Oxford University Press. See Introduction.

55. Ibid., p. 4.

56. Joe Flint. "ESPN anchor Sage Steele claimed Black colleagues excluded her from race special." *The Wall Street Journal.* July 21, 2020. Retrieved July 23, 2020, from https://www.wsj.com/articles/espn-anchor-sage-steele-claimed-black-colleagues-excluded-her-from-race-special-11595365089.

57. Jason Owens. "ESPN's Sage Steele says colleagues kept her off racial justice special claiming she isn't Black enough." *Yahoo Sports.* July 22, 2020. Retrieved July 23, 2020, from https://sports.yahoo.com/esp-ns-sage-steele-says-colleagues-kept-her-off-social-justice-special-claiming-she-isnt-black-enough-191732645.html.

58. Ibid.

59. Libby Emmons. "Watch: CNN analyst says all white people have virus of racism." *The Post Millennial.* May 30, 2020. Retrieved August 23, 2020, from https://thepostmillennial.com/watch-cnn-analyst-says-all-white-people-have-virus-of-racism.

60. Margaret Thaler Singer. *Cults in our midst: The continuing fight against their hidden menace*. 2003. San Francisco, CA: Jossey-Bass.

61. Ben Shapiro. "Not all Black lives matter to Black Lives Matter." *Pittsburgh Post-Gazette*. July 11, 2020. Retrieved August 23, 2020, from https://www.post-gazette.com/opinion/Op-Ed/2020/07/11/Ben-Shapiro-Black-lives-matter-hypocrisy-violence-Davon-McNeal/stories/202007110006. Cf. Mike Gonzalez and Andrew Olivastro. "The agenda of Black Lives Matter is far different from the slogan." *The Heritage Foundation*. July 3, 2020. Retrieved August 23, 2020, from https://www.heritage.org/progressivism/commentary/the-agenda-black-lives-matter-far-different-the-slogan.

62. Erica Buchanan-Rivera. "Identity-affirming schools need race-conscious educators." *Association for Supervision and Curriculum Development*. October 24, 2019. 15(4): 1–5. Retrieved June 4, 2020, from http://www.ascd.org/ascd-express/vol15/num04/identity-affirming-schools-need-race-conscious-educators.aspx.

63. Ibid.

64. Ibid.

65. Ibid.

66. Mohler, *The gathering storm*, p. 146.

67. Buchanan-Rivera. "Identity-affirming schools need race-conscious educators." *Association for Supervision and Curriculum Development*. 15(4): 1–5.

68. Emma Colton. "White people kneel and ask for forgiveness from Black community at George Floyd prayer gathering." *Washington Examiner*. June 2, 2020. Retrieved August 23, 2020, from https://www.washingtonexaminer.com/news/white-people-kneel-and-ask-for-forgiveness-from-black-community-at-george-floyd-prayer-gathering.

69. Juliana Menasce Horowitz and Gretchen Livingston. "How Americans view the Black Lives Matter movement." *Pew Research Center*. July 8, 2016. Retrieved August 23, 2020, from https://www.pewresearch.org/fact-tank/2016/07/08/how-americans-view-the-black-lives-matter-movement/.

70. Ibid.

71. Mohler, *The gathering storm*, p. 97.

72. Rebecca McLaughlin. "Going to church could save your life." *The Gospel Coalition*. May 29, 2020. Retrieved May 30, 2020, from https://www.thegospelcoalition.org/article/church-save-your-life/.

73. Sam Stringer. "Minister Creflo Dollar asks for $60 million in donations for a new jet." *CNN*. March 16, 2015. Retrieved August 23, 2020, from https://www.cnn.com/2015/03/13/living/creflo-dollar-jet-feat/index.html.

74. Jack Jenkins. "Prosperity gospel pastor is asking his church to buy him a $65 million jet." *Think Progress*. May 21, 2015. Retrieved August 23, 2020, from https://archive.thinkprogress.org/prosperity-gospel-pastor-is-asking-his-church-to-buy-him-a-65-million-jet-c1df63baa330/.

75. William Cummings. "Televangelist says God told him he needs 4th private plane." *USA Today*. May 30, 2018. Retrieved August 23, 2020, from https://www.usatoday.com/story/news/nation-now/2018/05/29/televangelist-wants-new-jet/653202002/.

76. Ernesto Soliven. "Kenneth Copeland net worth: Evangelist is richest pastor in the world." *International Business Times*. April 3, 2020. Retrieved August 23, 2020, from https://www.ibtimes.com/kenneth-copeland-net-worth-evangelist-richest-pastor-world-2951331.

77. Staff. "Top 15 richest and most successful pastors in the whole world." *ETI News*. August 23, 2019. Retrieved August 23, 2020, from https://www.etinside.com/top-15-richest-pastors-america-promise-1-will-shock/.

78. Costi Hinn. *God, Greed, and the (Prosperity) Gospel: How truth overwhelms a life built on lies*. 2019. Grand Rapids, MI: Zondervan Publishing.

79. William Michael Cunningham. "Black Lives Matter: Corporate America has pledged $1.678 billion so far." *Black Enterprise*. June 10, 2020. Retrieved August 23, 2020, from https://www.blackenterprise.com/black-lives-matter-corporate-america-has-pledged-1-678-billion-so-far/.

80. James Wellemeyer. "Want to know where all those corporate donations are going? Here's the list." *NBC News*. June 5, 2020. Retrieved August 23, 2020, from https://www.nbcnews.com/business/consumer/want-know-where-all-those-corporate-donations-blm-are-going-n1225371.

81. Charles Fillmore. *Prosperity*. 1960. Lee's Summit, MO: Unity School of Christianity, pp. 82, 86–87.

82. Emmet Fox. *Power through constructive thinking*. 1940. New York, NY: Harper and Brothers, pp. 265–66.

83. Ernest Holmes. *New Horizons* (Vol. 2). 1973. Los Angeles, CA: Science of Mind Publications, p. 56.

84. Mark Victor Hansen. *How to achieve total prosperity*. 1981. Newport Beach, CA: Mark Victor Hansen, Associates, p. 27.

85. Fillmore. *Prosperity*, pp. 33, 81.

86. C. S. Lewis. *God in the dock: Essays on theology and ethics*. (Edited by Walter Hooper) 1970. Grand Rapids, MI: William B. Eerdmans Publishing Company, p. 242.

87. Mohler, *The gathering storm*, p. 134.

Chapter 6

Is Public Education Too Far Gone?

> *If our universities are teaching students that their emotions can be used effectively as weapons—or at least as evidence in administrative proceedings—then they are teaching students to nurture a kind of hypersensitivity that will lead them into countless drawn-out conflicts in college and beyond. Schools may be training students in thinking styles that will damage their careers and friendships, along with their mental health.*[1]

Most people with any significant time spent in America's public learning institutions understand that cultural changes find their ways into classrooms, one way or another. Far too many times these changes are disruptive to the educational process. In fact, social media cultural news finds its way forward more quickly.

As all teachers are aware, schools and classrooms develop their own cultures over time. The recent coronavirus pandemic has changed so much of culture in America and it has changed education in so many ways. One of these ways is the way education is delivered. The model of education of the recent past will probably disappear into the vortex that was 2020.

The Internet now plays a major role in the dissemination of information to the masses. As a result, such a change will also alter the means of student learning and assessment of this learning for years to come. There is one thing that will probably remain constant. That is, those on the political left, along with progressive teachers, will be pushing for their American version of utopia to become a reality. Their utopia begins with a world without Donald Trump as president.

UTOPIA ON THE MIND

Utopian ideas are nothing new. From Thomas More, Francis Bacon, and Jean Jacques Rousseau, to Karl Marx and H. G. Wells, utopian ideas and utopian philosophies have been a mainstay in higher education studies. One of these ideas or philosophies is credited with producing failed states and destruction, and as a political model has been an abject failure throughout history. It is called by many names, including Marxism (although Marx was not especially supportive of utopian theory), and it has been associated with socialism and communism.

What the nation has experienced recently in its largest cities in the explosions of protests, riots, and leftist's support for looting and criminal destruction of property[2] is a clear example of methods used to move from the creation of dystopia to the establishment of utopia, or Shangri-La.

The battle for the minds and hearts of today's students is a serious one. The spread of popular ideas always encroaches upon society with the intent to evangelize. C. S. Lewis captures the essence of such a spread with the admonition, "The heart never takes the place of the head; but it can, and should obey it!"[3] Unfortunately, this is not the case today.

The message is clear whether discussing revolution or utopia, the one who can convince the hearts of a generation can overrule reason by emotion. It is no accident that public-learning institutions are consciously tailoring educational learning strategies for specific actions and their outcomes. What people are trained to do in thought cannot become a surprise when those trained in revolutionary rhetoric and tactics actually perform the tasks for which they prepared.

Accordingly, leading the way are social-emotional learning programs. These are making headway in American schools and the intent is to focus on growing children's social and emotional well-being.[4] The development of empathy toward people is wonderful in this age of social media, and is a focus upon which many people could benefit. But the program brings to the classrooms of America's public schools much more than its title. The programs place emotions at the center as strategies of reasoning and reactions.[5]

Social media has become at least as important as formal schooling. It has a schooling-type culture all unto its own and does little to emphasize any self-regulation of posted content. At present, the concern is with online education. Teachers do not want their students' parents sitting by and listening and watching what is taught and how students respond.

Certainly, with online there is a greater chance of accountability between parents and what teachers would be expecting from their students. By contrast, in the actual classroom, significant time would have been spent addressing ways to deal with various problems, where parents are not present. While at home, there is greater difficulty in addressing these points candidly with students. So, social media becomes another tool to input emotional stimuli into the brains of students.

Online Utopia

Education, as the nation has come to know it, has been extended by a cadre of online classes, from kindergarten through college. At some of these levels, the quality of online instruction consists of a patchwork of worksheets, YouTube videos, and readings and writing assignments. There is no stretch in saying that parents have a different appreciation for teachers now that they understand the complexities and difficulties of teaching more greatly than they did before. But students are being short shrift from the multitude of online classes and sessions.

One of the hazards of children going back to in-person schooling might well be the downturn in the quality, compared to the one-to-one attention they had probably received at home. In fact, some children might well have advanced academically, beyond what they could have, if they were sitting in a school room with thirty other students. There is the possibility that some students reason that being home for school is some form of personal paradise in learning—one's own educational utopia away from bullies, snide remarks, and in control of the learning environment.

The focus on social-emotional learning has leaned into social justice education. Certainly, most K–12 public educators think students will fall behind academically as a result of not meeting as a group in person. But will there be any downturn in the social and emotional development of the students if they are with their parents and siblings more often at home?

Adding to the concerns for teachers are the social-emotional aspects of family life for themselves and their students. Both are being severely challenged, and psychologists, physicians, and educators are worried about the long-term effects upon children. Students are not finding the outlets they need for positive, wholesome growth.

There are questions about whether a school can teach social and emotional lessons through online programs. Also under scrutiny is how do counselors and professionals meet the special needs of students and their families? As noticed in previous chapters of this book, some in higher education worry about parental authoritarianism while students are home learning online. Medical professionals fear the diminishing of students' mental health by not being able to join peers in person. Is online education the utopian model for schools?

Online programs as online instruction can only accomplish so much. Such instruction depends largely on the development of independent worker skills, if there is any hope for best outcomes. Public schooling, as it has been known, has morphed into something new. Maybe the time had come for a timeout. Possibly a serendipitous or even providential intervention occurred by way of China, to slow the spread of one thing, by way of another.

The direction in which American schooling was headed became more than a little concerning. On the one hand, the COVID-19 pandemic might have saved a generation from a year or two of wholesale indoctrination. On the other hand, we have lost so many people to death, and probably a year or so of educational, athletic, and social growth. Through it all, the unfortunate reality is that many of the nation's students will have fallen behind academically once again.

SLOGANEERING

More than a little outcry had resulted over classroom discussions and curriculum pertaining to issues that parents deemed questionably subversive, and highly offensive. Some of this subversion and offense are often reinforced by sloganeering. One of the simmering concerns in schools is the growing marginalization between the generations working side-by-side in the workplace. The taking of sides over issues that are now being forced upon schools by state and federal bureaucrats do not help matters.

There are clear generational differences between generations over issues, and these differences place wedges between people. Unfortunately, these differences are becoming more prominent, and the result is that sometimes teachers are placed at odds with colleagues, because of them.

Those unsupportive of public school racial and gender programs are assigned with "global negative traits,"[6] which are reserved for those who disagree with the social direction schools are heading. Every teacher knows parents tagged as problems. But this is more than a concern. The sole purpose of the label is to *red letter* people perceived as potentially troublesome to the liberal narrative experienced by children in classrooms. Even students are encouraged, accordingly, to be on guard for things they consider troublesome and to say something if they see something contrary within the walls of their classrooms,[7] and on their campuses.

WHAT IS UP WITH STUDENTS THESE DAYS?

One moment students are sullen and dispassionate. The next moment, after reading a text message, social media post, or newsfeed, they are headlong into the middle of tantrums. These reactions often border on hysteria and occur in the middle of what were once calm conversations. Students in twenty-first-century public-learning institutions, especially at the higher education levels, are causing professionals serious concern. The concern is not so much about their academics. Rather, the concern is about their mental health and their ability to cope with real-life circumstances, apart from their safe-space, protected environment.

A report from the *American Association of University Professors* (AAUP) notes habitual reactions that occur at greater intervals among students in college. Their conclusion is "The presumption that students need to be protected rather than challenged in a classroom is at once infantilizing and anti-intellectual."[8] As Mary Eberstadt eloquently asserts, social movements have placed in motion identity politics that claim victimhood as a means to answer the question, *Who am I?*[9]

Groups like Black Lives Matter and #MeToo are examples of using victimhood as a means to gain political identity. These groups are also reactions to events in both history and culture, which have become more important and more exclusive, it seems, than other historical events.

Educating the Whole Student?

Educating the whole student is a quaint parental assurance axiom. However, as a goal it is impractical and literally impossible to achieve, by all measures.

Who decides what a whole student education consists of and the measures to which any growth is attested?

The impractical side is the ridiculous claim that a teacher can educate all the students in one or more classes that run the range from self-contained to secondary, with special needs students mixed in? The impossible side of educating the whole student is the reality that children come to schools from impoverished backgrounds, broken and abusive homes, drug-addicted parents, single-parent households, and with special needs from birth and life-traumas.

What could teachers possibly accomplish toward educating the whole student with the prominence of such baggage? What, if anything, can teachers and schools do to deal with the problems of their students? Add in the distance learning and the whole student philosophy completely falls short.

First, it is important to decide what educating whole, complicated human beings even means. The question of whether students are even whole today, or whether education makes them whole is up for debate. Second, there are those who say education should be about academics and emotions, in order to meet the needs of all students. Whole student education is another well-meaning ideology that sprung from an Ivory Tower that was intended to sound empathetic and comprehensive to the basic needs of students. The phrase was little more than a *bumper sticker* and determining its meaning is like grasping a piece of the sky.

What is actually taking place under the whole student education banner is the molding of children's mindsets and beliefs. There is no better way to train students than by empowering them to use emotions and empathy when responding to questions.[10] Educators are trained to do just that.

Instead of the whole student education philosophy, others have come to the realization that what is more possible in American schools is the idea that *all children can learn*.[11] This is a safer maxim. Still, theorists do what they best: theorize. So, they have revised this to a newer "pivotal, powerful assumption."[12] The newer catch-phrase is *all students can learn at high levels*.[13] The definition and measuring of this aphorism will certainly be challenging.

As long as schools promote absolutes with terms such as "whole students" and "all children," while at the same time practicing contradictions, then rhetoric will not match what is actually taking place in the classroom. The public school moniker that all students can learn at higher levels is another mechanical, all-purpose educational phrase that comes across as an absolute, while stated as an assumption.

Parents communicate concerns about the nature and extent of their students' academic institutions. So, if schools care more about changing beliefs than academics, then parents must take a stand. They would be justified in their concerns and even with those concerns the humanists in schools still *believe* that in the face of the impossible moniker, and that humans can overcome just about anything with reason and hard work. Interestingly, humanists say they do not believe in the miraculous, but they claim students can be anything they want to be. This sounds quite similar to some of the humanistic feel-good teachings of some churches today.

HUMANISM TO THE RESCUE?

Humanists place faith in personal efforts. For humanists *all things are possible* with reason, science, and logic. In other words, they exercise faith. But faith always has an object. Having faith in faith is a mark of a religion that places humans as shapers of personal destiny.

If a student practices faith in a fundamental belief that a certain behavior or lifestyle is morally wrong, the humanist does not allow room for such a belief. The humanist would refer to the belief as being formed from religion. An illustration of this is exemplified in an anecdote that occurred recently in the United Kingdom. "A mother in the United Kingdom has taken formal legal action against her son's former elementary school after he was not permitted to opt out of an event in celebration of Pride Month."[14] The parent was told that permission to opt-out of the event was denied because the event "related to the spiritual, moral, cultural, mental and physical development of pupils."[15]

When schools decide which messages and programs are in the best interests of students, they usurp parental authority in so doing. In America, when states compel students to attend schools, then require them to learn behaviors and content that contradict the child's upbringing, then something is terribly wrong with the education system.

If anything in America is systemically broken, it is the education system that forces indoctrination upon all students—some of whom have beliefs contrary to the messages of humanism. Many of these requirements imposed upon children and families spring from the state-level politicians and their lobbyists,[16] who probably have spent no time working in classrooms with children and their families.

The school environment in the U.K. anecdote became toxic and the parent said she felt that the odds were already stacked against her. The head teacher's daughter, who was present at the meeting with the parent, was wearing a t-shirt that read, "Why be racist, sexist, homophobic, or transphobic, when you could just be quiet?"[17]

Forced attendance at rallies, assemblies, and other gatherings are not only happening in the United Kingdom. Wherever humanism's offshoots have taken root, these types of experiences can be found. Realistically, a person would be hard-pressed to find schools where these experiences are not found. American students are being forced to listen to stories about alternate lifestyles and pressured to rethink beliefs and practices that are against their personal and family beliefs.

Schooling in many schools in the United States comes across more like a bait-and-switch. This premise is the claim of educating the whole student, but demonstrating quite the opposite by focusing on politically correct teachings of social groups and serving as their apologists. The problem comes in select focal points that align with programs that consist of teachings that are opposite students' traditional family values.

This reality is not consistent with wholeness of all children. Is it any wonder that such conscious efforts are why public-learning institutions have been accused of indoctrinating children?[18] However, as long as there is no blowback from parents, or the community, the efforts to influence children will continue to press forward unabated.

An example of a Bakersfield, California, parent speaking up comes from a high school sophomore student's class. The parent was watching her son's AVID (Advancement Via Individual Determination) class, when she noticed the teacher had placed Black Lives Matter and LGBTQ+ posters in the direct range of the camera view. Students online were distracted by these posters, and the observing parent was furious. The values of both groups are not in line with her family's values and the parent argued that her child should not have to be triggered each day by these posters supporting the movements.

A similar situation occurred in Washington State, this time when a high school student was dismissed from Sports in Literature class for having a flag on his wall that read, "Trump 2020, No More Bullshit." This triggered parents and they complained to the school, and then to the district.[19]

Another student from Sacramento, California, was threatened to be removed from the class by his teacher for having a "Keep America Great" flag in his wall in his bedroom. Again, the reasons given for both these threats was the triggering of anger of anti-Trump parents and students.[20] Schools that claim inclusiveness demonstrate they want to control the messaging that students and parents see and hear. When people complain about schools indoctrinating their children, it is all about controlling the message.

Examples like these are not exceptions and are reasons why parents are curious about what their children are exposed to in schools. But this is also a reason why teachers and administrators are not copacetic toward parents watching their children's instructors in action, either in person or online.

EDUCATIONAL AND HISTORICAL REVISIONISM

Humanists are correct about one thing. Humans seem to have always had this fondness for self-determination. Western civilization can thank the European Renaissance for much of this interest. Hearkening back to the French philosopher, Rousseau, it becomes clear that he was sympathetic to the idea of civil religion. He reasoned that sovereignty of all citizens cannot be possible in any society apart from efforts made by governments seeking the outcome of a common good.[21] Thus, the nature of individual expression and the limitation of the individual for the good of many have always been at odds by the promotion of self over others.

But how does one compromise for the common good, particularly when a culture has decided one's autonomy and personal destiny are so intertwined? How can the common good be the focus when marginalization occurs from elevating groups based on external characteristics and identities?

Absent individual control of one's life, individuals are limited in what they can become and that does not fit the paradigm of self-worship. As a result, great revisions across American society have taken place. An example of the type of conflict between the self and the common good was on international display during the summer of 2020. When enough individuals discover others have similar beliefs, they find ways to join forces and a tribal group is formed.

The autonomous zones created in cities like Seattle and Portland demonstrated the folly of autonomous utopias. Questions arose like, (1) "Will they be planting their own gardens on land stolen from taxpayers?" (2) "How will they eat until the gardens grow?" (3) "Who will pay for their housing and medical care?" (4) "Will they have an economic policy for employment?" Cynically, (5) "Whose parents will be the first to drop off lunches over the chain link fence, like they did when the 'domestic invaders' were children?"

Creating an illegal zone from someone else's designated illegal territory is itself illegal. The irony is beyond them, but they do not care. They are making a point. There are followers and there are activists. The former seldom ask questions. The latter call the shots especially if they are paid to do so.[22]

These same autonomous groups were literally screaming that the settlers of the American colonies ransacked, stole, and pillaged the inhabitants of the areas they eventually colonized. The explorers are labeled murderers and tyrants by the history revisionists that focus heavily on social justice. There is an uncanny correlation here to those using hatred of the past which is what protesters call justifiable *tactics* to take over someone else's land. In fact, the accusers are invaders themselves, since they did not give back to a group they claimed were disenfranchised in the beginning. This point especially relates to the rhetoric of Black Lives Matter.

Today's young people, including the leaders of BLM,[23] are being either formally trained or informally guided in Marxism.[24] The purpose of this training is to prepare Blacks for new ideologies to follow and to unite in a social and political revolution,[25] as necessary. But this is not the only revolution that is taking place among the younger generations.

Generation Z leaders have organized an expanding group that appeals to disaffected Republican voters.[26] The newly formed group lays claim to being anti-Trump, but the Gen-Z-GOP is more than that. Many center-right conservatives "feel lost and without a home in the current political conversation, and a growing faction of the discontented is forming."[27]

Revising American History

Civics education in public schools has changed in recent years. Now, civic education has become civic activism and social justice, rather than the history of the Constitution and traditional American patriotism. Revisionism bias leads students to believe in some highly distorted perspectives about

American history. For example, the framers of the Constitution are portrayed by the late Howard Zinn as those exercising whiteness and privilege. They displayed this in their subjugation of indigenous people groups and imported Africans in order to retain this privilege. Zinn's history is highly controversial among history scholars and is worth examining to understand some of the reasons why contemporary public school students come away with certain viewpoints.

Zinn Educational Project (ZEP). According to Ursula Wolfe-Rocca of the Zinn Educational Project, "Too often, our curriculum teaches the Constitution as if it is a holy text (with the framers its prophets), that asks students to memorize what is legal more often than it asks them to grapple with what is just, and which privileges the mechanics of political institutions over the social movements that can transform them."[28]

The first point to observe is the progressive plea from the organization is dripping with incentives toward student social activism. Secondly, the Constitution is diminished in stature, sort of like the Bible is just a book of stories and the Constitution is just a document written by White men.

Then there is disrespect for the office and person of the forty-fifth president of the United States. The ZEP, in alignment with BLM, proclaims that White-American DNA is fraught with underlying endemic problems of hatred and bigotry. Thus, the next generation is encouraged to take to the streets and to act to correct injustices, by whatever means possible.[29]

The project also teaches that nearly 40 percent of those who supported Trump are tainted and systemically affected by the unjust past, even if they are not aware of it. As a result, "there is no pristine moment—no uncontaminated DNA—to which we can return to escape the evil of the present; indeed, the white supremacist, nativist, misogynist language we have heard spill from the lips of Donald Trump resonates with the 39 percent who steadfastly support him precisely because it has deep roots in U.S. history and politics."[30]

Now, as a means of convincing the public that the progressive ideology is revelatory, Wolfe-Rocca addresses the blind faith of students who are taught the Constitution. By not making certain to engage students in progressive action against injustice and endemic racism, teachers run the risk of being called out for their own bias. For example, "civics has meant challenging students' blind faith in our political DNA by introducing them to times when, if not for whistleblowers and lawbreakers, the unconstitutional use of state power would have proceeded unchecked, like the FBI's war on the Black Freedom Movement."[31]

What the Zinn Education Project does not address are the negatives and injustices perpetrated by activists and Marxists revolutionaries in America. It does not celebrate northerners who died to free slaves. The ZEP also leaves out key points, such as our nation was begun by White colonists fighting White British soldiers, all for White independence from Whites.

Another war was fought just eighty-four years later, and one of the major issues of that war was freeing Blacks from slavery. There were two nations on the soil of the United States after secession. There were also two armies, two constitutions, two currencies, and two uniforms. The south was primarily Democrat and that is the historical party of slavery and Jim Crow in the south. The ZEP seems to indict the north with the south during the Civil War, by painting all of America as a racist nation from the beginning.

What the left views as setting things straight and bringing justice to injustice, others claim the very opposite. For example, the ZEP celebrates actions that brought down President Trump, but is silent on the Hillary Clinton's scandals as Secretary of State. In addition, students do not learn about the Obama Administration's use of the Department of Justice, the FBI, and the Attorney General's Office as political tools under Eric Holder[32] and the FBI's James Comey,[33] but suffered through an impeachment process. If there is bias in American history, why then does the ZEP's revisionism resort to the same?

The very civics that students were to learn is that activism outside the Constitution is permissible and peaceable assembly, so called, can actually be violent. The actions it applauds are those which itself would not tolerate if brought against its own organization.

Justice becomes estranged from reality when a group believes in breaking the law to provide justice. The youth of America are easily swayed, it seems. There is no "small wonder that so many teenagers have liked him. But that describes a weakness of Zinn's book rather than a strength if mature historical insight is what one is looking for. Maturity and acne don't generally mix."[34]

American history is not perfect. But revisionists like Zinn and others want to change the past and rewrite it onto the minds of students in the present. Revising history to modify the past to make it appear so much worse than it was, affects students understanding in the present. But that is the aim, and it is also intellectually dishonest.

Revisionists assume they understand past human motivations when they attempt to interpret past events. They do this from a set of assumptions about a nation, but this is not history. These are preclusions looking for examples. It is an example of the bias and cancel culture prevalent in so much academe today. Fortunately, not everyone is taken in by the ZEP.

For example, Stanford professor of Education, Sam Wineburg, asserts: "Howard Zinn's *A People's History of the United States* offers bad lessons in historical thinking."[35] What revisionists fear most is being challenged. Focusing on perceived evils of humans to taint an entire nation is stoking anger and action. What the *tainters* do not reveal is that they also taint themselves in the process. Wolfe-Rocca demonstrates this as she explains that America is a nation with a history of "land theft, genocide, slavery, and the disenfranchisement of women and people of color."[36]

If these things are true, why hold today's American citizens accountable? America has a principle found in Article III of the United States Constitution that does not allow for the *corruption of blood*. If this principle is extended generally to modern families, then people today could not be held accountable for what their ancestors did in the past. Such a principle would circumvent the entire notion that Americans must pay the price for guilt of their predecessors.

For example, even if a family member had been convicted of something infamous against the government in the early days of America as a nation, there would be major legal challenges mounted today against anyone seeking to harm current offspring because of the past. In other words, the *no corruption of blood* principle could easily clear today's Whites from any of the BLM arguments of being accountable for slavery, and thus preclude the writing bills of attainder to hold them accountable, for what supposedly their ancestors committed. This would also take punitive reparations off the table. The reparations advocates would have an easier time securing reparations from businesses in the south that still exist from the Jim Crow era.

In any case, the ZEP makes every effort to lead by revisionist exemplars. "In 2017, they successfully pressured *Scholastic* to stop distributing positive books about President Trump. They conducted protests against the *Bill of Rights Institute*, including publicly at the 2014 *National Council for the Social Studies* annual meeting, and then claimed victory when the institute was absent in 2015. Due to *Southern Poverty Law Center* lobbying, Zinn's lessons on Reconstruction are taught throughout South Carolina."[37]

If the outcomes of social actions are viewed as part of the social reform and change desired, then the subjective morality is justified as right and good. If this is civics, and innocent children are taught to take sides and fight for something they do not understand and did not cause, then American civics is truly broken morally and ethically.

Political support for Zinn's progressive agenda resulted in the Obama Administration's rewrite of Advanced Placement education guidance in United States History. The change to far-left progressive standards caused more than a splash of controversy among teachers of AP U.S. History. Zinn's *A Young People's History of the United States* became a required and suggested text for extra reading by many teachers and professors in their history courses.[38]

To illustrate, what is quite telling is that during the summer of 2020, many cities were overrun by people between the ages of eighteen to thirty-five—the very generation to come through post-9/11 Bush and Obama years. The changes in education with *No Child Left Behind* (NCLB), the *Common Core*, and societal, racial, and gender tribal marginalization, set the stage for the nation to head in the current wrong direction.[39] Add to this the hatred of the forty-fifth president, Donald Trump, a viral pandemic, excessive government crackdowns and state governors' early prison releases of thousands and thousands of hardened criminals to the streets of America, and people were primed for action.

THE DOCTRINE OF SOCIAL JUSTICE

One of the main arguments used by social justice activists is that this nation was set up for the success by Whites for Whites, and cast aside all others. History is clear that it certainly did not include the slaves or women and children at the time. So, on that basis, there is the feeling that patriarchal White Supremacy which began the American experiment was codified in the founding documents and culture.

These same social justice activists then turn around and extrapolate that America is truly a racist nation and that White Supremacy is so ingrained in culture from the beginning that Whites are not even aware of it. In the words of CNN racial activist and commentator Van Jones, Whites have a virus in their brains that is switched on and off.

When asked about racism in other nations, particularly about tribal racism in Africa, or racism between Asians, Hispanics—or any other demographic—all such queries and discussions are muted. The reason they are muted is because no other race is granted a place of preeminence within the BLM political and social justice narratives.[40] Once again, there is the feeling that one race is superior over another.

What the social justice activists intentionally overlook is that the United States has made many society-altering changes. A good number of these changes were aimed at dismantling both the perception and reality of supremacy at the nation's inception. Some examples include The Emancipation Proclamation, many Supreme Court cases, equities in education, economics, and athletics are proof of many positive changes. In addition, owners of businesses, wealthy millionaires, and billionaires of color are reaping the benefits of the opportunities afforded to all Americans.

Add to this Historically Black Colleges and Universities (HBCSs), private schools, charter schools, and other schools of choice in urban communities, and it is not difficult to feel like opportunities for families and children of all races are more widely available today. A nation that recognizes changes, and makes those changes—so as to level the playing field—is not a racist nation. Still the "America is Racist" slogan persists.[41]

Certainly, the outcomes of these opportunities are sometimes vastly different and cities have a long way to go to make things better. The citizens of those cities might look to the political structures in place and consider what they might be able to do differently through elections to affect better educational and economic outcomes. They should also look to the cultures of inner cities to find areas that need to be changed so that crime is not more lucrative to residents than an honest career. Good schools and two-parent households can help to shape culture differently, and that is not White racist thinking. It is pure and simple common sense—the type that spans continents and recorded history.

Social Justice and Medicine

Schools of medicine in the United States are adding social justice to the medical training of their physicians. Some medical school students are now eligible to earn a *health justice* certificate, along with their diplomas. Physicians are now being reminded to make certain that patients of traditionally underserved and minority groups receive the same care as Whites. There is somehow this notion that the medical services consisting of highly trained doctors and nurses are disregarding or shunning people based on race.

The accusation that medical staff are making institutionalized decisions based on race is highly offensive and insulting. Any such assumption is evidence of a problem in thinking on the parts which make those who share this perception. That being said, the claim is that the medical professional is institutionally racist.[42]

Examples of pressing forward social justice political agenda are obvious in the trend of hiring of social scientists to assist as change agents. At the University of Southern California's Keck School of Medicine, social scientist Laura Mosqueda was hired to implement such change. The institution writes:

> The introduction of health justice to the medical school curriculum demonstrates the Keck School's deep commitment to equity, justice and structural transformation to ameliorate health disparities. It also recognizes that physicians trained in health justice will be best equipped to stand at the forefront of social change. After George Floyd was killed by a police officer in Minneapolis on May 25, Laura Mosqueda, MD, dean of the Keck School, wrote in a message that the death of Floyd and others 'are symptoms of the same inequalities that contribute to poorer health for people of color in the United States. . . . We were inspired by Dr. Mosqueda saying to us that she wants the Keck School to be known for social justice,' said Donna Elliott, MD, Ed.D, vice dean for medical education and chair of the Department of Medical Education.[43]

EVALUATION OF THE CLAIMS OF HUMANISM

The average humanist has a belief system and, as such, is open to evaluation. After each humanist tenet below, a brief evaluation is provided.

(1) "There are no supernatural beings."[44] Since this is a preclusion, there is nothing that a believer in the supernatural could suggest to qualify as supernatural, or miraculous, that would change the mind of a true humanist. One must question what is greater, the humanist's belief in self or the disbelief in a Supreme Being.

A human would have to possess all knowledge to be able to establish the humanist's preclusion as fact. There are no humans with this type of all-knowledge. Therefore, statements regarding the existence or lack of existence of a supernatural being, including God, would have to be taken on faith, by both claimants. This faith would be just as informed for the believer in the existence of God as well as a believer in the non-existence of God. They are both believers, and both place faith in their beliefs.

Out of necessity, faith and belief accompany both systems of thought. So, all things considered, which of the two systems in a competition over the moral high ground edges out the other in claiming god-like all-knowledge, hence omniscience?

Secondly, in the minds of humanists, (2) "the material universe is the only thing that exists."[45] The only way a humanist can prove this is to be everywhere present, which is impossible. Also, what else is impossible to know on the part of the humanist is the reality about their statement (3) "there is no after-life."[46] With these two statements, the humanist would like to attribute omnipresence and omniscience to humans.

In order for a person to accomplish this, and to justify the point that the material universe is the only thing that exists, one must be as God. This denial of afterlife is a slogan, which is self-defeating as a presupposition. Besides, the vast majority of humans would not agree with the humanist on this declarative.[47] Disagreement is not material, and neither are emotions. Life and death are materially scientific.

The humanist (4) elevates science as "the only reliable source of knowledge"[48] about the universe. Which branch science is elevated, depends on the humanist. Is it the astrophysics of Robert Jastrow, evolutionary biology of Richard Dawkins, or the Center for Science and Culture? In addition, humanists grant the scientific method and inquiry the power to help shape human experiences and personal destiny. However, this same scientific method and its usual reliable consistency is quite porous. Hypotheses and conclusions change all the time and science has not proven there is no God.

Thus, along with the humanist attributing the possibility of all-knowledge to the self, one would also have to ascribe the attribution of being everywhere present. Likewise, in order to negate a person's claim of both the existence of God and miracles, the humanist must be greater than a natural human; hence supernatural. In so being, such a person is outside the realm of humanity to know that these do not exist and cannot occur. But since humanists do not believe in an afterlife, the miracle of it is left to the believers. Humanists cannot simply dismiss out-of-hand any logic that they deem unfit to their worldview. Humanism rejects the supernatural and theism, yet ascribes the very nature of god-like actions to themselves and their cognitive-emotional presuppositions.

Among other belief tenets affirmed by humanists include (5) "human beings can live ethical lives without religious beliefs."[49] Is it also possible to live a religious life without ethical beliefs? In the case of the humanist, the rules for ethical behavior are set by presupposed standards. There is a high degree of likelihood that a humanist that tries to live a humanist ethical life falls short because there is no religious truth associated with the behaviors. In other words, this standard allows for subjective living that is considered beneficent or pleasurable to only the person living by those standards.

This open door of ethics presents no objectives and offers only truth-in-the-moment, subjectively. The fact is that humanists are adamant about human beings (6) deriving "their moral code from the lessons of history, personal experience, and thought."[50] The facts are that religion and faith are embedded in history and historic religious figures and cannot be excised without affecting those things upon which they were based.

Would humanists have developed education, medicine, and law in the United States, absent the Judeo-Christian ethics and heritage? The values and traditions of our nation have their genesis in the Christian religion. The very fact that this nation was formed by those fleeing tyranny, and a compact was formed favoring their community based on religious freedom, is no small historical point to discard.

One of the problems of developing a moral code from human reasoning is that the same faulty humans record history, interpret personal experiences differently, and think differently on so very many matters of life. So, what is the framework whereby humanists can judge history, since they reject religion in framing ethics? How can humanists properly interpret their experiences, without first knowing and understanding both context and content of others' experiences?

There is no corporate thinking on many issues in life and certainly the humanists' claim of morality and ethics without religion is spurious at best. For example, there are religious humanists and their claim about what they do, and why they do it, may not align with the strict secular humanist. In such cases, whose ethic plays out as truth in this type of contradictory, subjective ethical world?

BLM: A NEW RELIGIOUS CULT IN AMERICA

There is a new religion in the public square. Question it and reprisal results. Disagree with it and one is labeled. Lukianoff and Haidt explain the tactic of this new religion. "A claim that someone's words are offensive is not just an expression of one own subjective feeling of offendedness. It is, rather, a public charge that the speaker has done something objectively wrong. It is a demand that the speaker apologize or be published by some authority for committing an offense."[51]

We need look no farther that the headlines of news, where anyone disagreeing with the Black Lives Movement tenets is branded with one label or another. Some of the fallout for mentioning anything critical of the movement has resulted in (1) losses of sponsors for cable programs, (2) retractions of comments, (3) forced apologies on air and on social media, (4) reversals of policies under threats of boycotts, and (5) firings for mere disagreements over the tactics and strategies employed.[52]

BLM has all the earmarks of a religious cult and incorporates many elements of religious humanism into its platform. The empowerment of the organization has occurred by political bully tactics, mass protest, and violence. All over America, people are being shamed into apologies for their opinions, and even into bowing knees in asking public forgiveness. The confusing part to all of this is that this cult is allowed to proliferate in public schools and is supported by administrations. There is a new religion in town and it is being practiced in K–16 schools and colleges.

An aspect of this new cult is the inability to handle criticism. In fact, what the groups does not allow, they actually practice toward those unsupportive of their tactics. In the face of BLM's targeted demographic bullying, a question has been asked by more than one researcher: "What are we doing to our students if we encourage them to develop extra-thin skin just before they leave the cocoon of adult protection?"[53]

There is more than the appearance that our public-learning institutions have gone too far and now riots and destruction are becoming part of the expression of the newly emerging *anger culture*. When race is affiliated with humanism, and schools are the places to enlist recruits, horrific results can be expected. These, along with BLM's Marxism and its anti-family emphases, will be laid bare over time in the annals of history.

The Universal Declarative of Black Lives Matter

The Black Lives Matter moniker states an exclusive and universal declarative. Hundreds of millions of dollars have been given with billions more pledged to fight racial bias, as a result of the group's pressure on corporate America.[54] The organization is the recent wunderkind, in terms of capitalizing on amassed selective moral outrage, by both factional and political power. BLM's philosophy is appearing in more and more schools, and even among youth groups and churches once described as conservative and evangelical. Many times these organizations have not thought beyond the slick placards held by the group's activists. Slogans have a way of taking on a life of their own.

There is an all-out effort to sacralize BLM and to lift it to governmental sacrosanct status with impunity. Public education is welcoming it with open arms. One example recently shared with this author describes the infiltration of BLM and the new racial justice paradigm sweeping the nation.

> We had concerns about social justice overtaking theology in our church, and since we have a Christian school on our larger campus, we worried about the creep of the BLM message into the classrooms. But it's there already. The church we attended posted a black out on its website, in support of BLM. They did this while our son—a law enforcement officer—had just finished eight nights in a row on riot patrol. This was followed by an increase in sermon teaching of a social justice gospel, on Sundays. We don't believe that is biblical. To make matters worse, since our son, certain factions checked our son's high school record and found that he once dressed as Obama for a dress up day. As a result, our son was accused of racism at work. He was eventually cleared of this, but White officers are routinely accused of racism. He is no longer sure he wants to remain in law enforcement, since the powers-that-be are retreating from support more and more. What is happening to our world?

A quick view of the BLM website provides the reader with the tenets of the group and its intentions. However, regular visits to the site prove very interesting, as the organization regularly sanitizes its inflammatory rhetoric. For example, anyone following the website would have observed the removal of the straightforward vilification against Whites and the intentional attacks on the nuclear family.[55] These have been shifted to "softer" language. Nevertheless, the original statements truly represent the BLM organization and remain on the *Wayback Machine*, in media archives, and additional various retrieval systems.[56] Below is a list of original tenets from the BLM website[57] before it was sanitized:

- Black Lives Matter began as a call to action in response to state-sanctioned violence and anti-Black racism.
- The impetus for that commitment was, and still is, the rampant and deliberate violence inflicted on us by the state.
- We are unapologetically Black in our positioning. In affirming that Black Lives Matter, we need not qualify our position. To love and desire freedom and justice for ourselves is a prerequisite for wanting the same for others.
- We are guided by the fact that all Black lives matter, regardless of actual or perceived sexual identity, gender identity, gender expression, economic status, ability, disability, religious beliefs or disbeliefs, immigration status, or location.
- We make space for transgender brothers and sisters to participate and lead.
- We are self-reflexive and do the work required to dismantle cisgender privilege and uplift Black trans folk, especially Black trans women who continue to be disproportionately impacted by trans-antagonistic violence.
- We build a space that affirms Black women and is free from sexism, misogyny, and environments in which men are centered.
- We disrupt the western-prescribed nuclear family structure requirement by supporting each other as extended families and "villages" that collectively care for one another, especially our children, to the degree that mothers, parents, and children are comfortable.
- We foster a queer-affirming network. When we gather, we do so with the intention of freeing ourselves from the tight grip of heteronormative thinking, or rather, the belief that all in the world are heterosexual (unless s/he or they disclose otherwise).
- We embody and practice justice, liberation, and peace in our engagements with one another.

Activists and followers of BLM tend to be quicker to point to race when incidents occur upon people of color and conflate these incidents as proof of systemic issues. The problem is that BLM relies on false racial theories, and oft-repeated popular mantras. Nevertheless, allegiance to the cult is mounting across segments of American society.

The organization's intentions are to continue the refrain that America is a bad nation and has a terrible original sin that exists in every corner of American culture. As stated earlier, this original sin was slavery and, coupled with the accusation of White superiority and racism, the only way to fix the irredeemable nation and its White race is to overthrow it by revolution and start over.[58]

Differences in Theology and Philosophy

The following is a Facebook statement posted by this author, in response to a converted supporter of the Black Lives Matter movement. The supporter in question had an emotional reaction to an incident involving a police officer in a major city.

> There are major differences in what BLM and Antifa stand for, but there are also far too many similarities in tactics and methods to achieve their independent goals. But the main concern here is the "phrase" Black Lives Matter. Regardless what people immediately begin to exclaim about any criticism leveled at the group, or the rally cry of racism, nothing could be farther from the truth. No group and no message is above criticism.
>
> BLM does not refer to any OTHER black lives than those lost from real and perceived police brutality and injustice. Therefore, as a result of that, it does mean all lives do not matter. It also means not all black lives even matter. The premise that any black life lost to a white officer is racism on an entirely systemic level, yet there is no application of racism of same-group racial demographics, or Black on White crime, is quite myopic and wide open to reverse discrimination.
>
> The reality is that by strict BLM definition, when a White physician performs an abortion procedure on a Black woman, this should also be scrutinized as evidence of oppression and racism. This practice, after all, is institutionalized in America. Yet this is not considered racist and the lack of messaging from the group is quite troublesome.
>
> BLM is demonstrating selective moral outrage, and what is occurring now was bound to happen. The strategy is clear. It consists of (1) find an event, (2) marginalize one or more groups/individuals, (3) organize and mobilize, (4) protest and/or riot to send message of concern. Has anyone taken the time to read through the BLM website? It is clear the acronym BLM is no longer associated

with cries for help against injustice for select Black men. The organization is associated with a leftist, Marxist/Communist ideology that promotes violence, when necessary—and of this is clear from its leaders' interviews.

Radicals love mantras. They love to come up with short bumper sticker philosophies. People are attracted to supporting slogans, and their minds are allowed to fashion meaning out of slogans. Their emotions validate their feelings of the truth of the group's rhetoric. Slogans are often like advertisements for sales, attracting both the unwitting and the unquestioning. The costs for both are often unequal in outcome. If outcomes are the goal, then one should not complain when other groups form to state their own views. For example, as a counter to Black Lives Matter, White Lives Matter began to appear.

White Lives Matter was deemed racist, but to those whose minds thought something else about the slogan, it was no such thing. Then when police were being injured and killed by rioters and anarchists during the summer of 2020, Blue Lives Matter memes and gifs began popping up all over the Internet. Those were also labeled as racist.

Each of these additional monikers spawned a following, but only Black Lives Matter has a full-fledged set of goals to tear down the infrastructure of American culture, revamp law enforcement, do away with the nuclear family, and promote the LGBTQ+ in schools and communities. One might ask, how is that the mission of BLM, when it was initially formed to protest what it perceived as police excess use of force against Black men?

Nevertheless, no one questions this disconnect because the followers ascribe to the affirmation intended by the group's moniker. The leaders allow this disconnect between followers and the deeper mission, because numbers of followers speak volumes, even if the followers are blinded by their own perceptions. Any questioning of the phrase that identifies the group as anything other than what their propaganda asserts, and the wholesale response is to demonize the critic as an immediate racist. Again, this is Marxist and it is also a Saul Alinsky strategy used by radicals for decades.

What is missing here is the truth, and not some linguistic or rhetorical spin. Stating that Black Lives Matter in the midst of the larger American context that All Lives Matter, would bring with it more people into agreement. But because the group is based on radical leftists and claims that systemic racism is comprehensive and pervasive in every aspect of American life, the admission of alternate slogans cannot be acceptable, per se.

The accusation that all Whites are by nature implicitly biased and racist falls on deaf ears with a majority of the Americans. It's not that Americans do not care, but it's because their messaging is accusatory and not based in what most Americans understand as truth. Rewriting history with false premises that all Whites are racists is not unifying. Quite the contrary. False premises will not massage faulty predicates any closer to the truth. Still, BLM, Zinn's educational project, and the 1619 Project seek to supplant and rewrite it.

Saying White Lives Matter does not mean that all lives do not matter. They all mattered before BLM even existed. But by saying Black Lives Matter, their website makes it clear that only some of them do, even if they say they are not responsible to qualify their declarative. Therefore, All Lives Matter is an appropriate replacement to a group that thinks all of its own lives do not matter and covers more people under its umbrella. Lives matter and they are not any greater or lesser because of a flag or a sign. Life is sacred for all.

The religious-type movement that is BLM seems to have gained more than a grasp on American culture. Only history will be able to count the cost of this movement in American culture and its impact upon students in schools. Eberstadt illustrates a significant aspect of these types of movements and the dangers they pose. Writing about another movement, she exclaims, "the #MeToo movement exhibits in full what happens what great swaths of humanity are more socially illiterate than our forebears were, because the pool of those from whom we learn earliest and most naturally has diminished."[59] This is not only a slight upon movements, but it also an indictment of groups indoctrinating the American populace, in general.

Moreover, there is also an indictment of America's failure in public-learning institutions—the very places where academic learning is supposed to occur. Public-learning institutions in America have lost their ways and are demonstrating that, as a system, it is probably too far gone to save.[60] Therefore, maybe BLM and its cult of race is right in one particular area. It might be time to overthrow at least one institution in America and rebuild it from scratch. Can we begin this effort in the burned-out cities that are testimony to the new method of humanistic evangelism?

NOTES

1. Greg Lukianoff and Jonathan Haidt. "The coddling of the American mind." *The Atlantic*. September 2015. Retrieved June 9, 2020, from https://www.theatlantic.com/magazine/archive/2015/09/the-coddling-of-the-american-mind/99356/.

2. Natalie Escobar. "One author's argument 'in defense of looting.'" *NPR*. August 27, 2020. Retrieved September 1, 2020, from https://www.npr.org/sections/codeswitch/2020/08/27/906642178/one-authors-argument-in-defense-of-looting.

3. C. S. Lewis. *The abolition of man*. 1944. San Francisco, CA: HarperCollins Publishers, p. 19.

4. Joseph A. Durlak (Ed.), Celene E. Domitrovich, Roger P. Weissberg, et al. *Handbook of social and emotional learning: Research and practice*. 2015. New York, NY: Guilford Publications Inc.

5. Sara LaHayne. "5 reasons why social-emotional learning should be a daily routine." *Education Week*. October 29, 2018. Retrieved September 22, 2020, from https://blogs.edweek.org/edweek/learning_social_emotional/2018/10/5_reasons_why_social_emotional_learning_should_be_a_daily_routine.html.

6. Lukianoff and Haidt. "The coddling of the American mind." *The Atlantic*.

7. Daniel Fishel. "Hear something, say something: Navigating the world of racial awkwardness." *NPR*. September 28, 2016. Retrieved September 2, 2020, from https://www.npr.org/sections/codeswitch/2016/09/28/494881057/hear-something-say-something-navigating-the-world-of-racial-awkwardness.

8. Report by Subcommittee of Committee A on Academic Freedom and Tenure. "On trigger warnings." *American Association of University Professors*. August 2014. Retrieved June 12, 2020, from https://www.aaup.org/report/trigger-warnings.

9. Mary Eberstadt. *Primal screams: How the sexual revolution created identity politics*. 2019. West Conshohocken, PA: Templeton Press, p. 91.

10. Sarah Schwartz. "Teachers support social-emotional learning, but say students in distress strain their skills." *Education Week*. July 16, 2019. Retrieved December 27, 2019, from https://www.edweek.org/ew/articles/2019/07/17/teachers-support-social-emotional-learning-but-say-students.html.

11. Larry Leverett. "Closing the achievement gap: All children can learn." *Edutopia*. September 5, 2006. Retrieved August 25, 2020, from https://www.edutopia.org/closing-achievement-gap.

12. Mike Mattos. "A pivotal, powerful assumption: All students can learn at high levels." *Solution Tree Blog*. January 29, 2019. Retrieved August 25, 2020, from https://www.solutiontree.com/blog/assuming-all-students-can-learn/.

13. Ibid.

14. Heather Clark. "UK mother takes legal action against primary school for not allowing son to opt out of gay pride event." *Christian News*. March 26, 2019. Retrieved December 14, 2019, from https://christiannews.net/2019/03/26/uk-mother-takes-legal-action-against-primary-school-for-not-allowing-son-to-opt-out-of-gay-pride-event/?fbclid=IwAR3y1LcEYxUK-VY7znIuncouGPgLM4q60N31Omjvagby4S7ajednmXF53wk.

15. Ibid.

16. Staff. "The roles of the federal and state governments in education." *Find Law*. March 21, 2018. Retrieved September 2, 2020, from https://www.findlaw.com/education/curriculum-standards-school-funding/the-roles-of-federal-and-state-governments-in-education.html.

17. Clark. "UK mother takes legal action against primary school for not allowing son to opt out of gay pride event." *Christian News*.

18. Ilya Somin. "Public education as public indoctrination." *Reason*. January 12, 2020. Retrieved September 2, 2020, from https://reason.com/2020/01/12/public-education-as-public-indoctrination/. Cf. Auguste Meyrat. "How public schools indoctrinate kids without almost anyone noticing." *The Federalist*. October 26, 2018. Retrieved September 2, 2020, from https://thefederalist.com/2018/10/26/public-schools-indoctrinate-kids-without-almost-anyone-noticing/.

19. Elise Sole. "School report card: This week, parents flout pandemic rules and Trump flags cause controversy in virtual school." *Yahoo Lifestyle*. September 25, 2020. Retrieved September 25, 2020, from https://www.yahoo.com/lifestyle/school-report-card-parents-flout-pandemic-rules-trump-flags-controversy-virtual-school-181257495.html.

20. Ibid.

21. G. D. H. Cole (Trans.), J. H. Brumfitt and J. C. Hall (Eds.). *Jean-Jacques Rousseau: The social contract and the Discourses*. 1992 (1931). New York, NY: Alfred A. Knopf Publishers, pp. 192, 203, 258, and 295.

22. Legal Staff. "Are BLM rioters made up of paid protesters?" *Ehline Law Firm, Los Angeles, CA*. July 30, 2020. Retrieved September 14, 2020, from https://ehlinelaw.com/blog/blm-rioters-paid.

23. Daniel Payne. "Video resurfaces in which Black Lives Matter founder says groups' creators are 'trained Marxists.'" *Just the News*. June 20, 2020. Retrieved June 24, 2020, from https://justthenews.com/politics-policy/video-resurfaces-which-black-lives-matter-founder-says-groups-creators-are-trained.

24. Payne. "Video resurfaces in which Black Lives Matter founder says groups' creators are 'trained Marxists.'" *Just the News*.

25. See the *Black Lives Matter* website. https://blacklivesmatter.com/.

26. Kim Parker and Ruth Igielnik. "On the cusp of adulthood and facing an uncertain future: What we know about Gen Z so far." *Pew Research Center*. May 14, 2020. Retrieved September 3, 2020, from https://www.pewsocialtrends.org/essay/on-the-cusp-of-adulthood-and-facing-an-uncertain-future-what-we-know-about-gen-z-so-far/.

27. Rachel Janfaza. "Gen Z conservatives build new groups for Anti-Trump Republicans." *CNN*. September 2, 2020. Retrieved September 3, 2020, from https://www.cnn.com/2020/09/02/politics/gen-z-conservatives-anti-trump-groups/index.html?fbclid=IwAR3DU3PURDGQxpEPnxO-gf0OpXKFZkfVVwzWoJddCN6SEf0rg7xjFUrYocc.

28. Ursula Wolfe-Rocca. "Teaching more civics will not save us from Trump." *Zinn Education Project*. September 10, 2018. Retrieved May 11, 2020, from https://www.zinnedproject.org/if-we-knew-our-history/teaching-more-civics.

29. Brie Stimson. "Rep. Pressley calls for unrest in the streets over Trump-backing GOP members." *New York Post*. August 16, 2020. Retrieved August 25, 2020, from https://nypost.com/2020/08/16/rep-pressley-calls-for-unrest-in-the-streets-over-trump-backing-gop-members/. Cf. Jason Turesky. "Rep. Ayanna Pressley on police reform: This is a moment of reckoning." *WGBH News*. June 23, 2020. Retrieved

August 25, 2020, from https://www.wgbh.org/news/national-news/2020/06/23/rep-ayanna-pressley-on-police-reform-this-is-a-moment-of-reckoning.

30. Wolfe-Rocca. "Teaching more civics will not save us from Trump." *Zinn Education Project.*

31. Ibid.

32. John Bresnahan. "Holder held in contempt." *Politico.* June 28, 2012. Retrieved August 25, 2020, from https://www.politico.com/story/2012/06/holder-held-in-contempt-of-congress-077988.

33. Staff. "Report of investigation of former Bureau of Investigation director James Comey's disclosure of sensitive investigative information and handling of certain memoranda." *U.S. Department of Justice Office of the Inspector General.* August 2019. Retrieved August 25, 2020, from https://oig.justice.gov/reports/2019/o1902.pdf.

34. Wilfred McClay. "A radical pseudo-historian meets his match." *The James G. Martin Center for Academic Renewal.* April 15, 2020. Retrieved April 15, 2020, from https://www.jamesgmartin.center/2020/04/a-radical-pseudo-historian-meets-his-match/.

35. Sam Wineburg. "Undue certainty: Where Howard Zinn's a people's history falls short." *American Educator.* Winter, 2012–2013, pp. 27–34. Retrieved August 25, 2020, from https://www.aft.org/sites/default/files/periodicals/Wineburg.pdf. Cf. David Plotnikoff. "Zinn's influential history textbook has problems, says Stanford education expert." *Stanford News.* December 20, 2012. Retrieved August 25, 2020, from https://news.stanford.edu/news/2012/december/wineburg-historiography-zinn-122012.html.

36. Wolfe-Rocca. "Teaching more civics will not save us from Trump." *Zinn Education Project.*

37. Ibid.

38. Mary Grabar. "The Zinn Education Project: Teaching Trump-hate and other dogma." *The American Spectator.* January 6, 2020. Retrieved May 11, 2020, from https://spectator.org/the-zinn-education-project-teaching-trump-hate-and-other-dogma/.

39. Ernest J. Zarra III. *The wrong direction for today's schools.* 2015. Lanham, MD: Rowman & Littlefield Publishers.

40. Kristyn Martin. "Teachers across America are talking about racial injustice with 'fed up' students: They're sick of living in a world that's trash." *Yahoo Life.* June 11, 2020. Retrieved June 12, 2020, from https://www.yahoo.com/lifestyle/teachers-across-america-talking-racial-injustice-students-221101614.html.

41. Shayanne Gal, Andy Kieraz, Michelle Mark, et al. "26 simple charts to show friends and family who aren't convinced racism is still a problem in America." *Business Insider.* July 8. 2020. Retrieved September 25, 2020, from https://www.businessinsider.com/us-systemic-racism-in-charts-graphs-data-2020-6. Cf. Ward Connerly. "America isn't a racist country. *Wall Street Journal.* July 24, 2020. Retrieved September 25, 2020, from https://www.wsj.com/articles/america-isnt-a-racist-country-11595628914.

42. Aaron E. Carroll. "Doctors and racial bias: Still a long way to go." *New York Times.* February 25, 2019. Retrieved September 25, 2020, from https://www.nytimes

.com/2019/02/25/upshot/doctors-and-racial-bias-still-a-long-way-to-go.html. Cf. Ayotomiwa Ojo. "Racism in medicine isn't an abstract notion. It's happening all around us, every day." *WBUR.* June 14, 2020. Retrieved September 20, 2020, from https://www.wbur.org/cognoscenti/2020/06/12/anti-racism-in-medicine-hospitals-ayotomiwa-ojo.

43. Landon Hall. "The Keck School adds health justice to curriculum." *HSC News of University of Southern California.* July 14, 2020. Retrieved July 16, 2020, from https://hscnews.usc.edu/the-keck-school-adds-health-justice-to-curriculum.

44. Robert Ashby. "Humanism: A positive approach to life." *BBC.* October 27, 2009. Retrieved May 29, 2020, from https://www.bbc.co.uk/religion/religions/atheism/types/humanism.shtml.

45. Ibid.

46. Ibid.

47. Staff. "Most Americans believe in the afterlife." *Rasmussen Reports.* June 8, 2017. Retrieved August 25, 2020, from https://www.rasmussenreports.com/public_content/lifestyle/general_lifestyle/june_2017/most_americans_believe_in_the_afterlife.

48. Ashby. "Humanism: A positive approach to life." *BBC.*

49. Ibid.

50. Ibid.

51. Lukianoff and Haidt. "The coddling of the American mind." *The Atlantic.*

52. Curtis Renee and John Sloan III. "Opinion: What we mean when we say Black Lives Matter." *The Detroit News.* June 15, 2020. Retrieved June 24, 2020, from https://www.detroitnews.com/story/opinion/2020/06/16/opinion-what-we-mean-when-we-say-black-lives-matter/3190936001/.

53. Lukianoff and Haidt. "The coddling of the American mind." *The Atlantic.*

54. Staff. "Bank of America pledges $1 billion to address racial, economic, equality." *Reuters.* June 2, 2020. Retrieved September 25, 2020, from https://www.reuters.com/article/us-minneapolis-police-bank-of-america/bank-of-america-pledges-1-billion-to-address-racial-economic-inequality-idUSKBN2391NO.

55. Bradford Betz. "Black Lives Matter organization deletes pages calling for 'disruption' of nuclear family." *Fox News.* September 21, 2020. Retrieved September 22, 2020, from https://www.foxnews.com/us/blm-deletes-page-disruption-nuclear-family.

56. Ibid.

57. *Black Lives Matter.* https://blacklivesmatter.com/.

58. Mike Gonzalez. "Marxist NLM is committed to overthrowing America's system." *Real Clear Politics.* September 2, 2020. Retrieved September 21, 2020, from https://www.realclearpolitics.com/2020/09/02/marxist_blm_is_committed_to_overthrowing_americas_system_522215.html. Cf. Ryan James. "Black Lives Matter Marxist plot to overthrow America's founding." *Freedom Wire.* July 23, 2020. Retrieved August 5, 2020, from https://freedomwire.com/blm-marxist-plot/.

59. Eberstadt. *Primal screams: How the sexual revolution created identity politics,* p. 91.

60. Annie Murphy Paul. "Diane Ravitch declares the education reform movement dead." *New York Times*. January 21, 2020. Retrieved May 23, 2020, from https://www.nytimes.com/2020/01/21/books/review/slaying-goliath-diane-ravitch.html. Cf. Editorial Staff. "Is public education dead?" *Harvard Graduate School of Education*. March 10, 2014. Retrieved September 20, 2020, from https://www.gse.harvard.edu/news/14/03/public-education-dead.

Index

ableism, 50
abortion, 114
Abrams, Meyer Howard, 14–15
actions as religion, 14
active partisan polarization, 49
activists seek converts, 61
adolescent brains, 24
Alinsky, Saul, xiii, 175
all children can learn, 158
all words matter, 61
America: accusations against, 115–16; as racist nation, 106, 166
American, xviii, xix; Association of University Professors (AAUP), 157; culture, xviii, xix; patriotism, 162; of sex, 130; society, xviii
American colonies, 38
American Humanist Association v. United States Federal Bureau of Prisons (2014), 17
Ames, Aaron, 46
anger culture, 171
anti-Blackness, 95
anti-Christian doctrine of man, 63
antifa, 47, 101–2, 174
apocalyptic destiny, 16
Apostle Paul, 28, 38
Asian monarchs, 76
Asians, 167

atheists, 115; and beliefs, 51
attire as triggers, 52
autonomous zones, 162
A Young People's History of the United States. *See* Zinn, Howard

Bacon, Francis, 154
Bailey, Ronald, 115
Bakersfield, California, 160
Baptists, 85
Barr, Bill, 100
Bartholet, Elizabeth, 96
battle for minds, 134
Beatles, 15
belief system, xviii
beware of truth that changes, 50
Bible, xviii, 28, 76, 85, 163; passages of, 28–29, 75
biblical account of creation, 39
biblical worldview, 123
Biden, Joe, 107
bill of attainder, 165
Black, 142; on Black crime, 142; churches, 112; communities, 106–7; privilege, 108; students, 107; voters, 101; wealth, 108
Blackboard, 2
Black Lives Matter, xii, xvii, xx, 47, 50, 58, 83–84, 101, 110, 124–25,

141–45, 160, 162, 165, 175–76; capitalizing on deaths, 141–42; caught by the *Wayback Machine*, 173–74; as cult, 124, 140–41, 171, 176; and destruction of nuclear family, 175; goal of Marxist revolution, 125, 174; as Marxists, 110, 124, 141, 175; myopia of, 174; for the overthrow of Whites, 174; practices of shaming, 84; and selective Black lives, 174; softens language online, 172–73; supports revolution, 58; tenets of, 171–72; universal declarative of, 172; and the use of victimhood, 157; woke to, 85. *See also* Marxist, cult
blind beliefs, 7
blind faith, 27, 163
Blob, 89
bogus history, 96
Bolsheviks, 102
born-again, 73, 85
boyish-girls, 86
brain, 24; chemistry, 24; sequencing in students, 71
Bramfeld, Theodore, 40
Bray, Mark, 102
Buchanan, Rivera, Erica, 142–44
bullying, 98
bumper-sticker philosophies, 61
Bush, George W., 25, 166
Butler, Nicholas Murray, 42

Campbell, W. Keith, 82
cancel culture, 17; affecting people, 97; tactics, 98
canvas, 2
Carson, Ben, 107
caste system, 98
Center for Human Values, 115
Center for Science and Culture, 169
children, 84; assigned bias, 116; born as haters, 84; exploited, 134; oversexualized, 136
Christian, x; activists, 20; apologetics, xx; conversations, xxiii; theism, 14

Christianity, xix, 51, 96–97; as myth, 41; patrimony, 44; as religion of White man, 17
church, x; challenges, 86; denominations, x, xx; of Satan, 15
citizenship participation, xviii
civic, education, xviii, 49, 162, 164, 166
civil, 25; disobedience, 58; rights movement, 25; rights struggles, 111–12; religion, 64; Rights Act of 1964, 133; society and activism, 26; War, 164
Claiborne, Shane, 26
Claremont Institute, 100
Clark, Chloe, 50
classism, 50
classroom discipline, 3
Clay, Lacy, 125
Cleveland abortion clinic, 114
Cline, Austin, 21, 30
Cline, Monica, 30
CNN, 166
colonization, xiv
Columbia University, 110
Columbus, Christopher. *See* Zinn, Howard
Comer, James, 71
come to Jesus moment, 146
Comey, James, 164
common, 39; good, 161; school, 39; sense, 105
Common Core State Standards, 2
competition, 51; between worldviews, 51; over classrooms, 52
Comte, August, 64
conservatives, 97–98
Constitutional Amendments, 114, 162–63
conversion experiences, 24, 73, 137
Cooper, Brittany, 100–101
Copeland, Kenneth, 144
correction of injustices, 63
corruption of blood, 165
Coulter, Ann, 97–114
counter culture, 17

COVID-19, 29, 55, 99, 101, 125–26
Crain, Natasha, 87
creationism, 41
creator, 16
critical theories, xix, 99; about race, 5, 81–82; banned by Trump, 84; definitions of, 81
Crow, Jim, 134, 164–65
cult, xiv, 124; characteristics of, 128–29; definition of, 124; and evangelism, xix; of gender, 132; groups, xiv, 5, 6; leaders, 141; of personality, 15, 76; of race, xix, 140; recruitment model, 126–27; religious, 23; of sex, 131; stirring of national rebellion, 143; tactics of, 127–28; and violence, 23
cultural progressives, 31
Cuties, 134

Danbury Baptists, 7
Darwin, Charles, 40, 114
Datskovska, Stacia, 63; disenchanted, 63; leaves church, 63; loses feelings of hope, 63
Dawkins, Richard, 169
dearth of historical knowledge, 125
debates forbidden, 58
deceptive narrative, 5
Declaration of Independence, 56
deconstructionism, 31
Descarte, Rene, 84
Democrats, 104; in California, 105; in the south, 164
Denton, Melinda Lundquist, 139–40
detached generation. *See* Generation Z
Devil and Daniel Webster, 85
Dewey, John, xix, 40, 42, 64
Diallo, Nkechi, 79
DiAngelo, Robin. *See* White fragility
disappearing sex differences, 89
Discovery Institute, 15
disunity in schools, 61
divine wokeness, 48
DNA of Whites, 27

Dolezal, Rachel, 79
Dollar, Creflo, 144
domestic terrorism, 145
dominionist, 12
downplaying of beliefs, 62
drug addiction, 74
drunk on exclusivity, 98
DuPlantis, Jesse, 144

eastern religions, 15
Eberstadt, Mary, 14, 38–39, 75–76, 103, 108, 137, 157, 176
ebony towers, 101
echo chambers, 95
Economic State Board of Black Americans in 2020, 107
education: based on children's goodness, 63; definitions, 37–39; as messiah, 40; reformation, xviii; is religion, 37, 63; as savior, 10; and spiritual formation, 43; used as recruitment for souls, 10
educational, 11; messianism, 11; psychology, 2
effects of religious humanism, 62
Eichner, Edward, 114
Eighty Years' War, 13
elevation of self, 74
elite professoriate, 98
Ellis, John, 103–4
Ellul, Jacques, 16–17
Emancipation Proclamation, 167
emotional, 70–71; escalation, 73; gospel, 71; intelligence, 70; reasoning, 84
entitlement-splaining, xi, 98
environment is god-like, 139
Epperson v. Arkansas (1968), 15
Equality Act, 132
Equal Protection Clause, 17
Espinoza v. Montana Department of Revenue (2020), 19
ESPN, 140
establishing a religion, 5
Establishment Clause, 17

ethnic groups, 4
eugenics, 115
Euro-centric thinking, 72
European, 12; monarchs, 76; nation states, 12
evaluating claims of humanism, 168–70
Evangelical Environmental Network, 138
evangelicals, xx, 25; are to be quiet, 62; and elections, 25; common elements with humanists, 27; churches, 11; concerns about immigration, 25; neo-, 25; on gay marriage, 25; and poverty, 25; regarding stewardship of the earth, 26; and the Republican Party, 25; and science, 26; as secularists, 26; shunning church, 146; withdraw from culture, 112
Evergreen College, 98
Everson v. Board of Education (1947), 15
evolution, 41, 115

Facebook, 101
Fairfax County, Virginia. *See* Heizer, Rachna Sizemore
faith, 26; adapted to culture, 26; in humanism, 159; placed in self, 144; in religious secularism, 42
Faith and Reason Institute, 103
family, 28; alternate, 54; and emotions, 54; is not family, 53; nuclear, 53; redefined, 28, 53
Fasching, Darrell, 16
fascist cult. *See* antifa
fear of speaking out, 41
Federalist, 18
feel good teachings at church, 159
feminism, 86
Fenker, Suzanne, 87; and feminism, 87; and womanhood, 87
Fillmore, Charles, 145
finding oneself, xix
First Amendment, 8, 17, 133

Floyd, George, 78; death of, 78; and group utopianism, 78; and the media, 78; and racial tribalism, 78
fluidity, 22; of gender, 22; of self, 75; of sexuality, 22
follow the cash, 145
formation of new Christian culture, 113
fostering of global consciousness, 142
Fox, Emmet, 145
free speech, 50; limited, 50; and restricted words and phrases, 54, 97
Freud, Sigmund, 40–41
Friedrich, Rebecca, 135
Fulton, Brad, 62

Galloway, Scott, 98
gatekeepers of facts, 96
gay marriage, 50
Geisler, Norman, 7
gender, xvii; differences, 86; identity, 3; phobic, 5; programs, 157; theories, 5
generational differences, 156
Generation Z, xviii, 138, 162; called the therapy generation, 70, 124; detached, 23; dumbed down, 85; leaving the churches, 63; as the post-Christian generation, 63
genocide, xiii
Ginsburg, Ruth Bader, 29
girlish boys, 86
Gitlin, Todd, 110
God, xviii, 55; and the astronomers. *See* Jastrow, Robert; of humankind, 41; of self, xix, 69
good, 11; news, 11; stewardship, 26
gospel of Goleman, 70
Graham, Billy, 15, 73
Great, 3, 113; Depression, 113; Recession, 3
great scattering, 75
Greenfield, Larry, 100
Grigson, Stephanie, 134
Groseclose, Tim, 100
group favoritism, 52
Guevara, Che, xiii

Haidt, Jonathan, 83, 171
Hammer, Josh, 31
Hamon, JoBeth, 56
Hansen, Kenneth, 63
Hansen, Mark Victor, 145
Hare Krishna, 15
Harris, Kamala, 107, 141
Harvard University, 24, 48, 96
hate, 49; lists, 135; speech, 104; as worship, 49
Hayden, Tom, 109–10
HBCUs. *See* Historically Black Colleges and Universities
heaven, 139
Heizer, Rachna Sizemore, 56
hero figures, 125
heteronormative, 72
hippie, xi, 15
Hispanics, 167
Historically Black Colleges and Universities (HBCUs), 167
historical revisionism, xix
Holder, Eric, 164
Holmes, Ernest, 145
Holy Writ, x, 27
homophobia, 50
Hopkins, Maggie, 102
Horowitz, David, 97
human, 18; deity, 41; dignity, 18; life as property, 114; reason, 41; sexuality in schools, 72
humanism, xiv, xviii, 4, 8; defining truth with, 43; beliefs of, 18; definition of, 9; diversity within, 21; in early American education, 40; exclusive claims of, 42; and faith, 26; intersecting with religion, 138; lens of, 43; philosophy behind, 42, 49; in post-Christian America, 16; religious, xiv, 19–21, 26; as repackaged religion, 4; and taking sides, 42
humanistic: culture, x; departments at college, 98; doctrines, xix; evangelism, 22, 176; optimism, 42; pessimism, 42; religious awakening, 21; tenets, xviii, 56; worldview, 7
Humanist Manifest I, 41
humanists, 9, 169; all-knowing, 169–70; all-powerful, 169–70; blended, 9; as center of universe, 55; differences between, 21; functional, 9; manifestos, 18; moral code, 170; recovery groups, 31; religious, 21; strict, 9

identitarianism, 81; foundation of, 81; leads to multiculturalism, 81; partisan, 103
identity, xi, 24; movement, 142; without biology, 20
implicit bias, 47, 49
inclusive environment, xii
Indiana University, 101–2
indoctrination, xii, 2, 6, 11
Inglehart, Ronald, 20
intelligent design, 15
international relations, 12
intolerance is intolerance, 52
intolerant, 41; beliefs, 41; of Christianity, 46
Islam, 12
it takes a village, 40
ivory tower, xx, 73, 81, 89, 95–97; cracks in, 99–101, 113, 115, 158
Ivy League seminaries, 38

Jastrow, Robert, 55, 169
Jefferson, Thomas, 7–8, 17, 64
Jesus Christ, 28, 44, 73, 85, 141
Jesus movement, 15
Jews, 115
Johnson, Lyndon B., 106
Jones, Van, 166
Judaism, 51
Judeo-Christian, 5, 53, 96, 170; teachings, 14

Keck School of Medicine, 23–24, 168
Kelsen, Hans, 19–20

King, Martin Luther, 112
knee-taking compliance, 103
Knott, Kim, 28
Krason, Stephen, 26–27
Kurtz, Paul, 42

Lancaster University. *See* Knott, Kim
LaVey, Anton Szandor, 15
law enforcement, 141; elimination of Blacks, 141; racist, 142
laws regarding property, 145
Leary, Timothy, 24
Legislative Branch, 8
Lewis, C. S., 145–46, 154
Lewis, John, 25
Lewis and Clark College, 98
LGBTQ+, xii, xx, 47, 49, 129–30, 132–33, 160, 175
liberal, 96; bad manners, 100; moral unrest, 96; violence, 100; worship of god of equality, 100
liberalization of churches, 112
Lindsay, James, 96
lobbyists, 1
losing oneself to find oneself, xx, 74–75
lost values, 76
love, 49; is about choices, 50; is love, 49; of self, 49; as worship, 49
LSD, 24
Lukianoff, Greg, 83, 171
Lutherans, 85
Lynch, Gordon, 9

Machen, J. Gresham, 112–13
Magna Carta, ix
Manhattan Institute, 106
Mann, Horace, xix, 38–40
marginalization, xii, 61, 166
marriage redefined, 28
Marriott, John, 87; and deconversion, 87
Marx, Karl, 154
Marxist, xii; cult, 80; devotees, 110, 116, 171; goes too far, 171; ideology, 109, 154, 162; professors, 104
masculinity under fire, 89
May, Samantha, 12–13

McClay, Wilfred, 57; critique of Zinn, 57; exposes fallacies of 1619 Project, 57–58
McDonald, Heather, 97, 106
McWhorter, John, 82
medical profession racist, 168
melting pot, 80. *See also* Zangwill, Israel
MeToo movement used as victimhood in society, xi, 39, 143, 157
microaggression, 5, 111–12
Middlebury College, 97
millennials as the therapy generation, xviii, 70, 138
mind-altering, 5
miraculous, 17
mocking, 50
Mohler, Albert, 9, 132–33
monergism, 48
Moonies, 15
moral changes by reprogramming, 51, 72
moralistic therapeutic deism, 139; and positive confession, 144
More, Thomas, 154
Mormon Church, 8
Mosqueda, Laura, 168
multicultural education, 80
Murray, Charles, 97
Muslim terrorist, 26

narcissism, 5, 70, 77; epidemic of, 82
National Council for the Social Studies (NCSS), 165
National Education Association (NEA), 130
Nazis, 115
Nazism, 102
NCSS. *See* National Council for the Social Studies
NEA. *See* National Education Association
new creatures in Christ, 73
new family paradigm, 136
New Jersey, 3
New Testament, 28
New York Times 1619 Project, 5, 15, 56–58; and changing the

Amendments to the Constitution, 114; dismissal of Declaration of Independence, 56; teaching of falsehoods, 57; and White supremacy, 57
New York University, 98
Nicolosi, Joseph, 134
No Child Left Behind, 2, 166
non-binary, 86
non-relational deity, 139
norms as taboo, 61
Norris, Pippa, 20
not Black enough, 140–41

Obama, Barack, x, 25, 166; and narcissism, 76, 106, 141
obesophobia, 95
Oklahoma City Council. *See* Hamon, JoBeth
old school altar call, 146
one flesh, 29
one with Christ, 45
online education, 155–56, 160
opioid addiction, 23
opportunity, 107; as privilege, 107; for success, 108; zones, 107
Orwell, George, 84, 103, 105
Osteen, Joel, 11, 144

Paley, William, 139; intelligent designer, 139–40; the Watchmaker, 139
Pally, Marcia, 10, 14, 26, 63, 137–38
pandemic, 2
parental support, 2
Parler, 101
PCUSA. *See* Presbyterian Church of the United States
Peace of Westphalia. *See* Westphalia
Peale, Norman Vincent, 145
Pearcey, Nancy, 96
People's Temple, 15
persons of color, 3
Planned Parenthood, 29; clinics on school campuses, 29; and COVID-19, 29; of Los Angeles County, 29; and sex education, 29–30

Pluckrose, Helen, 96
political activism, 96, 104
political correctness, 45; has become cult-like, 46; as religious expression, 45–46; as sacred practice for humanists, 46
politics and tribalism, 79
polygamy, 8
Portland, Oregon, 102; avoidance of Christian doctrine, 62; serving the city through work initiative, 62; social work of evangelism, 62
positive confession gospel, 144; creating own wealth, 144; and faith, 144
post-Christian, 11, 16; America, 17, 30; spirituality, 11, 16; theology, 16
post-religious era, 11
post-traumatic stress disorder (PTSD), 112
practicing exclusivity, 77
Presbyterian Church of the United States (PCUSA), 85
presidential election of 2020, 99
pride, 77
primary socialization, 51
pro-choice, 114
professional, 1, 2, 97; development leader, 1; learning communities, 2; untouchability, 97
profile of cult recruits, 126
Promise Keepers, 73
proselytizing professors, 97
prosperity teachers, 144–45
protected groups, 111
PTSD. *See* post-traumatic stress disorder
public learning institutions, 43, 153; have gone too far, 171; lost their way, 176; worship at, 48
public schools, xvii, xix
Pullman, Joy, 19

race, 79; becomes a god, 83; consciousness, 142; and divisions, 79, 105; and harmony, 108
Race to the Top, 2
racism as systemic and institutional, 47, 50

racists, xv, xvii, 3–5
radicalism, 48
Rasmussen, Eric, 101–2
reason is king, 30
recapturing history, 111
Reddit, 101
redefinition of family and norms, 28, 53
religion, xv; becomes secular, 144; definition of, 37; as education, 13; influence of, 11; without God, 20
religious, xv; beliefs, xv; denominations, 18; donations, 19; experiences and feelings, 43; humanism, 30–32, 127; humanism as replacement for Christianity, 127; movement, xx; nature of, 30–32; schools of the past, 48; separatism, 13
removal of common sense, 55
Renaissance, 9–10, 76
Republicans, 104
reshaping minds, 69; through emotions, 69–70; using emotional reasoning, 69–70
revelations, 126
revisionism, 161–65; assumes historical motivation, 165; of education, 161; of history, 161
ridicule, 51
rise of negative personalities, 82
Roe v. Wade (1973), 29
Roman Empire, 13
Roman Emperors, 76
romantic apocalypticism, 14
romanticism, 1
Rousseau, Jean Jacques, 64, 154, 161
rude liberals, 99
Rushdoony, Rousas, 12, 40, 43, 47, 63
Rutgers University, 100

sacred beliefs, 47
sacredness of marriage, 137
sacrifice of innocence, 130–31
safe spaces, 103–4
same-sex attraction, 27
Santa Claus, 45

Schaeffer Center for Health Policy and Economics, 23–24
Scholastic, 165
schools, xix
Schuller, Robert, 145
Scientology, 114
Scott, Tim, 107
secular, xi; becomes sacred, xiii, xvi, 45; definition of, 9; humanism, xi, xii, xvi; humanist evangelical, 63; idol, 138; religion, 11, 100
secularism, xvi, 14, 20
secularization of American religion, 40, 123
selective truth, 31
self as deity, 22, 134
sensitivity training, 47
separation of church and state, 5, 7–8, 15, 17
September 11, 2001, 26
sex education, 72, 129; advertisements, 72; California, 131–34; curriculum, 72, 130; leads to personal autonomy, 73
sexism, 50
sexual, 3, 74; abuse, 112; activism in schools, 130; children, 134; confusion, 135; differences, 86; experimentation, 135; exploitation of children, 136; guide for teenagers, 135; harassment of teachers, 129; identity, 74; innocence, 136; orientation, 3; victimization, 136
sexuality, xvii
sexualization of children supported by, 134; American Civil Liberties Union (ACLU), 135; Gay Lesbian and Straight Education Network (GLSEN), 135; National Association for the Advancement of Colored People (NAACP), 135; National Center for Trans-Equality, Human Rights Campaign (NCTEHRC), 135; National Education Association (NEA), 135; Southern Poverty Law Center (SPLC), 135

shaming, 51
Shapiro, Ben, 97
shared beliefs, 27
Singer, Peter, 115
Sisyphus, 84
skin color, 4
slanted views, 61
slavery, 106, 165
sloganeering, 156
Smith, Christian, 139
Smith, Kurt, 50
social, xvi, xvii; activists, 54; conditioning, xvi; divisiveness, 61; and emotional well-being, 154; evils, 43; gospel, 14, 38, 113, 115, 139; justice, as religious crusade, 58; justice education, 155, 166–67; media and influences, xvii, 28, 51, 102, 154
social-emotional learning, xvi, 71
socialization, 51; primary, 51–52; secondary, 52
Sommers, Christina Hoff, 98
sorophobia, 50
soteriology, 43
soul-searching, 139–40
South Carolina, 165
Southern Baptists, 11, 132
Southern Poverty Law Center, 105
speech, xx; as anti-American, xx; hateful, xx
stalking professor, 99
Stanger, Alison, 97
state economic punishments, 52
Steele, Sage, 140
Strings, Sabrina, 95
students, 21–23; brains and emotions, 21; as captive audience, 46; confusion, 21; for a Democratic Society (SDS), 109; mental health, 156–57; as objects of worship, 48; radicalized, 109; self-worship, 76; suicide rates, 23, 74, 135; verbally assaulted, 52; with special needs, 158

subjective truth, xvii, 61, 126, 146
Sullivan, Andrew, 78
Sunday schools, 85
supreme being, 28
Supreme Court of the United States, ix, 133, 167
swearing-in ceremony. *See* Hamon, JoBeth; Heizer, Rachna Sizemore
synergism, 48
systemic racism, 126

teachers, 54; blacklisted, 61; excommunicated, 61; fired, 61; as surrogate parents, 54
temptation of humans, 87–89
tenure, 100
theological absolutes, 11
theology, 53
Thiessen, Joel, 51
Thirty Years' War, 13
Thomas More Society, 15
threatening students, 54
Torcaso v. Watkins (1961), ix
traditional moral values, 72, 160
traditions of America, 96
transcendence, 19
transformation of learning, 69
transgender, 31
transphobia, 50
Treaty of Westphalia. *See* Westphalia
tribalism, 77–78; acronyms of, 77; definition of, 77; headed in wrong direction, 79; and marginalization, 166; and worship, 77
triggers of arguments and violence, 59–61, 103, 111–12
Trump, Donald, 70, 100, 102, 154, 163–65; administration of, 107; flag of, 160–61
Turley, Jonathan, 103
Twenge, Jean, 82
twentieth century empires, 76; German, 76; Japanese, 76; North Korean, 76; Soviet Union, 76
Twitter weaponized, 100–102

types of families, 27
tyranny of the majority, 137

unconscious bias, 48
unfair social media, 100
United Kingdom, ix, 159; children forced to participate in offensive lessons, 159–60; with LGBTQ+ pride month, 159; and parent complaints, 159
United Methodist Church, 85
United States v. Reynolds (1879), 8
universities replace churches, 109
University of California, Berkeley, 97
University of California at Los Angeles (UCLA), 97
University of Southern California (USC), 23, 168
utopia, 153; in America, 153–56; online, 155

value creep, 49
value of life, 29
van Roermund, Bert, 20
Vietnam War and protests, xx, 111
viral pandemic, 166
Vogelin, Eric, 20

Wall Street Journal, 124
waning of American church, 138
War on Poverty, 106
Warren, Elizabeth, 79
Washington State, 160
Watkins, William, 7
Weinstein, Brett, 98

Wells, H. G., 154
western civilization, 95
Westphalia, 12–13
White, 27, 81; American DNA, 163; Christian privilege, 81; oppressors, 105; privilege, 85, 106–8, 114; students, 105; supremacy, xiii, 27, 58, 84, 108, 166; virus, 141–66
White fragility, xvii, xix, 82
Whitehead, Alfred North, 43
Whites, xvii
whole child education approach, 39, 157–58
Wilson, Erin, 12
Wineburg, Sam, 165
winning at all cost, 27
woke, 6, 55, 76, 142
wokeness, xix, 44, 125
Wolfe-Rocca, Ursula, 163
worldviews, 7, 97
worship of self, xviii, 75

Yale Divinity School, 48
Yiannopoulos, Milo, 97
YouTube, 42, 155

Zangwill, Israel, 80
Zinn, Howard, xii, 56–58, 163–65; attack on Christopher Columbus, 56; Educational Project, xii, 5, 110, 163–65, 175; erroneous history, 56; political agenda of, 166; and racial anxiety, 56; *A Young People's History of America*, xii, 56, 166
Zoom, 2, 129, 160

About the Author

Ernest J. Zarra III, PhD, is a retired assistant professor of teacher education at Lewis-Clark State College. Zarra has five earned degrees and holds a PhD from the University of Southern California, in teaching and learning theory, with cognates in psychology and technology. He has a storied forty-two-year career in teaching at all levels, with most of his classroom experience in the teaching of seniors' U.S. Government and Politics and Economics.

Ernie is a former Christian College First Team All-American soccer player, high school and club soccer coach, former teacher of the year for a prestigious California public school, and was awarded the top student in graduate education from the California State University at Bakersfield, California. He is the father of two outstanding, professional, and accomplished adult children, a daughter and a son.

Dr. Zarra has written thirteen books, several of which earned awards, and authored more than a dozen journal articles. He has designed professional development programs, is a national conference presenter, former district professional development leader for the largest high school district in California, adjunct university instructor, and a member of several national honor societies. He also participated as a speaker of the Idaho Speakers Bureau, as well as presenter in the Lewis-Clark Presents program, bringing special topics to high school students.

Originally from New Jersey, he and his wife Suzi, also a retired California public school teacher, live in Washington State and enjoy spending time with family, cooking, church ministry, yard work, and finding energy to keep up with their grandchildren.

www.ingramcontent.com/pod-product-compliance
Lightning Source LLC
Chambersburg PA
CBHW031550300426
44111CB00006BA/256